Prestel Museum Guide

The Austrian National Library

Irina Kubadinow

Prestel

Munich · Berlin · London · New York

© 2004 Prestel Verlag, Munich · Berlin · London · New York
This publication has been made possible by the generous support
of the Society of Friends of the Austrian National Library.

Photographic acknowledgements
Photos by Pez Hejduk (title, p. 4/5, 6, 11, 26/27, 30 b, 31, 34/35,
38–53, 136–147), Sabine Hauswirth (p. 8) as well as Ingrid Oentrich,
Jean-Pierre Weiner, Picture Archive of the Austrian National Library

Concept and editing: Irina Kubadinow
In collaboration with Alfred Schmidt

Austrian National Library
Josefsplatz 1, A-1010 Vienna
Tel.: (+43–(0)1) 534 10–0
onb@onb.ac.at
www.onb.ac.at

The Library of Conress Cataloguing-in-Publication data is available;
British Library Cataloguing-in-Publication data: a catologue record for
this book is available from the British Library; Deutsche Bibliothek
holds a record of this publication in the Deutsche Nationalbibliografie;
detailed bibliographical data can be found under: http://dnb.ddb.de

Prestel Verlag
Königinstraße 9, 80539 Munich
Tel.: (+49–(0)89) 381 70 90
Fax.: (+49–(0)89) 381 70 935
info@prestel.de
www.prestel.de

Prestel Publishing Ltd.
4, Bloomsbury Place, London WC1A 2QA
Tel.: +44–(020) 7323–5004
Fax: +44–(020) 7636–8004

Prestel Publishing
900 Broadway, Suite 603, New York, NY 10003
Tel.: +1–(212) 995–2720
Fax: +1–(212) 995–2733
www.prestel.com

Prestel books are available worldwide. Please contact your nearest
bookseller or one of the above addresses for information concerning
your local distributor.

Project coordinated by Victoria Salley
Copy-edited by Anne Heritage
Translated from the German by Elisabeth Clegg
Designed and produced by a.visus, Michael Hempel, Munich
Lithography by Reproline mediateam, Munich
Printed and bound by Passavia Druckservice GmbH, Passau

Printed in Germany on acid-free paper

ISBN 3-7913-3148-5 (English edition)
ISBN 3-7913-3099-3 (German edition)
ISBN 3-7913-3225-2 (Italian edition)
ISBN 3-7913-3226-0 (French edition)

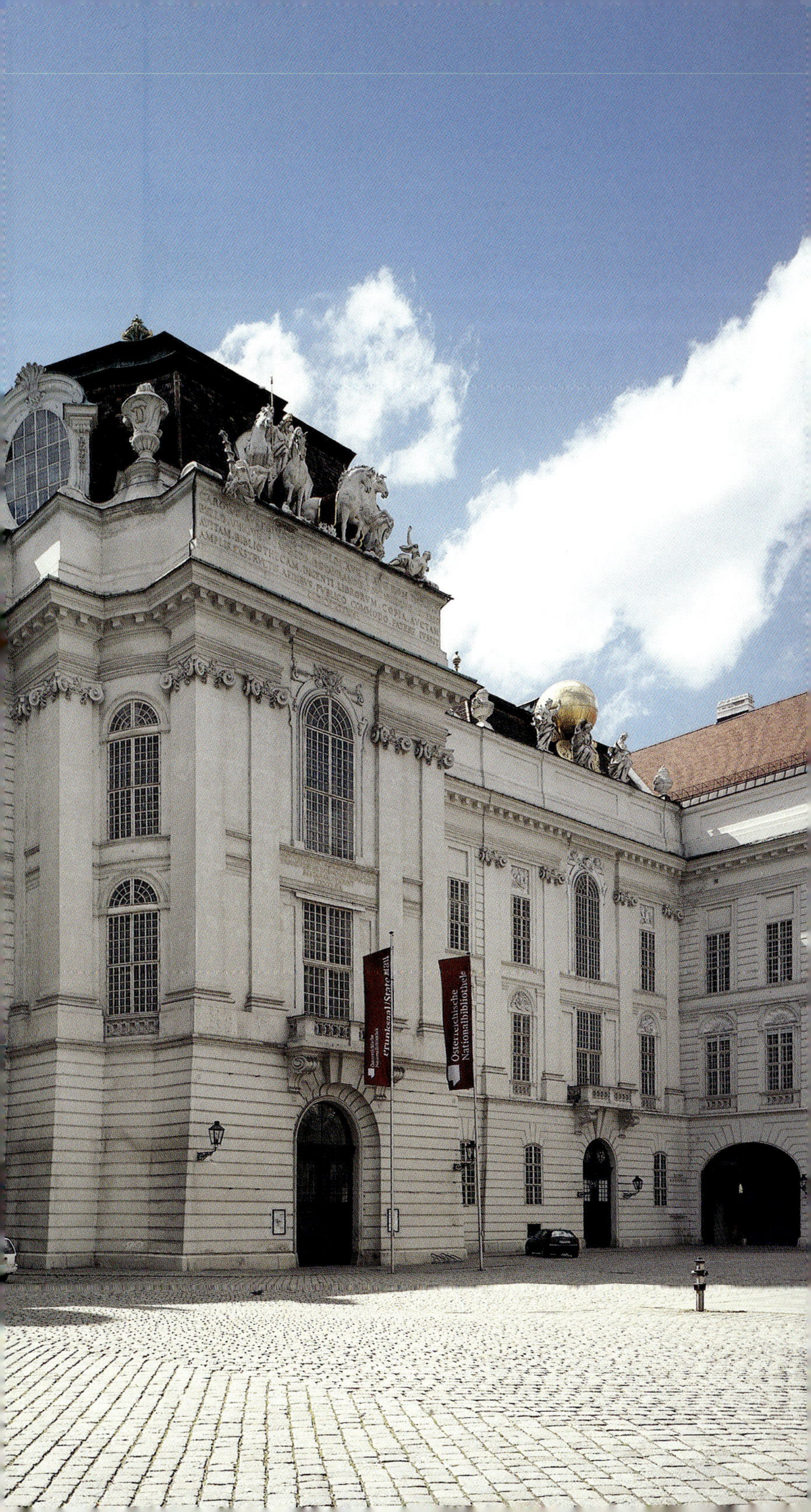

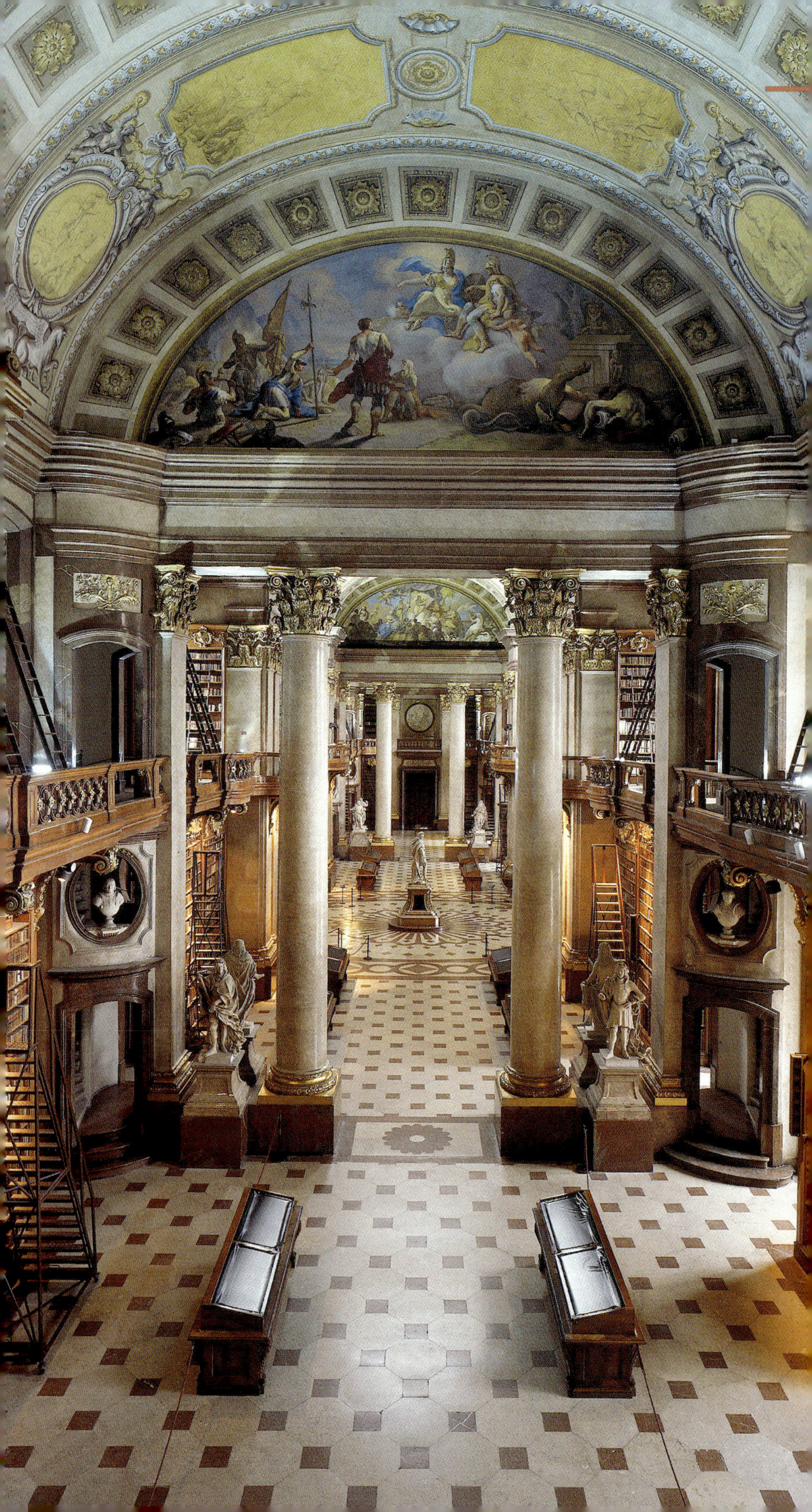

CONTENT

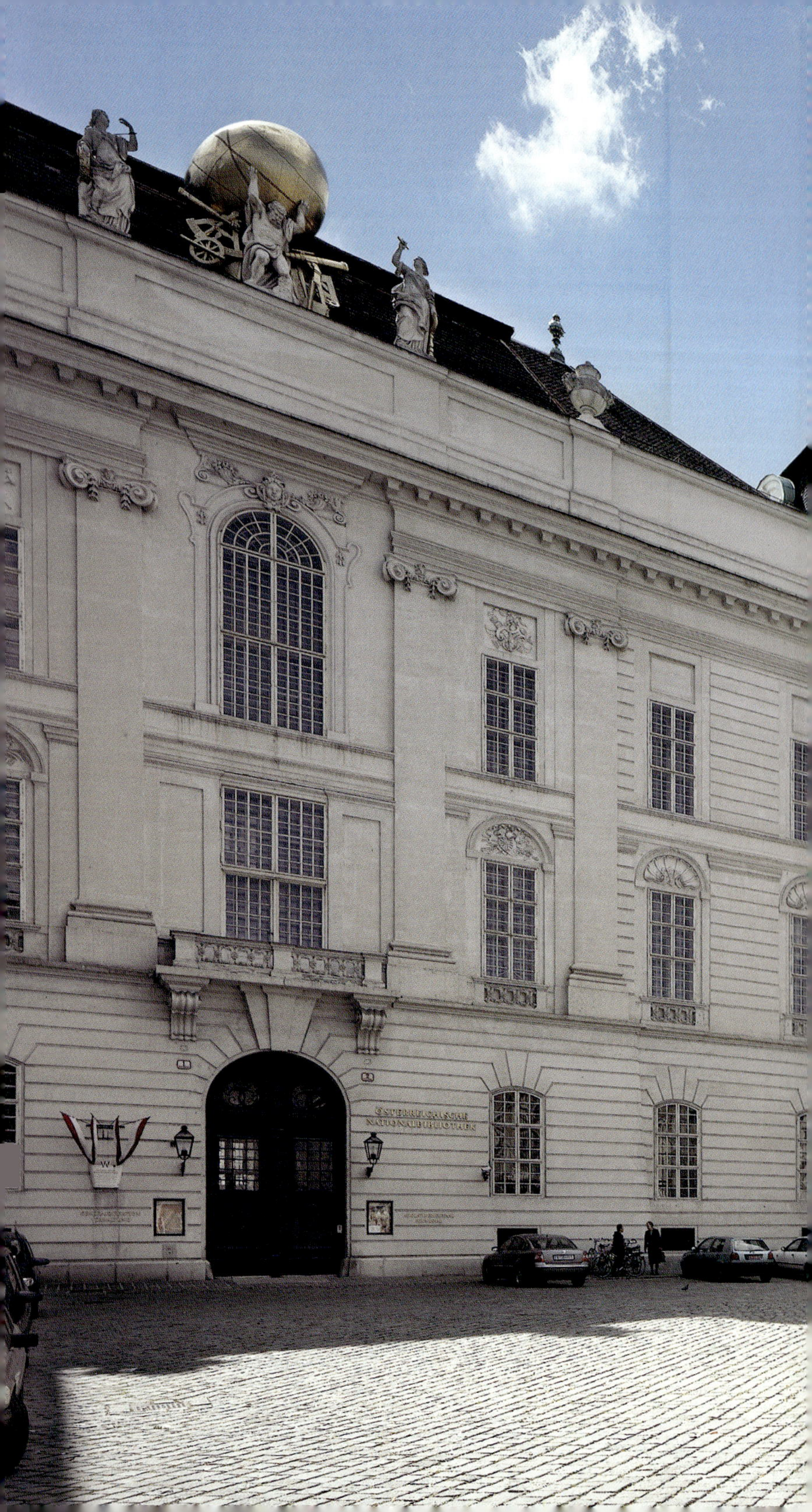

The Austrian National Library – Tradition and Innovation

Johanna Rachinger

The Austrian National Library in Its Own Estimation

The Austrian National Library, the principal academic institution of its type in the Republic of Austria, is extremely rich in tradition, having a history that dates back to the fourteenth century. Today, the Library serves as a bridge between the rich legacy of the past and the demands of our own future-oriented 'information society'. The Austrian National Library now sees itself as

| *a centre for the provision of information and the encouragement of research;*

| *the nation's prime institution for documenting and preserving the past; and*

| *a multi-faceted centre of both education and culture.*

As a centre for the provision of information, the Austrian National Library offers its users access not only to over 7.3 million objects in its own collection but also to data gathered from a range of international sources. In addition, its staff carry out commissioned research projects and provide detailed bibliographical documentation on specific areas, for example, on literature related to women. With the advent of digitalization, an increasing percentage of these services are available online via the Austrian National Library website at **www.onb.ac.at**.

The Legacy of the Past

The Austrian National Library is one of Europe's most historically important libraries. Even today its distinctive character is, to a large extent, still determined by its long history, especially as regards the immense cultural value of its special collections. For centuries the principal library of the Holy Roman Empire and later of the Austrian Empire, it became the Imperial Royal Court Library of the Danubian Monarchy and assumed its present form in 1920. The oldest book in the possession of the

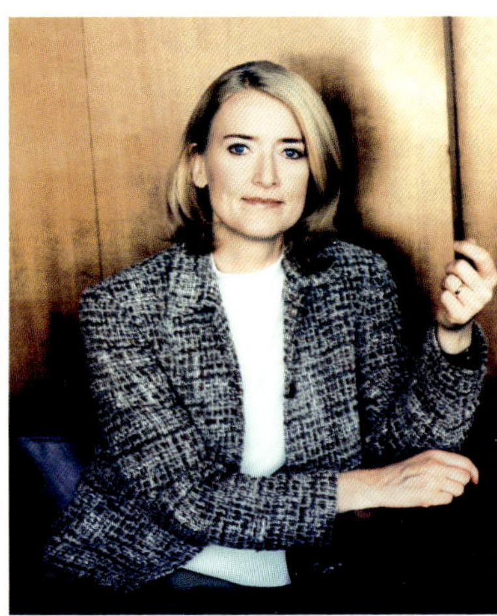

Dr. Johanna Rachinger
director-general of
the Austrian National
Library

Austrian National Library dates from 1368. In 1575 the Habsburg emperor Maximilian II

(b. 1527, r. 1564–76) formally appointed the Dutch scholar Hugo Blotius as prefect of the Court Library. To date, Blotius has had twenty-nine successors: further prefects and, more recently, directors-general, both male and female, among them many important scholars from across Europe.

It was only with the construction of the splendid Baroque edifice on Josefsplatz that the Library acquired a home of its own. This building, erected between 1723 and 1726 to the plans of Johann Bernhard Fischer von Erlach and his son, Josef Emanuel, is regarded as one of the most important examples of profane Baroque architecture in Austria and is widely seen as one of the most beautiful library buildings ever constructed. It should not, however, be forgotten that, for all its Baroque splendour, the Viennese Court Library was in all probability the first great library in Europe to be explicitly intended – as testified by an inscription above the main entrance on Josefsplatz – for the use of the public ('publico commodo patere jussit').

A substantial proportion of the older holdings of the Imperial Court Library is now preserved in the special collections of the Austrian National Library.

The Ten Special Collections

Although the Austrian National Library has become a symbol of Austrian cultural identity, above all that of the Second Austrian Republic established after the end of the Second World War, in its earlier history as the Imperial Court Library it was never limited to amassing a 'national cultural heritage', least of all as this might be defined in relation to the present-day national frontiers. The Austrian National Library houses 'world heritage documents' in the broadest sense of the term. Several of its holdings have been included by UNESCO in its *Memory of the World* register of such 'world heritage documents'. This is the case, for example, with the collection in the **Department of Papyri**, which with over 180,000 objects is the largest of its type in the world. Around 95% of these derive from the private collection of papyri amassed by the archduke Rainer (1827 until 1913) and presented in 1899 to the emperor Francis Joseph I (b. 1830, r. 1848–1916).

In 1998 the celebrated *Viennese Dioscurides* – a richly illustrated botanical and pharmacological manuscript – was recognized as a 'world heritage document' by UNESCO, along with the other Greek manuscripts in the Austrian National Library's **Department of Manuscripts, Autographs and Closed Collections**. In addition to its Greek manuscripts, this collection embraces codices of almost all the world's script cultures, autograph texts by celebrated individuals, and the literary estates of Austrian writers.

The holdings of the **Map Department**, comprising over 260,000 maps, among them outstanding historical rarities, and the affiliated **Globe Museum** (the only one in the world to be publicly accessible), with around 380 terrestrial and celestial spheres, relate to an area far larger than that of the present-day Austrian Republic. In 2004 the *Blaeu-Van der Hem Atlas*, dating from the Baroque era, was added to the aforementioned UNESCO register.

In the **Department of Music**, on the other hand, with its valuable autograph scores – including, for example, the largest collection of scores by Anton Bruckner – Austrian material dominates. **The Department of Incunabula, Old and Precious Books**, with over 8,000 examples of early printed material dating to before 1500, is regarded as one of the most important in the world. The Austrian National Library's holdings of printed material dating from before 1850 reflect not only the ethnic and linguistic diversity of the Danubian Monarchy but also the generally pan-European character of collecting activity at the Imperial Court Library. The holdings of material in Slavic languages are especially notable.

In its **Picture Archive**, the Austrian National Library preserves an extensive collection of visual documents in a wide range of media, including the largest Austrian collection of photographic documentation (a total of over two million images).

The **Department of Broadsheets, Posters and Ex Libris**, established as a separate section only in 1995, and the Austrian **Literary Archives**, founded in 1989, are among the more recent collections within the Austrian National Library.

The Library's ten special collections also include the **Department of Planned Languages**, with its world-renowned **Esperanto Museum**, and the **Archives of the Austrian Folk Music Society**, which was incorporated in 1994.

THE AUSTRIAN NATIONAL LIBRARY TODAY

In addition to housing its ten special collections, the Austrian National Library is a modern academic institution, in which printed matter and other media dating from 1851 onwards are preserved and new acquisitions processed. By Austrian media law, the Austrian National Library receives a copy of every item published in the country (be it in print or electronically). In addition, the Library regularly collects foreign publications relating to Austria as well as literature on the humanities, above all those with a particular relevance to the holdings of its own ten special collections.

From 1 January 2002 the Austrian National Library has been formally registered in the Austrian Republic as an academic institution with the status of a fully incorporated society. Both the Library and its holdings are owned in their entirety by the state, which guarantees their continued existence through an endowment. This status assures the Austrian National Library of considerable flexibility and adaptability in the allocation of its financial resources and serves as a spur to new initiatives. The Austrian National Library generates additional funds by hiring out its historic rooms, licensing objects in its possession, collecting fees for reproduction services, and seeking out sponsors and partnerships.

As a fully incorporated society, the Austrian National Library is managed to the highest standards as an academic institution and centre for information so as to be equipped in every respect to meet the demands of the twenty-first century.

One of the Library's principal goals with regard to modern information technologies is the transformation of all the catalogues of its holdings into electronic databases that may be searched via the internet. Since 2003 the catalogues of all the Austrian National Library's holdings of printed matter dating from 1501 to the present day (over three million books) have become accessible via the internet. From 2005 these will be joined by the catalogues of the Library's ten special collections.

Alongside the digitalization of its catalogues, the Austrian National Library has also risen to the challenge of the new information technologies, in particular with regard to the digitalization of objects

> | *digital Picture Archive: www.bildarchiv.at*
> | *digitalization of old newspapers: http://anno.onb.ac.at*
> | *digital collection of Austrian posters:*
>   *www.onb.ac.at/sammlungen/plakate/index.htm*

and the archival storage of new media.

The Austrian National Library continues to strive for improvement in the services offered to its users and to those visiting its museum collections. At the same time it seeks to extend the number and range of both users and visitors by achieving maximum accessibility to an ever-increasing constituency of interested individuals. The following activities contribute to a high-profile public presence for the Austrian National Library: regular exhibitions as a means of publicizing its collections; event series such as the ANL Literary and Musical Salons; participation in the 'Long Night of the Museums', organization of an 'Open Door Day' to mark the Austrian National Holiday on 26 October; presentations; symposia; concerts; guided tours; and above all hiring out its historic rooms for both corporate and private functions. In the totality of its activities the Austrian National Library fulfils its legal obligations as an educational institution, but, in doing so, it also asserts its role as a multi-faceted centre of culture.

Modern Library, Heldenplatz entrance

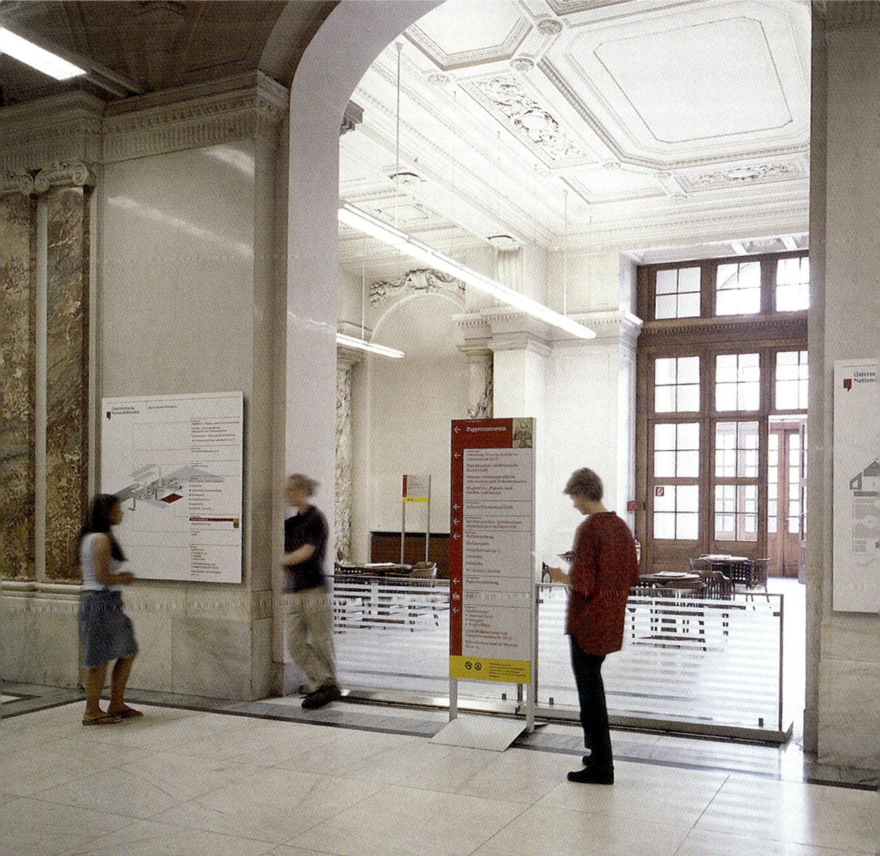

The History

Prefects and Directors-General of the Bibliotheca Palatina Vindobonensis

The first formally appointed imperial librarian was Hugo Blotius. Even before his appointment, however, there were several scholars who made their mark in the service of the Bibliotheca Palatina Vindobonensis – the name refers to the celebrated library founded by Emperor Augustus on the Palatine Hill in Rome. Portraits of these five preceding scholars, the thirty-two prefects and directors-general, and the two interim directors are arranged in a row at the top of the pages of this chapter. As some of the portraits are no longer extant, only the names have been listed.

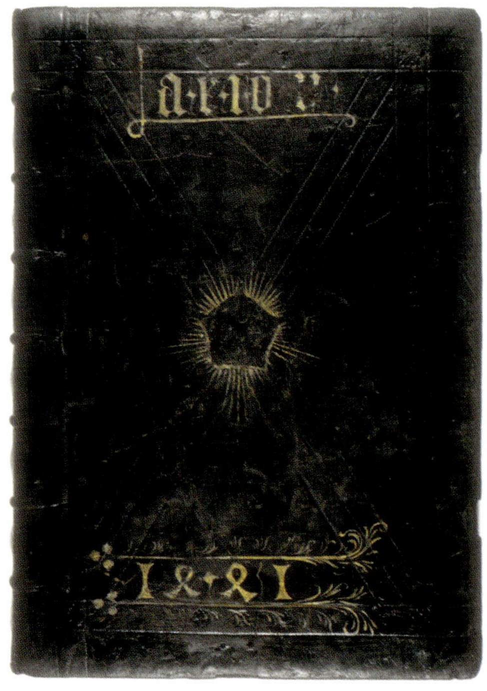

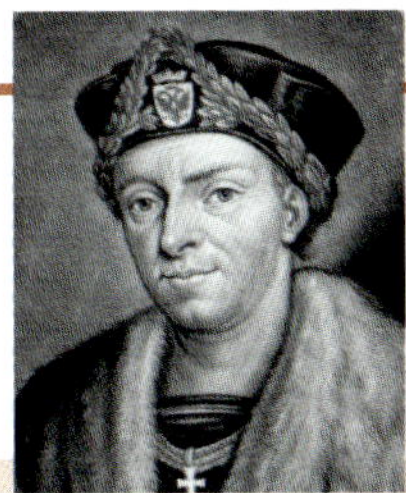

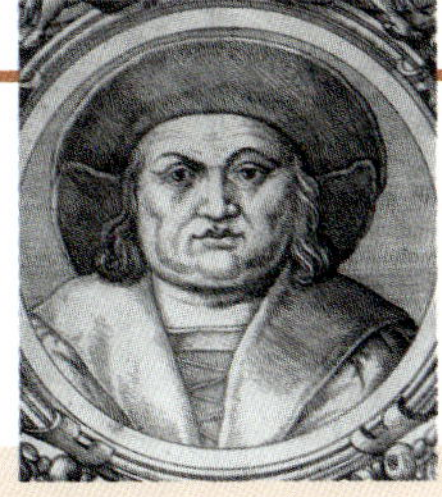

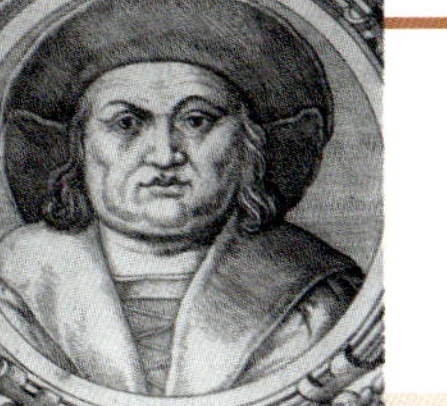

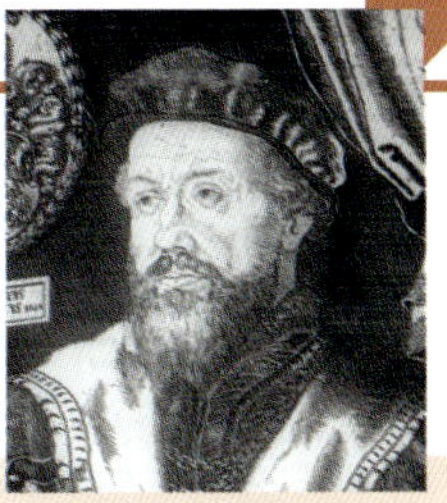

Conrad CELTES 1497–1508	Johann CUSPINIAN 1508–1529	1550–1557	Wolfgang LAZIUS 1557–1565

THE TREASURES OF THE MEDIEVAL ERA

The beginnings of the Imperial Library, the predecessor of today's Austrian National Library, date back to medieval Europe. The oldest book in the Library's possession was originally owned by the archduke Albert III (1350–95), a bibliophile who commissioned numerous manuscripts: it is a sumptuous Evangelary made in 1368 by Johannes von Troppau, a canon from Brünn and a priest in Landskron. This volume is now to be found in the Department of Manuscripts, Autographs and Closed Collections and is the so-called founding codex of the Austrian National Library (see p. 88).

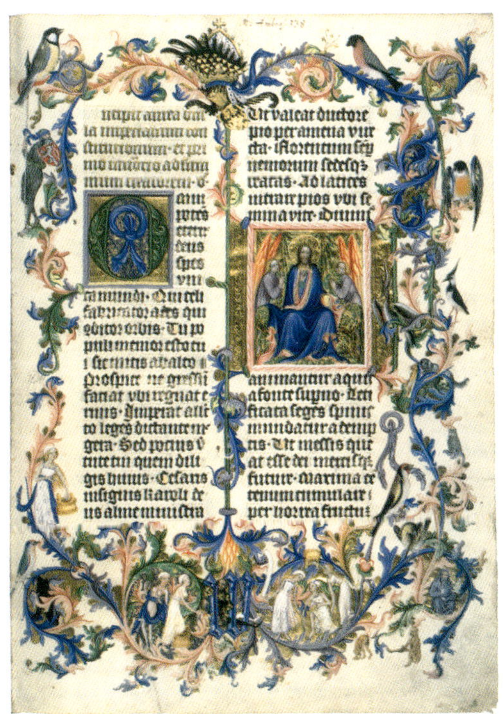

The Golden Bull cover (opposite) and one leaf

An exquisitely decorated transcript of the imperial edict issued in 1356 by Emperor Charles IV of the Luxembourg dynasty. It was made after 1400 for King Wenceslas I.

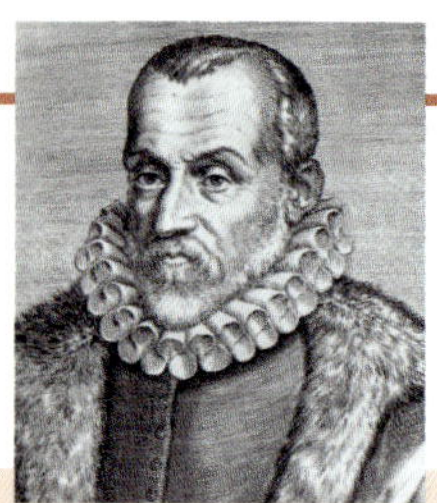

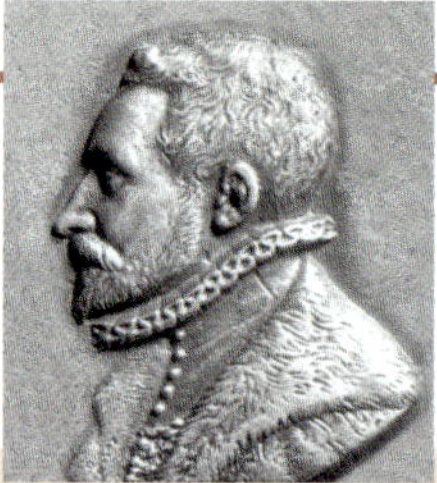

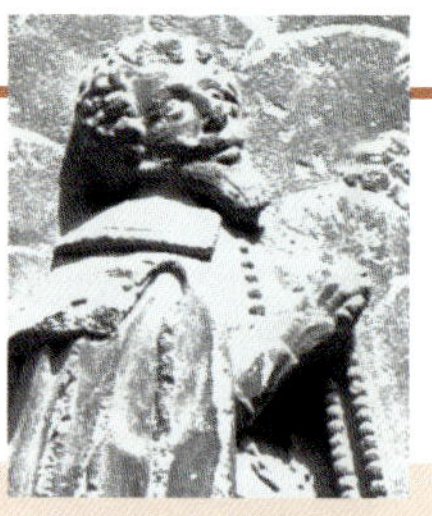

Augerius
Ghislain v. BUSBECKE
1565–1570

Hugo BLOTIUS
1575–1608

Sebastian TENGNAGEL
1608–1636

1636–1650

THE EMPEROR FREDERICK III

The first step towards the creation of an Imperial Library was taken in the reign of the emperor Frederick III (b. 1415, r. 1452–93), who had 110 especially valuable works brought to his castle at Wiener Neustadt, among them the Habsburg inheritance from Bohemia, which included the manuscripts collected in Prague by King Wenceslas I (IV) (b. 1361, r. 1378–1419). One of these was the *Wenceslas Bible*. Another precious item was the *Golden Bull*, a transcript of the emperial edict concerning the election of the German king, issued in 1356 by Emperor Charles IV of the Luxembourg dynasty (b. 1316, r. 1355–78). When, in 1400, the German electors deposed King Wenceslas I, he had the *Golden Bull* transcribed and exquisitely illuminated as a form of protest (for, according to its wording, he had been legally elected German king). Frederick III (1415/1452–1493), who inherited the manuscript, had a new binding made which bore the motto 'A.E.I.O.U.' (Austria est imperare orbi universo – The entire world is subject to Austria; see p. 13).

THE EMPEROR MAXIMILIAN I

Maximilian I (b. 1459, r. 1508–19), son of Frederick III, was himself an author and collaborated on works concerned with the history of his own life. He systematically enlarged the library amassed by his father. Through his marriage to Maria of Burgundy, some of the most important examples of Burgundian and northern French manuscript illumination entered the Habsburg collections. Magnificent manuscripts such as the *Book of Hours of Maria of Burgundy*, the *Chronicles of Jerusalem* or the *Statute Book of the Order of the Golden Fleece* derive from the Burgundian collections. Travelling by way of Brussels and Prague to Vienna, they were initially housed in the Treasury and were only later transferred to the Court Library.

Maximilian's second wife was Bianca Maria Sforza (1472–1510). Masterpieces of Italian manuscript illumination deriving from her own collection were soon added to the treasures of the Habsburg Library.

By this time the Library contained outstanding examples of work in the most important traditions of European manuscript illumination –

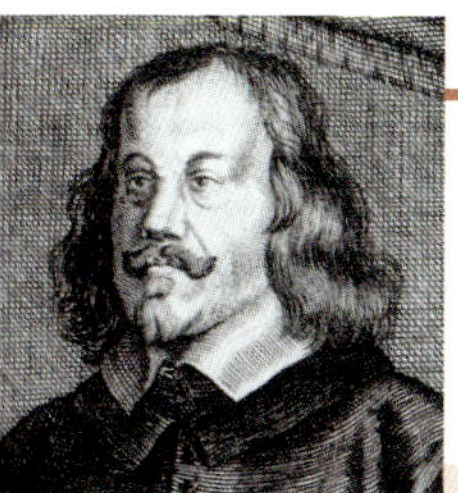

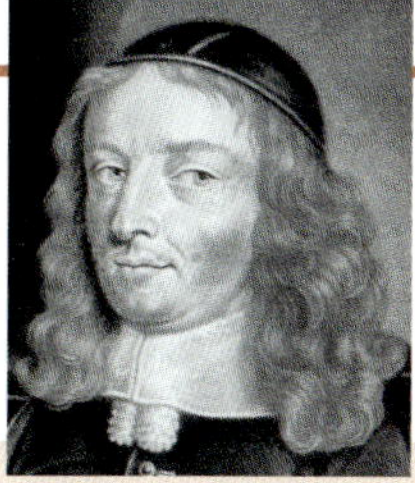

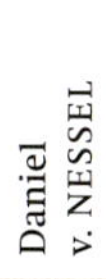

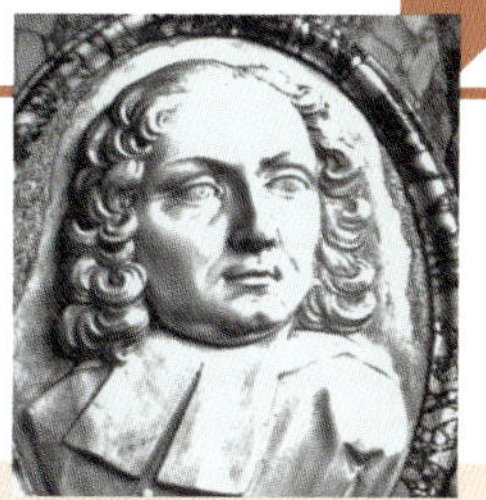

Matthäus MAUCHTER
1650–1663

Peter LAMBECK
1663–1680

1680–1700

Johann Benedict
GENTILOTTI
von Engelsbrunn
1705–1723

Bohemian, French and Italian – in addition to splendid Austrian work produced by the Habsburg Court's own illuminators. But this by no means signified an end to the Library's expansion. Maximilian I housed some of its holdings in the castle at Wiener Neustadt, some in the Viennese Hofburg and, from around 1500, some in Innsbruck, where after his death in 1519 it was moved to Schloss Ambras.

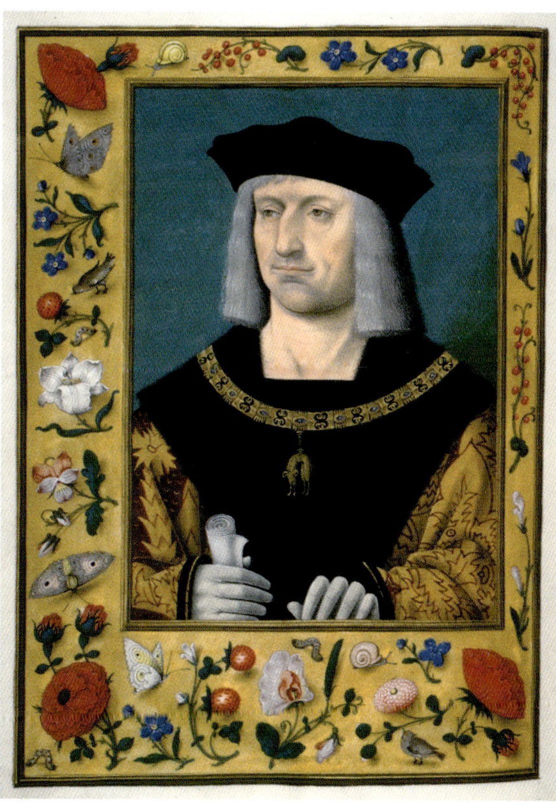

Emperor Maximilian I b. 1459, r. 1508–19

From the *Book of Statutes of the Order of the Golden Fleece* Bruges 1518/19

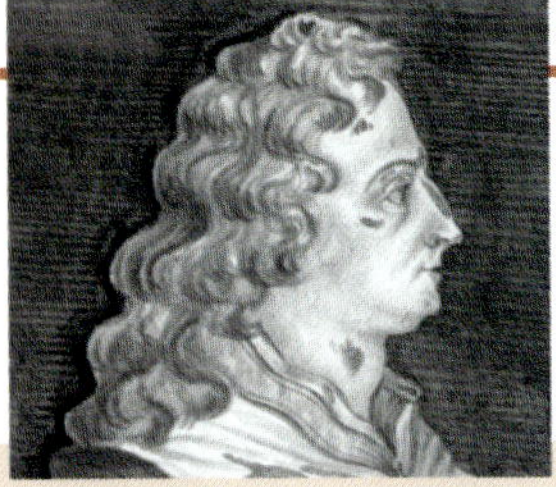

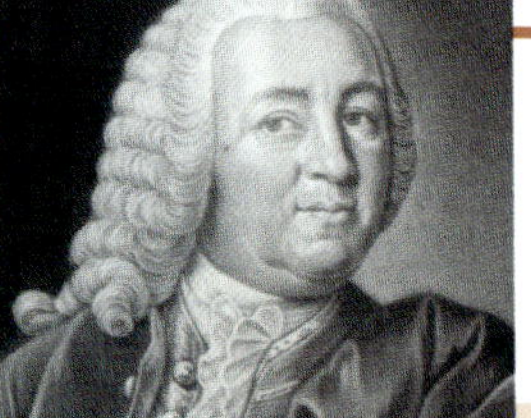

**Pius Nicolaus
v. GARELLI
1723–1739**

**Gerhard Freiherr
van SWIETEN
1745–1772**

1723–1725   1739–1745   1745–1772

BIBLIOTHECA REGIA

Those items in the Library collection that were perceived as especially valuable – its Medieval treasures – were always housed so as to be easily accessible to the emperor, whereas those that had been moved to the Hofburg in Vienna were of a scientific or schorlarly character. During the course of the sixteenth century these were joined by the libraries of scholars and by works produced in printed form. In 1504 the humanist Conradus Celtes (1459–1508), who had arranged and enlarged the Library at the request of the emperor, was the first to refer to it as the *Bibliotheca Regia*.

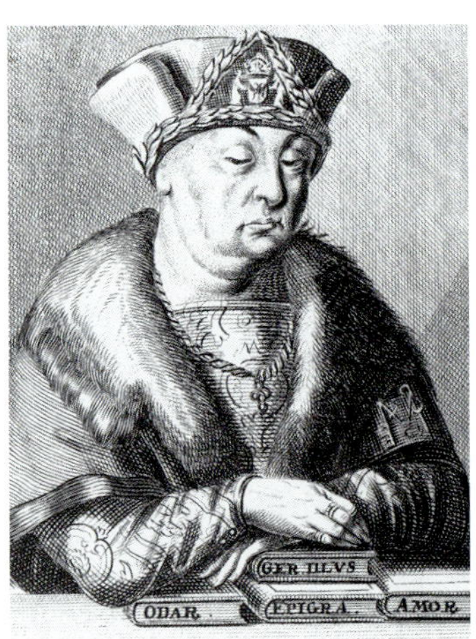

Conradus Celtes 1459–1508

In 1504 the Humanist Conradus Celtes referred to the collections he arranged and enlarged at the request of the emperor as *Bibliotheca Regia*.

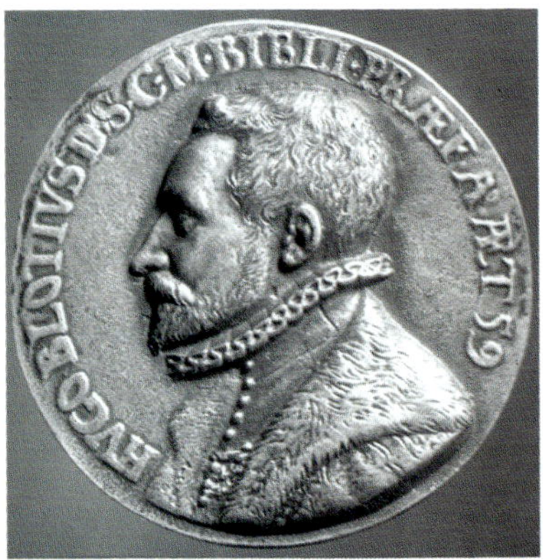

Hugo Blotius 1533–1608

In 1575 this Dutch scholar was the first individual to be formally appointed imperial librarian.

SCHOLARS AND THEIR OWN LIBRARIES

Among the scholars who were to be closely connected with the Court Library over the next seventy years were celebrated individuals such as Wolfgang Lazius (1514–65), who was professor of medicine at the University of Vienna and was appointed official historian to Emperor

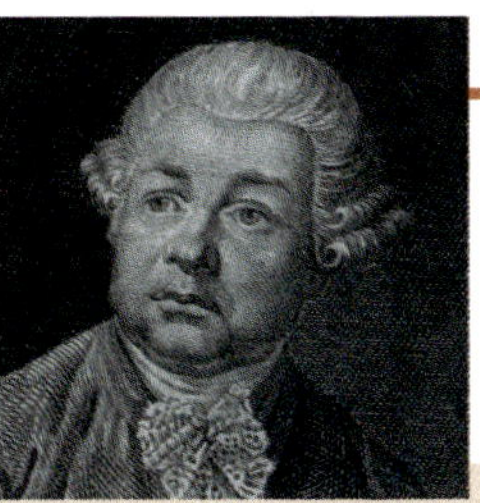

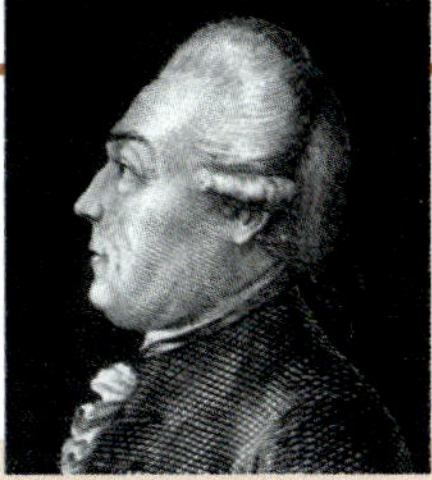

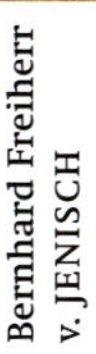

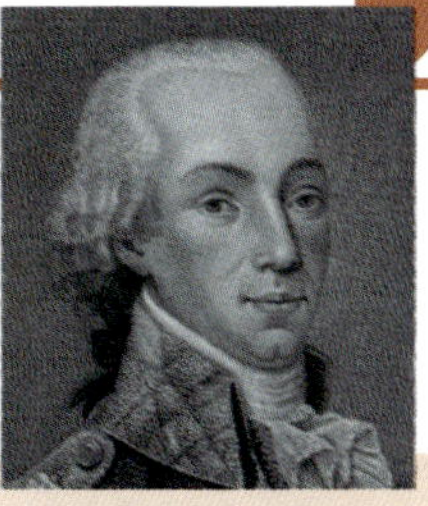

Adam Franz KOLLÁR
v. Keresztén
1772–1777

Gottfried Freiherr
van SWIETEN
1777–1803

Bernhard Freiherr v. JENISCH
1803–1807

Franz Maria Freiherr
v. CARNEA-STEFFANEO
1807–1809

Ferdinand I (b. 1503, r. 1558–64). Lazius undertook three strenuous book-collecting tours around the libraries of the Habsburg territories, visiting Admont, Seckau, St Lambrecht, Friesach, Gurk, St Paul, Cilli, Krain and the surrounding districts, and returned to Vienna with substantial spoils. After his death his collection was absorbed into the Court Library in Vienna.

Since the regency of Maximilian I there had been a growing recognition of the significance of printing, and consequently of the specialized fields of the sciences and of history, genealogy, heraldry and iconology, as potential tools in the legitimization of claims to power. While serving as Ambassador to Constantinople, the diplomat Ghislain de Busbecq (1522–92) acquired valuable Greek manuscripts, of which over 270 have been preserved. Over 560 Greek and Latin manuscripts derive from the collecting activity of Johannes Sambucus (1531–84) in Italy. The catalogue of the collection of Hans Derschwamm (1494–1568), administrator of the Neusohl copper mines leased to the Fuggers by the emperor, lists 651 works. After Derschwamm's death these were sold to the Imperial Library in Vienna.

HUGO BLOTIUS, IMPERIAL COURT LIBRARIAN

It is understandable, given the development of the sciences and of learning in the era of Humanism, that the emperor Maximilian II (b. 1527, r. 1564–76) should in 1575 appoint Hugo Blotius (1534–1608), one of the most widely travelled Dutch scholars of his age, as the first formally recognized Imperial Librarian. When Blotius took up this post, the Imperial Library was housed in a single room at the Minorite monastery not far from the Viennese Hofburg and consisted of around 9,000 items, both manuscripts and printed texts. His principal task was to draw up an inventory of these holdings. To this end, he prepared an index, listing each item by its author; but he also created a thematic catalogue embracing all the items that concerned Turkish history and culture. In 1576 he dedicated this to the new emperor, Rudolf II (b. 1552, r. 1576–1612), on the assumption that it would be of assistance in providing information on the Turks – at that time the most dangerous enemy of the Holy Roman

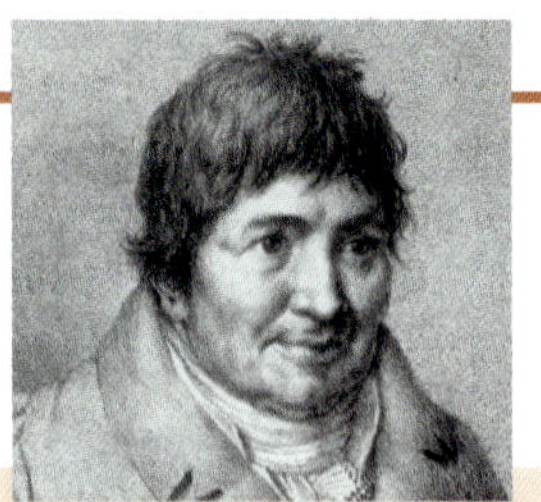

Joseph Maximilian Graf
von TENCZYN OSSOLIŃSKI
1809–1826

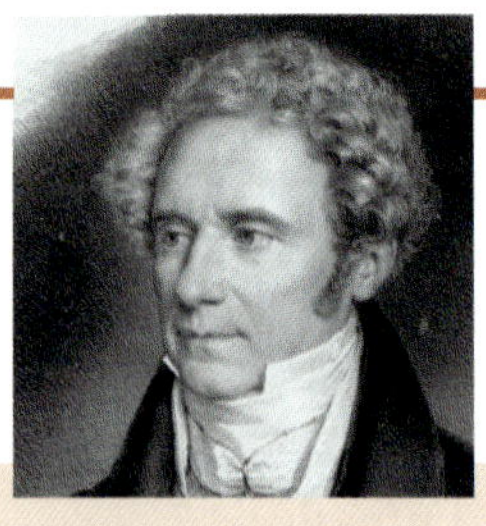

Moritz Joseph Graf
v. DIETRICHSTEIN-
PROSKAU-LESLIE
1826–1845

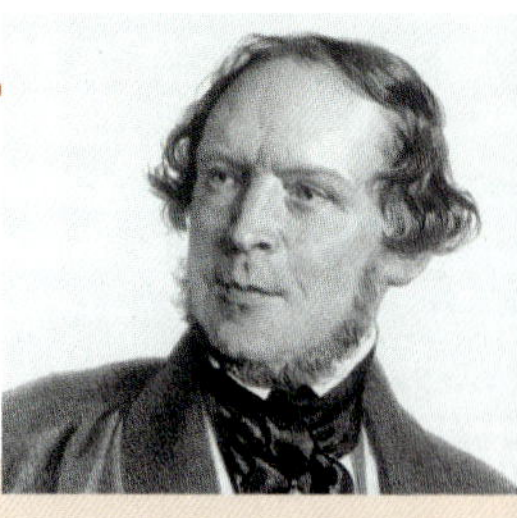

Eligius Franz Joseph Freiherr
MÜNCH v. BELLINGHAUSEN
(known as Friedrich Halm)
1845–1871

Empire. Over the following years this more or less political function of the Court Library was underlined in a series of decrees imposing on publishers in the Habsburg territories the obligation to supply the imperial court in Vienna, free of charge, with a copy of every work that appeared.

Without these sixteenth-century rulings, the Court Library would not have acquired such an astonishing abundance of publications on the most diverse range of scientific and academic disciplines. The prefects of the Court Library were, nonetheless, to complain for centuries of the failure of printers and booksellers to adhere to this obligation. Endeavouring to fill unfortunate gaps through later purchases proved expensive and also cut into an acquisitions budget intended for new foreign publications.

An event of particular significance for the Imperial Court Library was the transfer to Vienna in 1665 of the collections preserved at Schloss Ambras. It was here that the archduke Ferdinand II of Austria-Tyrol (1529–95) installed a veritable chamber of art and curiosities in a museum which is now regarded as the oldest purpose-built structure of its type north of the Alps. After the Tyrolean branch of the Habsburg dynasty died out, the archduke's valuable collection – including manuscripts and printed works amassed by Maximilian I, weapons, armour, paintings, dinner services, and curiosities of every kind – passed to the emperor Leopold I (b. 1640, r. 1658–1705) and thus came to Vienna. It is now preserved in the Kunsthistorisches Museum and in the Austrian National Library.

Also worthy of mention among the great sixteenth- and seventeenth-century collections of books that in the course of time entered the Court Library, is that of Philipp Eduard Fugger (1546–1618), a scion of the banking and trading house. This collection was acquired by the Court Library in 1654 for 15,000 gilders, although it took two years to reach Vienna from Augsburg because its last owner, Albert Fugger (1624–92), was so deeply in debt that the municipal authorities initially delayed its departure, thinking to hold it as collateral. The library comprised 15,000 books, approximately 300 of them in manuscript, but was also notable for its 27 volumes (a total of around 17,000 pages) of summaries of current events, the 'Fugger News-Letters'. These are now of great interest for historians researching communications in the early modern period.

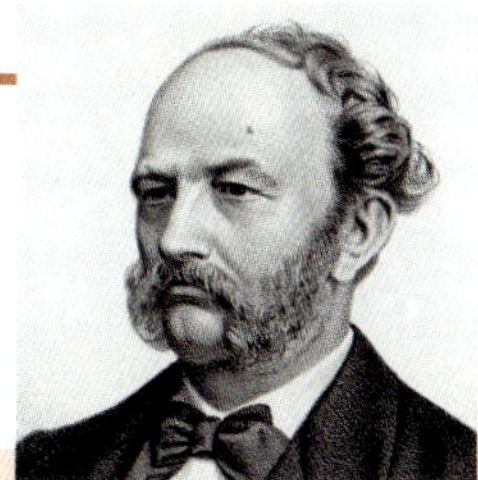

Ernst Ritter v. BIRK
1871–1891

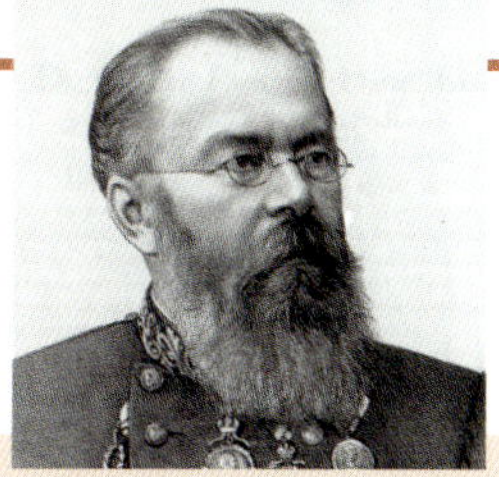

Wilhelm Ritter
v. HARTEL
1891–1896

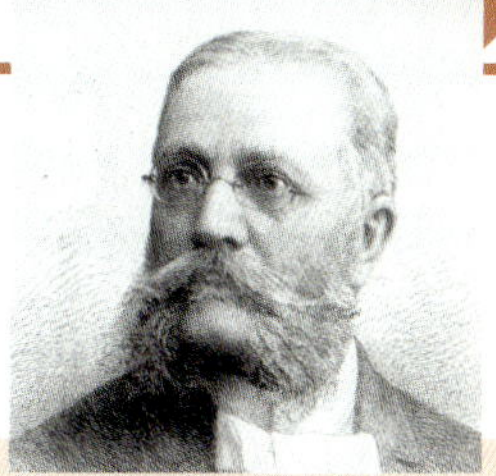

Heinrich Ritter
v. ZEISSBERG
1896–1899

CONSTRUCTION OF THE STATE HALL

The crucial turning-point in the history of the Court Library occurred in the eighteenth century. In 1722 the emperor Charles VI (b. 1685, r. 1711–40) ordered the construction of a library building on what is now Josefsplatz, thereby realizing a scheme devised by his father, Leopold I, but delayed by the Spanish War of Succession and then the

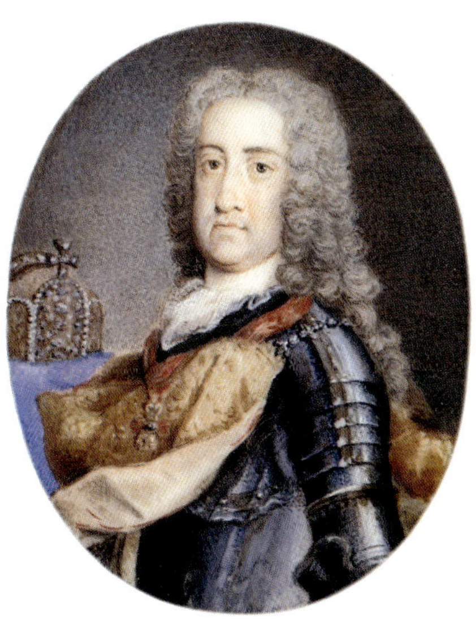

Emperor Charles VI
b. 1685, r. 1711–40
miniature of an
unknown artist.

In 1722 Charles VI ordered the construction of a new building to house the Library.

continuing wars against the Turks. Designed by Johann Bernhard Fischer von Erlach, the new library was built between 1723 and 1726 under the supervision of his son, Josef Emanuel. Work on its decoration continued until 1730, including the frescos in its State Hall, which was to become the Baroque showpiece of this first real home of the Imperial Court Library. From 1730 until well into the nineteenth century, the State Hall housed the Library's entire collection of manuscripts, incunabula, printed material, maps, globes, manuscript and printed musical scores, autographs, drawings and prints.

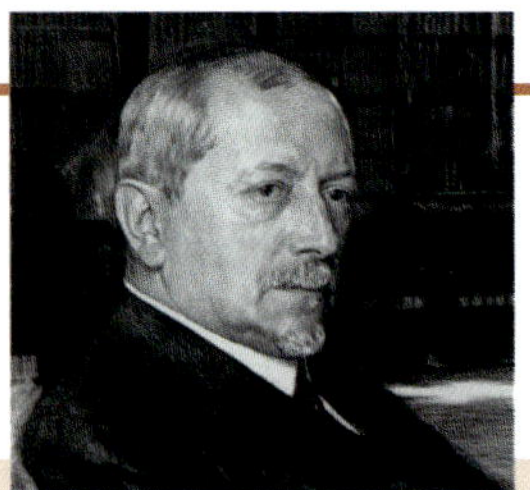

Josef Ritter v. KARABAČEK
1899–1917

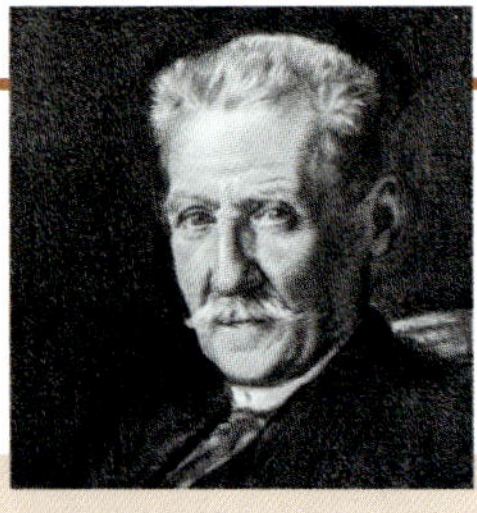

Josef DONABAUM
1917–1922

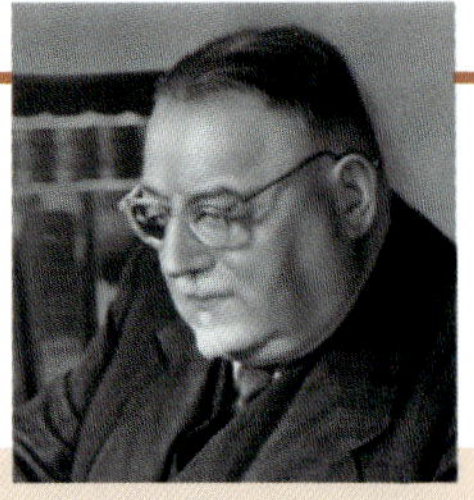

Josef BICK
1923–1938 und 1945–1949

Even at this relatively early date the Library was open to the public, between 8 and 12 in the morning. The emperor's 'instructions for users' read as follows:

Emperor Charles, son of the sublime emperor Leopold, Augustus, has determined that his library shall be for general use. No one is to enter unannounced or to touch the bookcases. Each reader must formally request the book he requires, use it and not tamper with it, that is to say not damage it by tearing or cutting it or adding scribbled notes. Bookmarks may, however, be used and excerpts of texts may be copied out. Readers must not lean on the book they are consulting, nor write on paper that is resting on it. Ink and pounce must be kept well away from the book. The ignorant, servants, layabouts, gossip-mongers and idlers should keep out. Silence must be observed. Users should take care not to disturb others by reading aloud. When one wishes to leave the library, one should close the book that has been consulted. If it is small, it should be returned to the attendant; if it is large, it is to be left on the table and the attention of the attendant drawn to it. Those using the library need pay nothing; departing richer than when they arrived, they will return the more often.

Primarily, however, the Court Library served in the eighteenth century as a showcase for imperial self-representation.

Gerhard and Gottfried van Swieten

In 1745 the empress Maria Theresia (b. 1717, r. 1745–80), daughter of Charles VI, appointed Gerhard van Swieten (who later became her personal physician) to the post of prefect of the Court Library in Vienna. In Holland he had become familiar with modern publishing practice, and in Leiden in particular he had the opportunity to learn about modern approaches to library science. Installed in his new post, he significantly modernized the process of making new acquisitions at the Court Library: utilizing his contacts with booksellers in Paris, Venice and Leiden, he amassed a collection of contemporary scientific literature from across western Europe. But Gerhard van Swieten also presided over a committee charged with the censorship of books, and he censored numerous works by leading representatives of the French Enlightenment. The Austrian

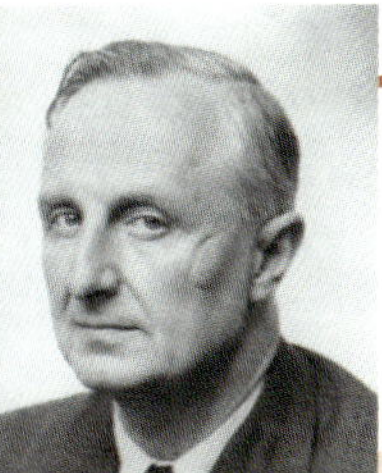

Paul HEIGL
1938–1945

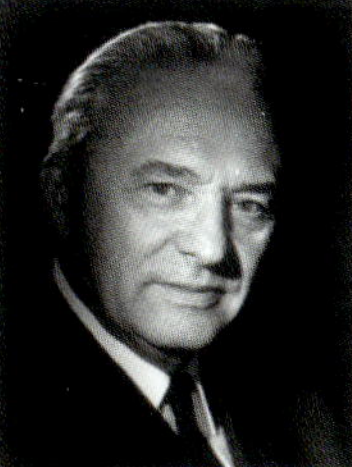

Hugo HÄUSLE
1945 – appointed interim director

Josef STUMMVOLL
1949–1967

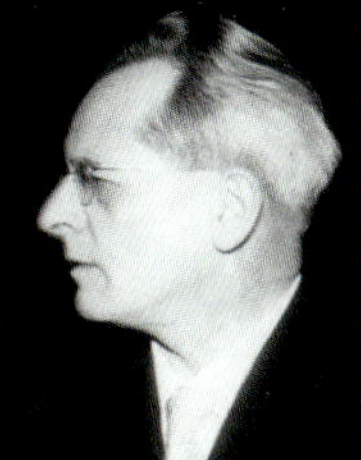

Leopold NOWAK
1968 – appointed director for two months

National Library still has in its possession a manuscript volume in which Gerhard van Swieten commented on the books he censored.

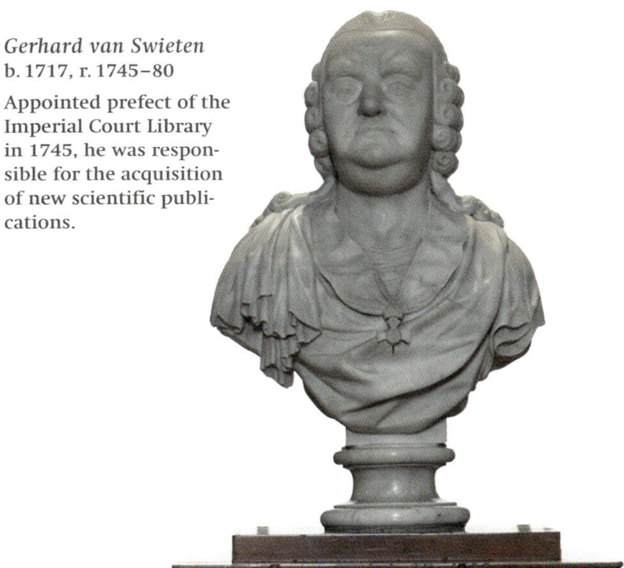

Gerhard van Swieten
b. 1717, r. 1745–80

Appointed prefect of the Imperial Court Library in 1745, he was responsible for the acquisition of new scientific publications.

THE WORLD'S FIRST CARD CATALOGUE

Gottfried van Swieten, the son of Gerhard, served as prefect of the Court Library from 1777 to 1803. It was in this period that the emperor Joseph II (b. 1741, r. 1765–90), the son of Maria Theresia, dissolved most of the monasteries in the Habsburg territories. As a result, around 300 manuscripts, 3,000 printed works and 5,000 charters came into the possession of the Court Library. Gottfried van Swieten also made a significant contribution to the organizational development of the Court Library. In 1780 he initiated the creation of what proved to be the world's first card catalogue for a library. Earlier library catalogues were self-contained volumes unsuited to keeping track of an expanding collection. The card catalogue was the first technical means of maintaining records that were up to date.

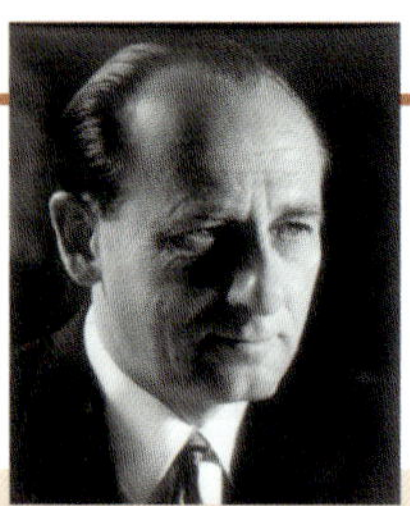

Rudolf FIEDLER
1968–1977

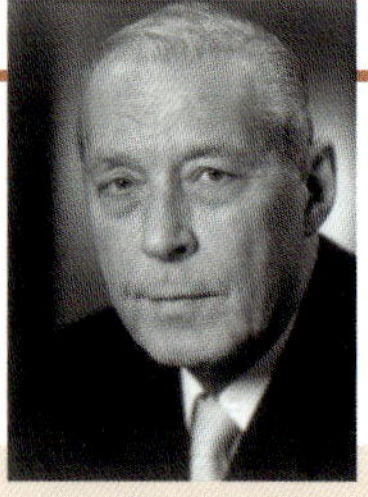

Karl KAMMEL
1978–1979

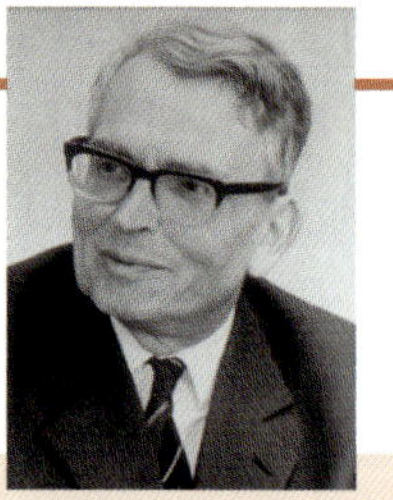

Josef ZESSNER-
SPITZENBERG
1980–1983

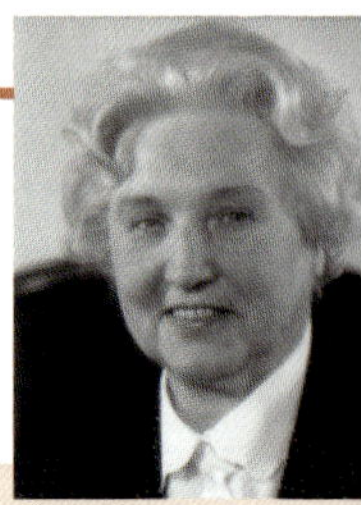

Magda STREBL
1983–1993

THE NATIONAL LIBRARY OF THE AUSTRIAN EMPIRE

In early 1807 the Curator Paul Strattmann penned the following programmatic description of the principal tasks of the Court Library: 'The Imperial Court Library … is the library for the educated class in the capital … It is the national library of the Austrian Empire. … Finally, it is the library of the Imperial Court, from which it takes its name.' The role the Court Library was to play until the end of 1918 – that of national library for the Austrian Empire – was thereby defined for the first time.

During the nineteenth century a number of important Slavic scholars played a significant role at the Court Library, among them Bartholomäus Kopitar, the Slovene founder of Slavic and Balkan studies in Vienna. Today, the Austrian National Library possesses around 300,000 printed works and 200 manuscripts in Slavic languages, making it one of the largest and most important Slavic collections to be found outside the Slavic language area.

The development of the Library from the nineteenth century onwards is distinguished by the foundation of separate special collections in order that distinct groups of objects, such as papyri, manuscripts, maps, scores and other musical material, portraits and prints, be better and more scientifically preserved and processed. It was above all Moritz Graf von Dietrichstein, in charge of the Library between 1826 and 1845, who recognized the scientific value of a specifically targeted collecting policy. During the first half of the nineteenth century the collecting activity of the Court Library was finally able to free itself from its overriding task of imperial self-representation. This was largely a by-product of the intellectual history of the nineteenth century, in particular the rise of the universities and the institutionalization of scholarly research.

THE ERA OF READING

In 1848, the year of revolution, when Vienna was shelled by Imperial troops, there was a fire at the Hofburg and the Court Library had to be temporarily moved. After the defeat of the revolutionaries and the accession of the emperor Francis Joseph I (r. 1848–1916), on 2 December

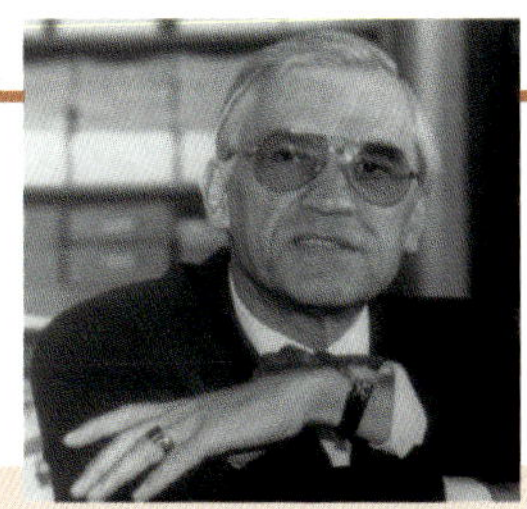

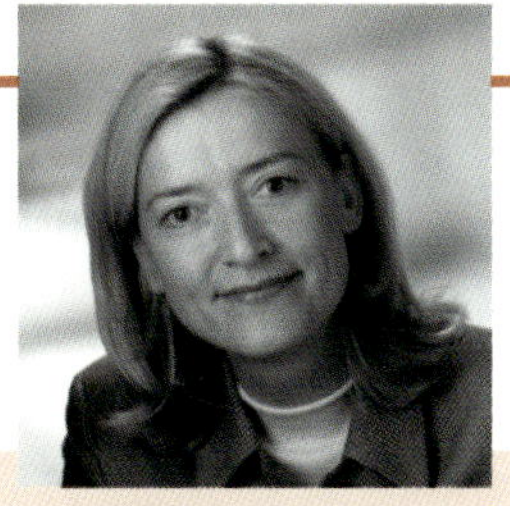

Hans MARTE
1993–2001

Johanna RACHINGER
from June 2001

1848, it became politically expedient to re-open the Court Library to read-ers. In 1848 a request that the opening hours be extended to the evening was granted.

Ernst von Birk, prefect from 1871 to 1891, had been, since 1846, in charge of a 27-year project to re-catalogue the entire holdings of printed material in the Court Library. The catalogue he initiated, eventually embracing items published between 1501 and 1929, is still in use today.

Birk's successor, Wilhelm von Hartel, who served from 1891 to 1896, was a scholar who greatly improved conditions for the Library's users, by mak-ing accessible to them more of the library's holdings and introducing cards on which books could be ordered.

In 1906, with the opening of the Augustinerlesersaal, the Court Library acquired a reading room of its own.

From Court Library to National Library

1918 brought the dissolution of he Austro-Hungarian monar-chy and, with it, the end of an era in European history. An unambiguous democratization of the cultural legacy of the Habsburgs was now required, as well as the re-arrangement of their collections, which had become state property. In 1919 the Imperial Library passed into the con-trol of the state, and in 1920 it was formally re-named the National Library.

After the end of the monarchy the Austrian Republic sought a national identity not in Austria but, rather, in Germany. It is notable that the col-lecting policy of the Library in the inter-war years was distinctly slanted towards German publications, and was in this respect quite out of keep-ing with the traditions of the national library of the Austrian Empire. Over the course of several centuries, scholars from all over Europe worked in one capacity or another at the Library. And its history and its holdings were, and are, a reflection of the diversity of the Austria and of its multi-national legacy.

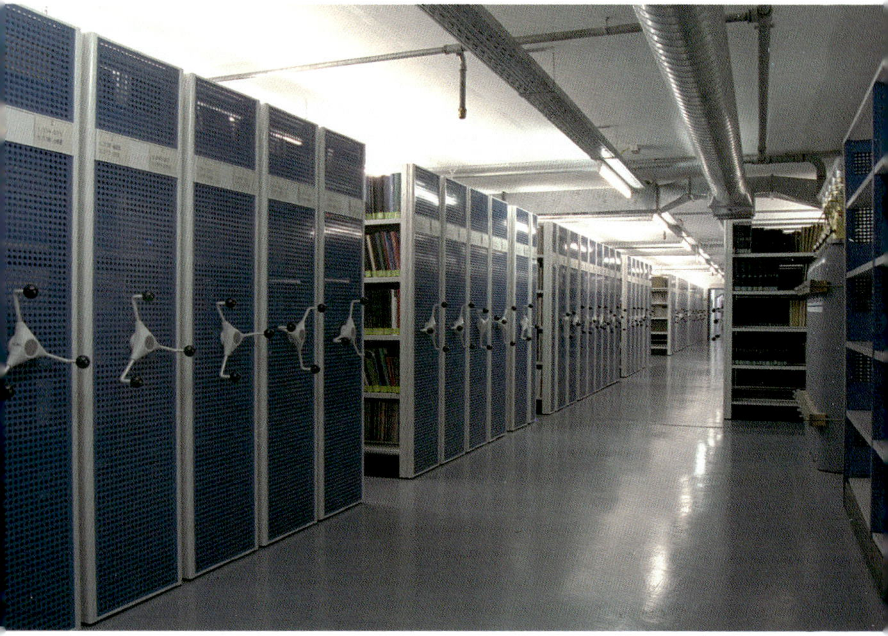

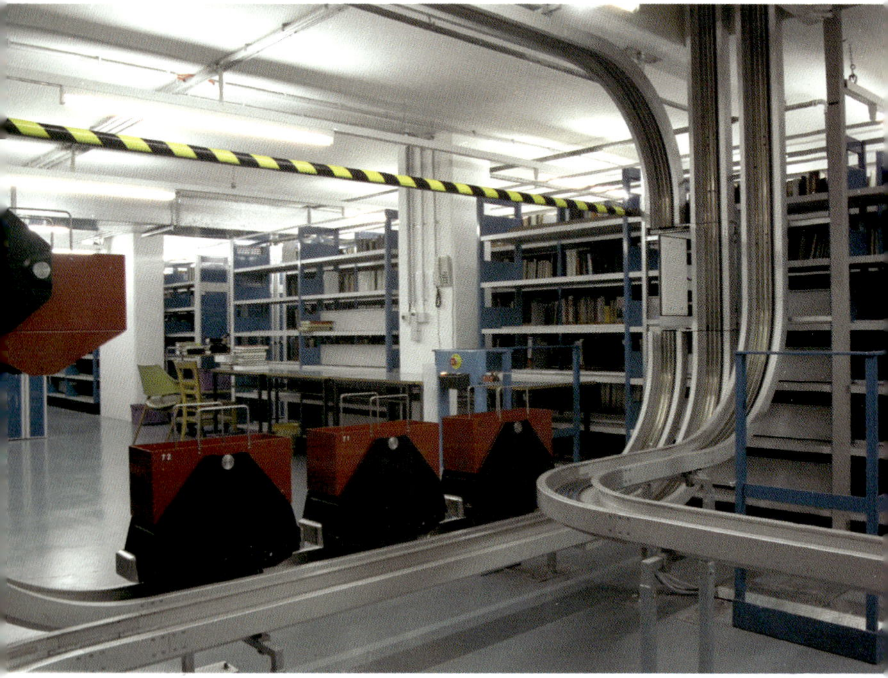

Modern underground storage

Opened in 1992, this facility is used as up-to-date
library storage space.

With the annexation of Austria to Hitler's National Socialist Germany in March 1938 the Library entered on a distinctly unhappy chapter of its history. Within a few days of the *Anschluss*, the director-general, Josef Bick (1880–1952), was arrested and his post assumed by Paul Heigl (1887–1945). From the start, Heigl, a committed National Socialist, used his elevated political position to implement an aggressive acquisitions policy. Entire libraries and collections belonging, above all, to Jewish victims of the National Socialist regime and to others being persecuted on political grounds, entered the Library at this time as booty. A substantial amount of this was given or sold to other institutions in the German Empire; so that at the end of the war it was no longer possible, in many cases, to achieve a full restitution of illegally seized material. Only with the publication, in December 2003, of the results of an enquiry into the provenance of these acquisitions was the Austrian National Library able definitively to close this sad chapter in its history.

THE AUSTRIAN NATIONAL LIBRARY IN THE SECOND AUSTRIAN REPUBLIC

After 1945, in keeping with the socio-political development of the state as a whole, the Austrian National Library, as it was now officially called, was able to assume its role as a symbol of the Austrian nation and, as such, to contribute to the emergence of a new national identity.

In 1966 the Library was again able to expand, by moving into substantial sections of the Neue Hofburg, where the Main Reading Room still in use today was installed. In 2004 the old reading rooms on Heldenplatz were renovated, the Main Reading Room and the Newspaper Reading Room connected with a glazed lift, and further re-building undertaken so as to provide access for the disabled. A newly furnished readers' lounge in the Hall of Columns has also been installed as an additional service to users.

The opening in 1992 of new underground storage space not only solved a storage problem but also provided an additional space for the use of new media and outsize printed matter. However, with the addition of around 60,000 volumes each year, this underground storage space will have reached its full capacity by 2010. The creation of new underground storage space below Heldenplatz has therefore been planned.

A significant shift in the focus of the Library as a building was achieved in 1999 with the extension of the ground floor, so as to provide a multi-functional area for organized events. A project currently being implemented, and due for completion in 2005, is the renovation and adaptation of Palais Mollard to house the Department of Music, the Globe Museum, the Esperanto Museum and the department of Planned Languages.

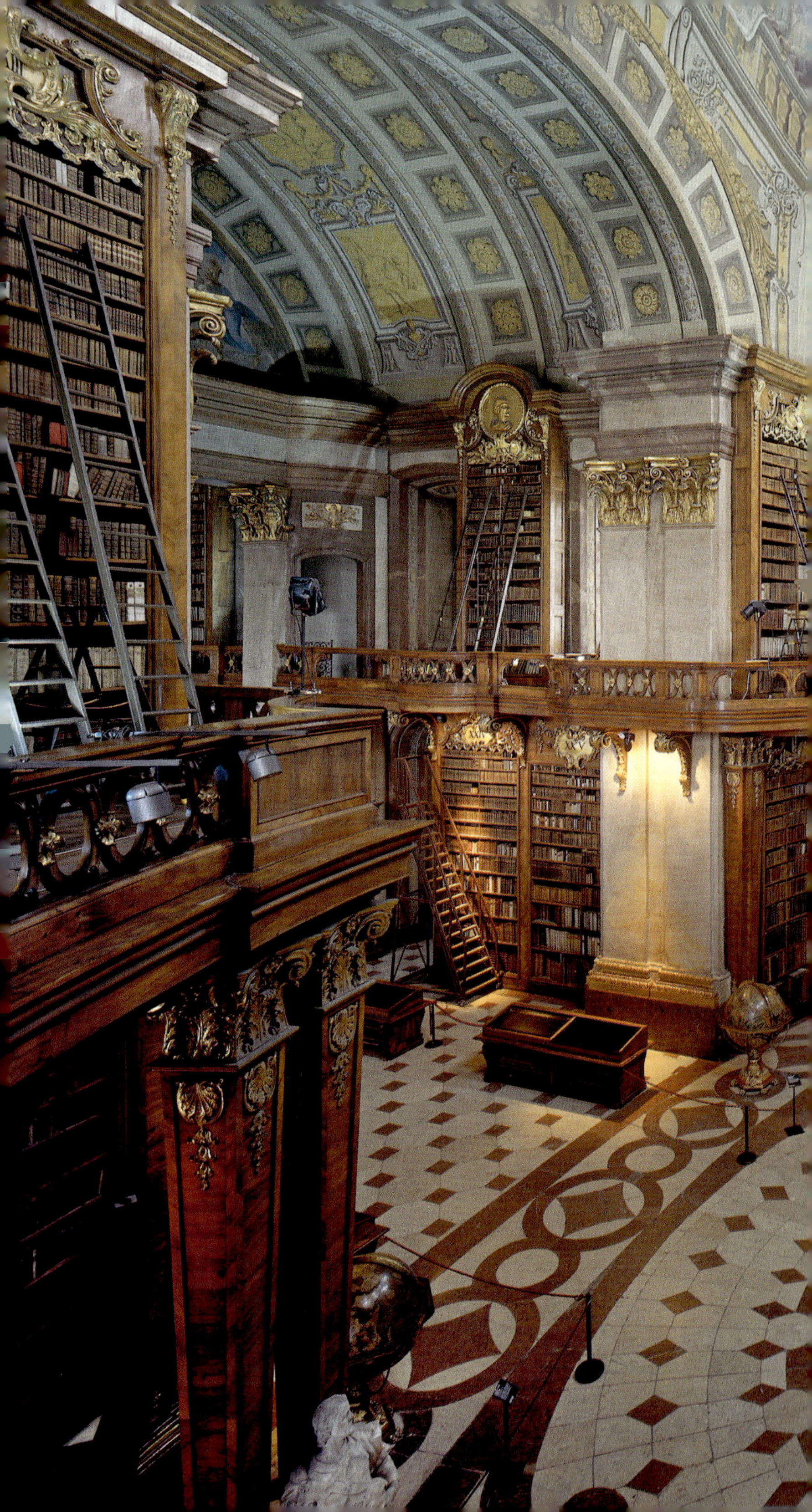

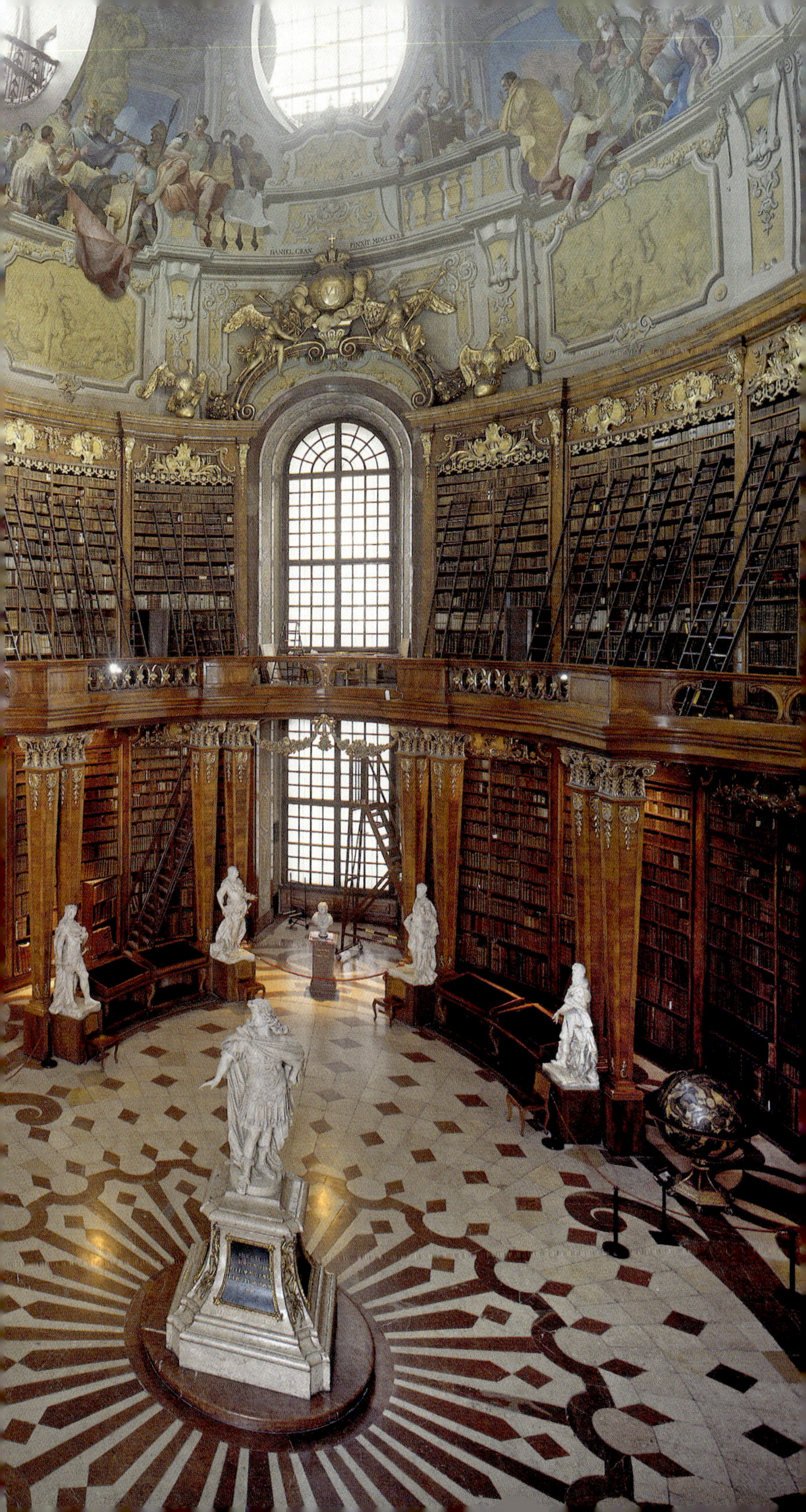

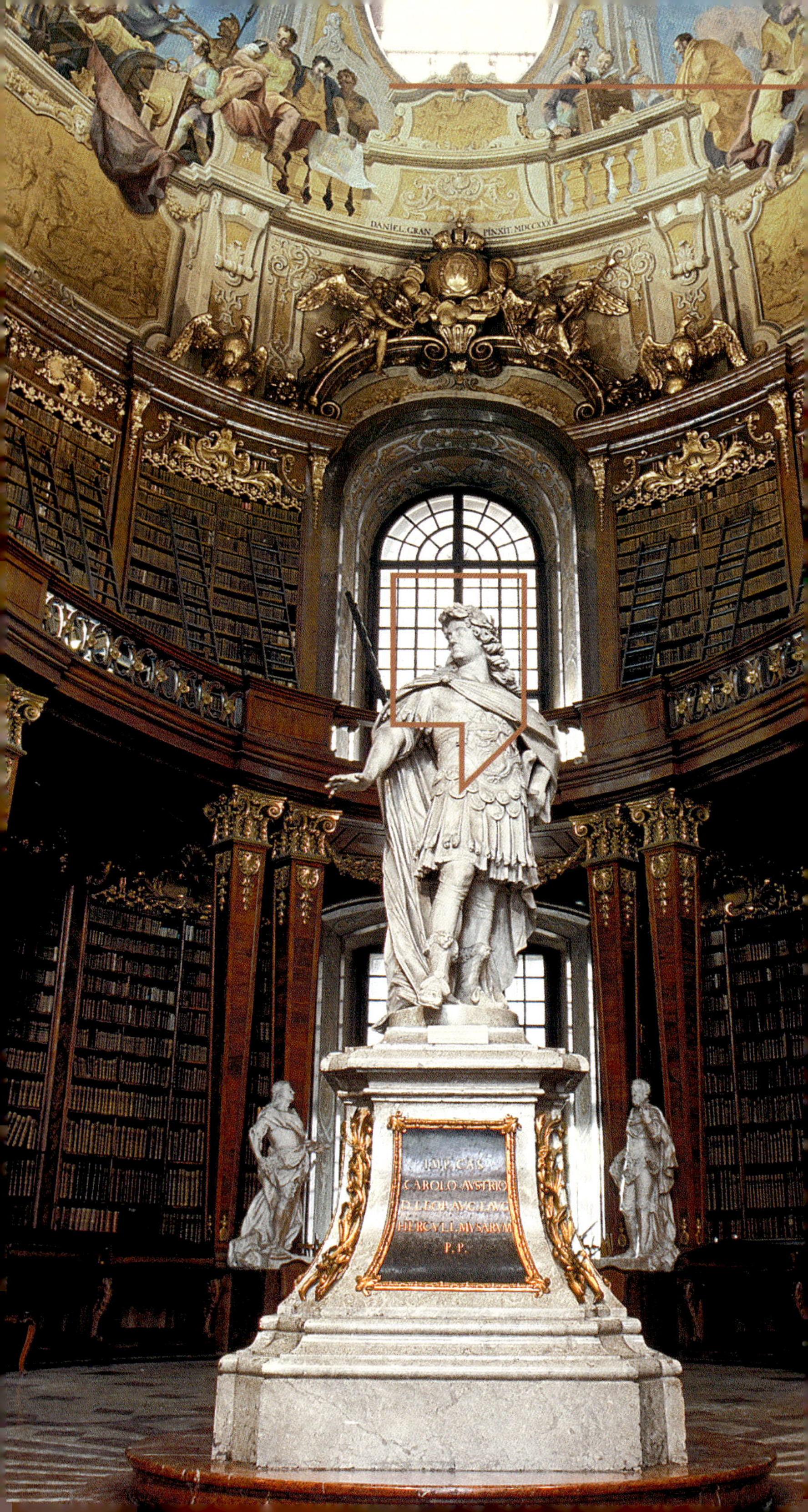

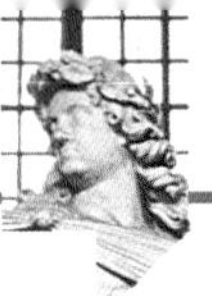

State Hall

At the time when Hugo Blotius (1575–1608) served as the first appointed prefect, the Imperial Court Library was housed in the Minorite Monastery. The well-house of the complex, situated adjacent to the monastery, produced, however, an atmosphere that was so humid as to compromise the safe preservation of the Library's valuable holdings. Between 1623 and 1630, therefore, the collection was stored in the Hofburg (in the area more or less corresponding to the present-day Imperial Chancellery Wing). Subsequently they were moved to the Harrach House, which had been acquired by the emperor, but there was soon so little space that the erection of a building to house the Library came to be seen as absolutely indispensable.

In 1681 the emperor Leopold I resolved that a building should be erected on the Tummelplatz (the later Josefsplatz), its ground floor to serve as an indoor riding arena and its first floor as library storage space. Shortly before the work was completed, however, this building was so severely damaged during the second Turkish siege of Vienna that the planned library storage was never installed.

It was only forty years later, after the Spanish War of Succession and the last of the wars against the Turks, that the emperor Charles VI ordered the construction of the library that survives to this day as the State Hall. This was built between 1723 and 1726 to the plans of Johann Bernhard Fischer von Erlach (1665–1723) by his son Josef Emanuel (1693–1742). Work on the decoration of the State Hall, including its frescoes, continued until 1730.

To cover the costs of this project, Charles VI instituted a new temporary tax on printers, to be paid on every sale of a calendar. He also imposed a

Statue of Emperor Charles VI as Hercules Musarum, protector and patron of the arts and sciences (left)

Oval cupola of the State Hall with its wooden bookcases, see pp. 26/27

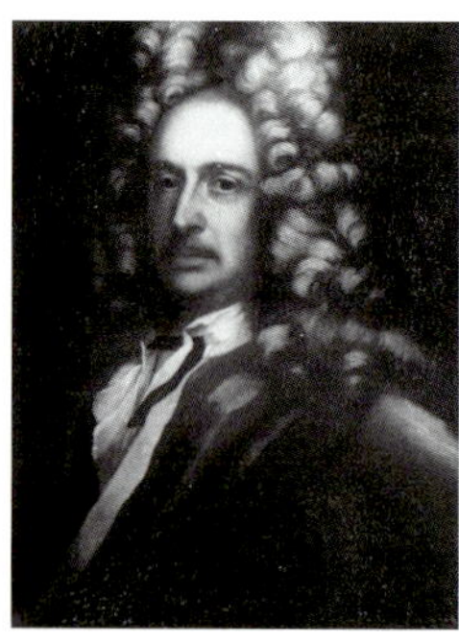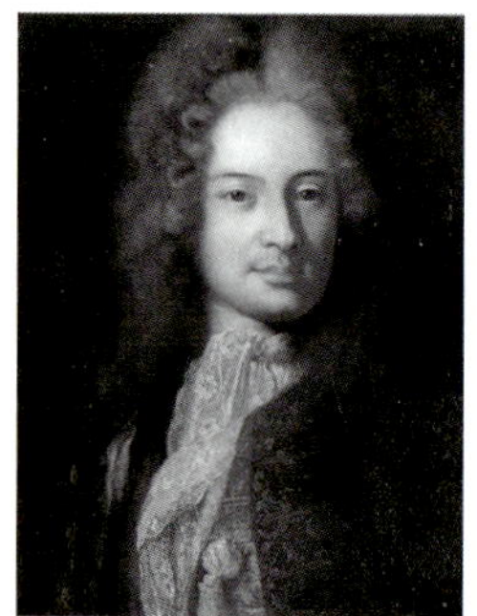

Johann Bernhard Fischer von Erlach 1665–1723 (left)

His son, Josef Emanuel 1693–1742 (right)

Oil paintings of an unknown artist in the Camera praefecti

tax on newspapers. Even before the completion of building work, however, he resolved that the newspaper tax should remain 'in perpetuum' so that its proceeds might in future provide funds for acquisitions and maintenance of the Library.

THE BUILDING

The State Hall spans the entire façade facing the north-east on Josefsplatz, thereby linking the Hofburg with the Augustinerkirche and the Albertina. Fourteen Ionic columns aligned along the ground floor, are punctuated by three grand entrances. An attic above the central entrance bears the following inscription:

Lorenzo Mattielli *Minerva with a quadriga* c. 1726

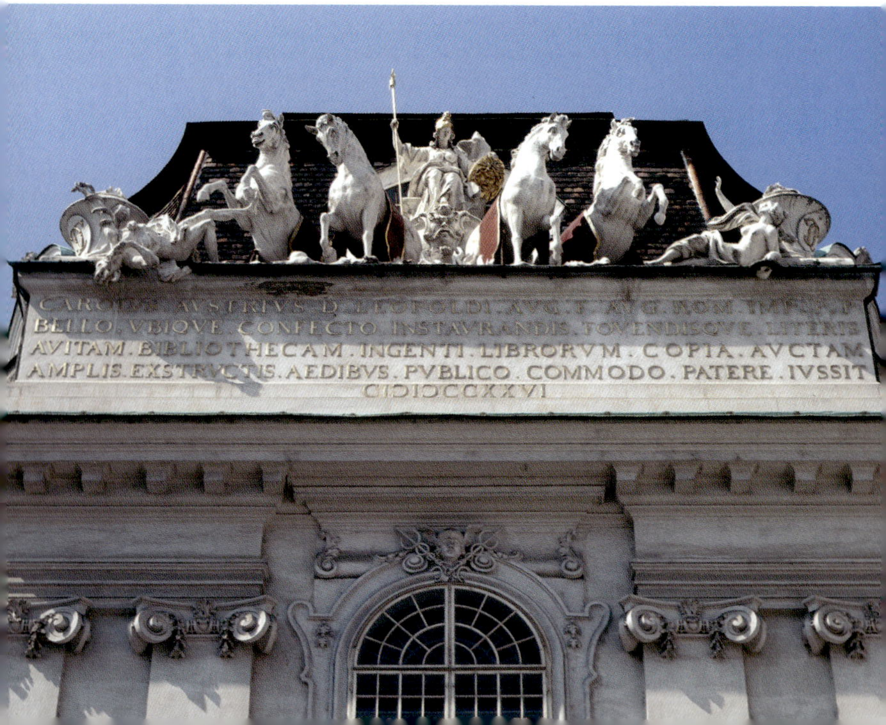

CAROLUS AUSTRIUS D. LEOPOLDI AUG. F. AUG. ROM. IMP. P. P.
BELLO UBIQUE CONFECTO INSTAURANDIS FOVENDISQUE LITERIS
AVITAM BIBLIOTHECAM INGENTI LIBRORUM COPIA AUCTAM
AMPLIS EXTRUCTIS AEDIBUS PUBLICO COMMODO PATERE IUSSIT.
MDCCXXVI

Charles of Austria, Son of the immortal emperor Leopold, Roman Emperor, father of the nation, after a general end to war has substantially enlarged the library inherited by him for the perpetual promotion of the sciences and has housed it in a spacious new building for the use of the public. 1726

Above the attic we find a group of figures in stone by Lorenzo Mattielli (1688–1748): the goddess Minerva/Pallas Athena with a quadriga is shown triumphing over the fallen figures of Envy and Ignorance. Above the lateral wing to the right we find Tellus or Gaea bearing a terrestrial globe, accompanied by Geometry and Geography. The counterpart to this group, above the lateral wing to the left, comprises Atlas, shouldering an enormous celestial sphere, accompanied by Astronomy and Astrology.

Both lateral wings were built between 1767 and 1773 by Nikolaus Parcassi (1716–90). That on the right houses the Redoutensäle (Ballroom and Banqueting Hall) and part of the Spanish Riding School; that on the left initially held the Imperial Collection of Naturalia, which was later moved to the purpose-built Natural History Museum. The spaces thus vacated were then allocated to the Court Library. It was only in 1748 that Josefs-

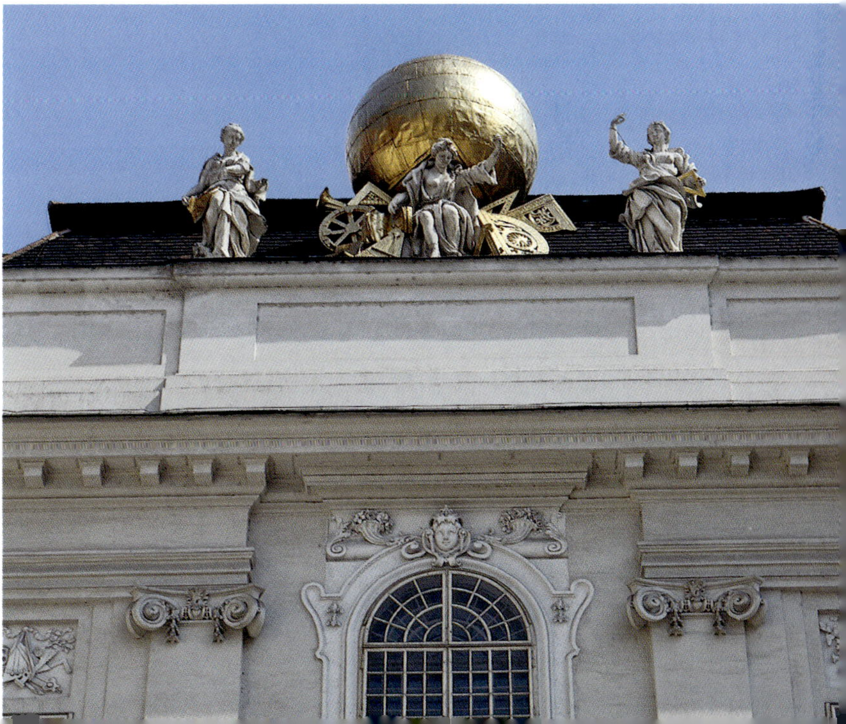

Lorenzo Mattielli *Tellus bearing a terrestrial globe, accompanied by Geometry and Geography* c. 1726

platz assumed its present-day appearance, following adaptations ordered by Joseph II (b. 1741, r. 1765–90). On account of its architectonically self-contained character, it is now regarded as one of the most beautiful squares in Vienna. The equestrian monument to Joseph II that stands at the centre of the square was made between 1795 and 1807 by the sculptor Franz Anton Zauner.

The State Hall is 77.7 metres in length, 14.2 metres in breadth, and 19.6 metres in height. It has an essentially tripartite structure, with two long bays divided by a central, taller section (of 29.2 metres) crowned by an oval cupola, and this is further emphasized by the scheme of frescoed decoration devised by Daniel Gran (1694–1757). The result is an outstanding example of profane architecture that has consciously incorporated elements of a sacred nature.

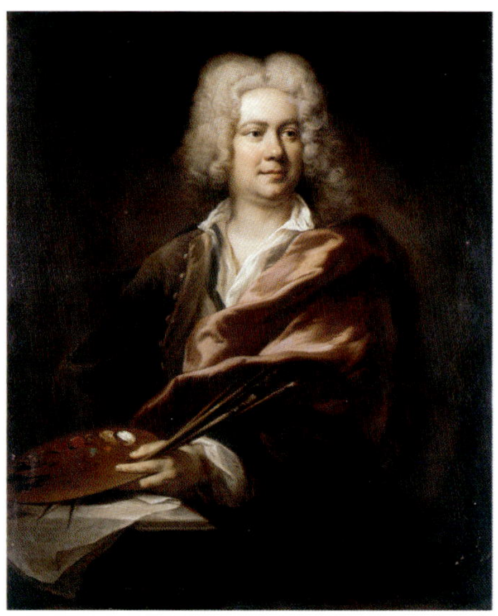

Daniel Gran 1694–1757 oil painting of an unknown artist in the Camera praefecti

The Austrian Baroque painter was the creator of the cupola fresco in the State Hall.

At the centre of the space beneath the cupola (see pp. 26–27) stands a life-size marble figure of Charles VI as Roman imperator, one of a total of sixteen figures of imperial predecessors, Austrian statesmen and victorious military leaders to be found in the State Hall, all of these the work of Paul and Peter Strudel (respectively, 1648–1708 and 1660–1714). Placed at the 'sacred' centre of the State Hall, the emperor is here identified as Hercules Musarum, the protector and patron of the sciences and the arts. The Library becomes thus the embodiment of the victor's claim to universal power.

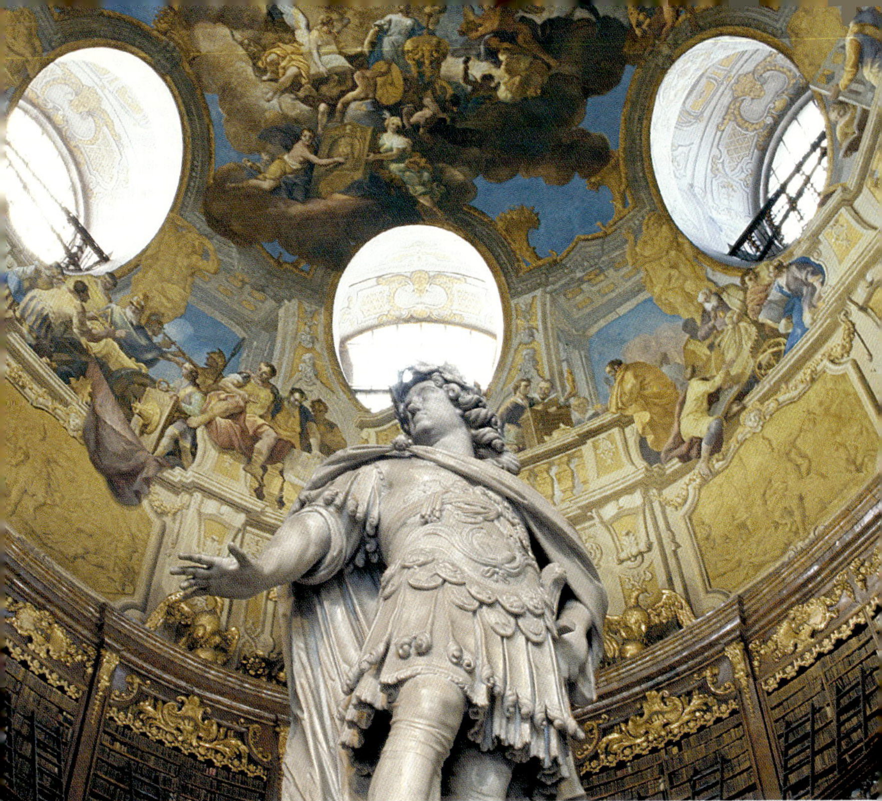

View of the cupola
Statue of Charles VI as Roman imperator

The oval cupola itself measures 18 by 29.2 metres. Its base is marked off from the bays extending to each side by two pairs of columns in stucco lustro, representing the pillars of Hercules and thereby alluding both to Charles VI's motto, 'constantia et fortitudine' (Steadfastness and Strength), and to his claims to Spain.

The fresco decoration in the bay facing Josefsplatz, where visitors now enter the State Hall, depicts profane and military themes, whereas the opposite bay adjoining the Hofburg (the entrance formerly reserved for the emperor and his court) shows allegorical representations of the heavens and of peace. The emperor, effectively placed in the centre, holds the balance between war and peace. He is both a war hero and a heroic peace-maker.

The fresco in the cupola combines an apotheosis of Charles VI with an allegory of the history of the construction of the library building. The Baroque scheme for the fresco decoration in honour of the emperor as a powerful ruler was devised by Conrad Adolph von Albrecht (1682–1751), a scholar attached to the imperial court. His programme is recorded in two manuscripts now to be found in the Austrian National Library (Codex No. 7853 and Codex No. 8334, while a third, shorter account is preserved in the Archive of the Monastery of St Florian in Upper Austria.

THE FRESCOES ON THE THEME OF WAR

On entering the State Hall, one sees, in the lunette above the first pair of columns, the figure of Cadmus, who was commanded by Minerva to sow the earth with the teeth of a slain dragon. From these 'seeds', warriors sprang forth. According to the myth, it was Cadmus who gave man the alphabet. As a result of his mastery of the practical arts, including the art of war, he was able to save Harmony and Universal Order.

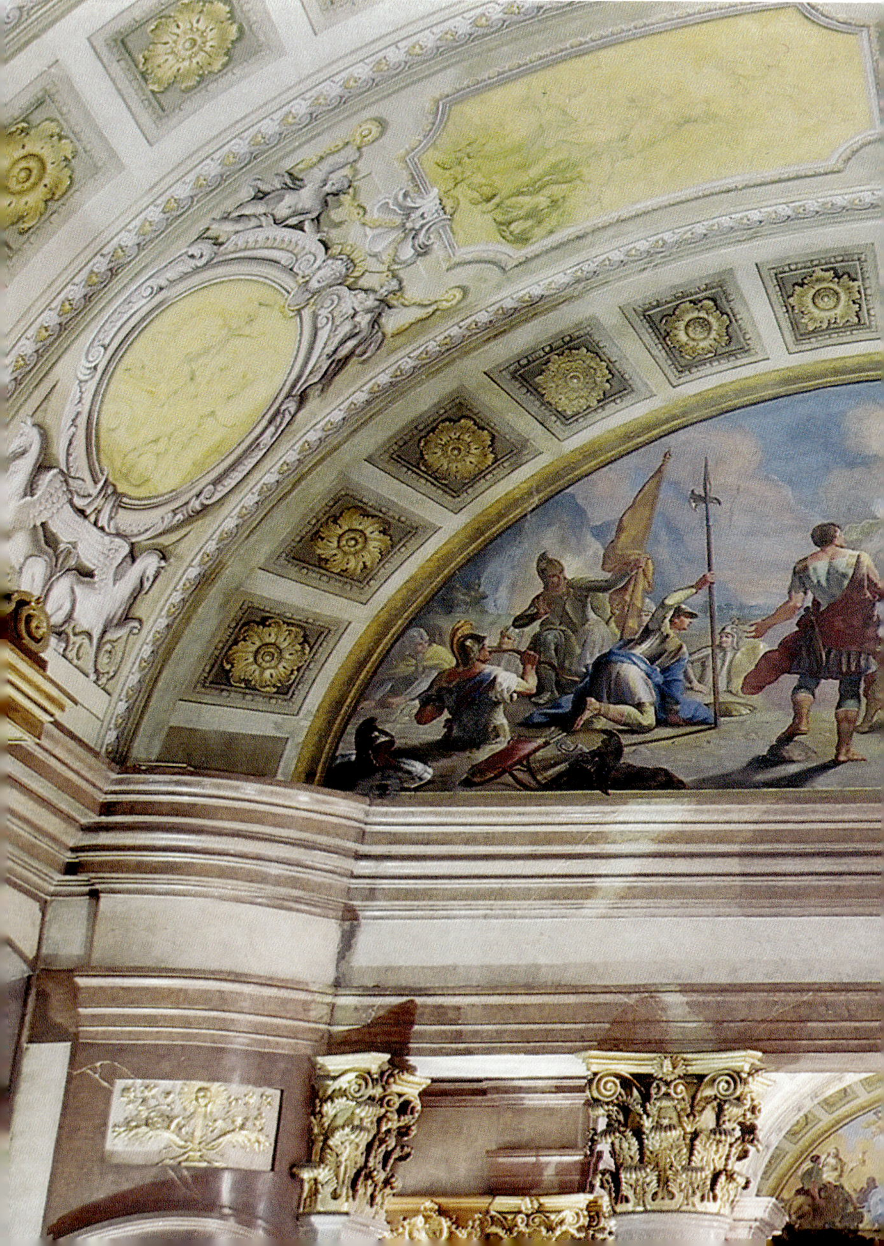

At the centre of the ceiling fresco in this bay is the allegorical figure of
Vigilance, accompanied by Hygiene and Agriculture. Beneath the lower
edge of the principal scene there are allegories of the Mechanical Arts and
the Art of Defence.

Cadmus sowing the dragon's teeth, fresco on the theme of war
in the lunette above the first pair of columns

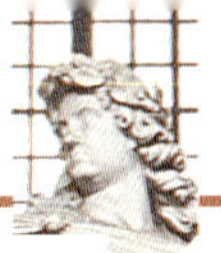

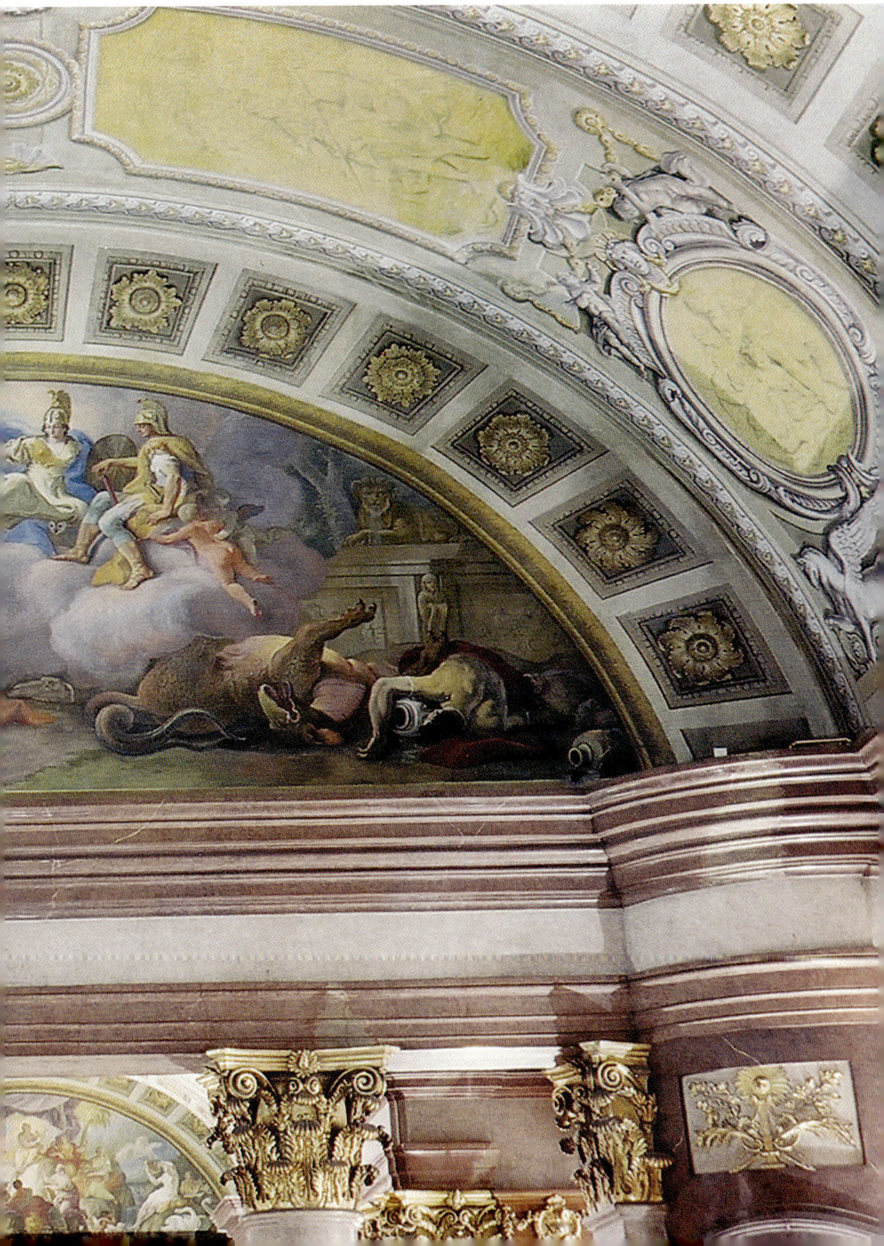

The fresco on the cupola side of the aforementioned lunette shows the forge of Vulcan. An allegorical figure representing the Quest for Knowledge is alarmed by the sound of weapons but in time of war is accompanied by the Genii of Valour. As the visitor progresses through the State Hall the Arts of War give way to the Arts of Peace. In the Baroque iconography of power the allegorical representations of War and Peace, of the earthly and the heavenly spheres, of Strength and Wisdom, do not signal opposites but, rather, the complementary facets of a perfectly ordered world, which finds its centre in the figure of the ruler. The sole task of

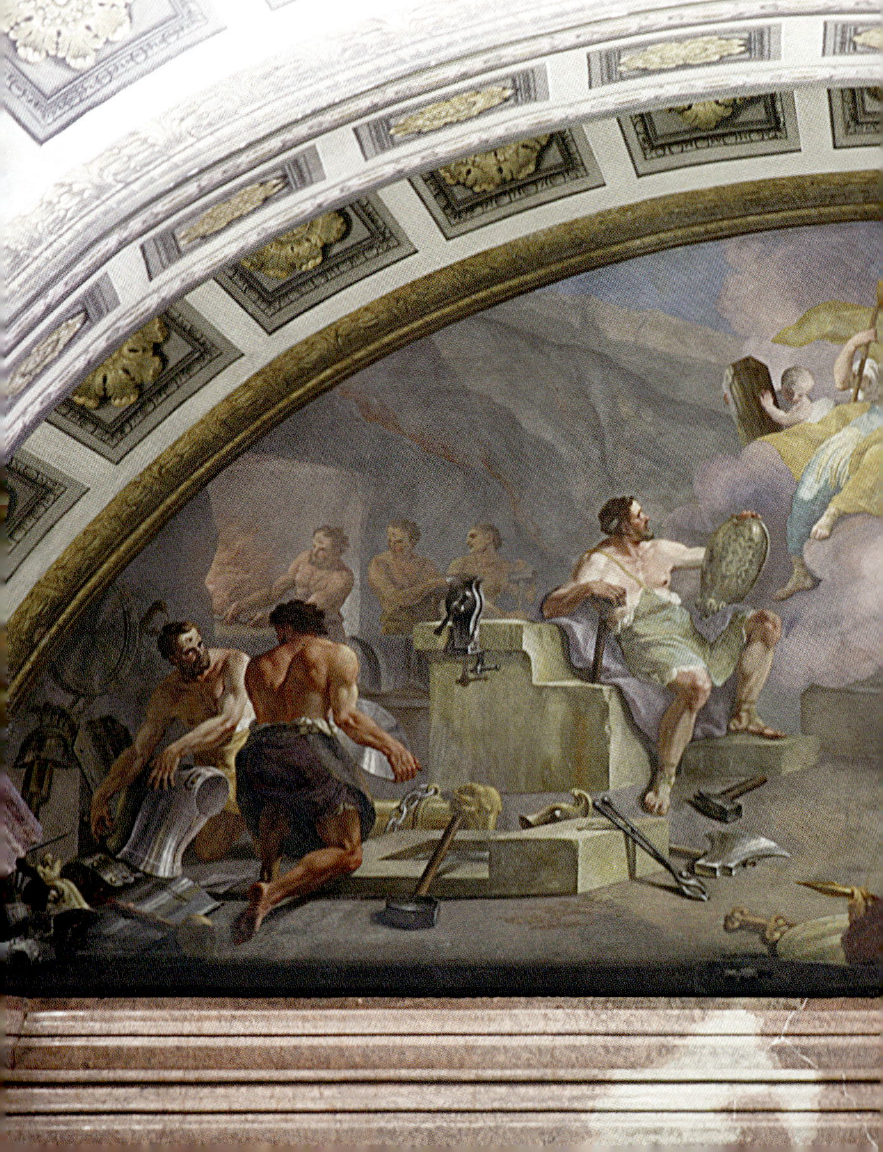

learning and the sciences is to preserve this perfectly ordered world for
posterity.

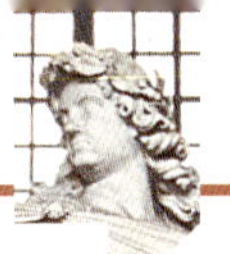

Vulcan's forge
fresco on the theme of war in the lunette above
the first pair of columns on the cupola side

Cupola fresco in the State Hall
(pp. 38/39)

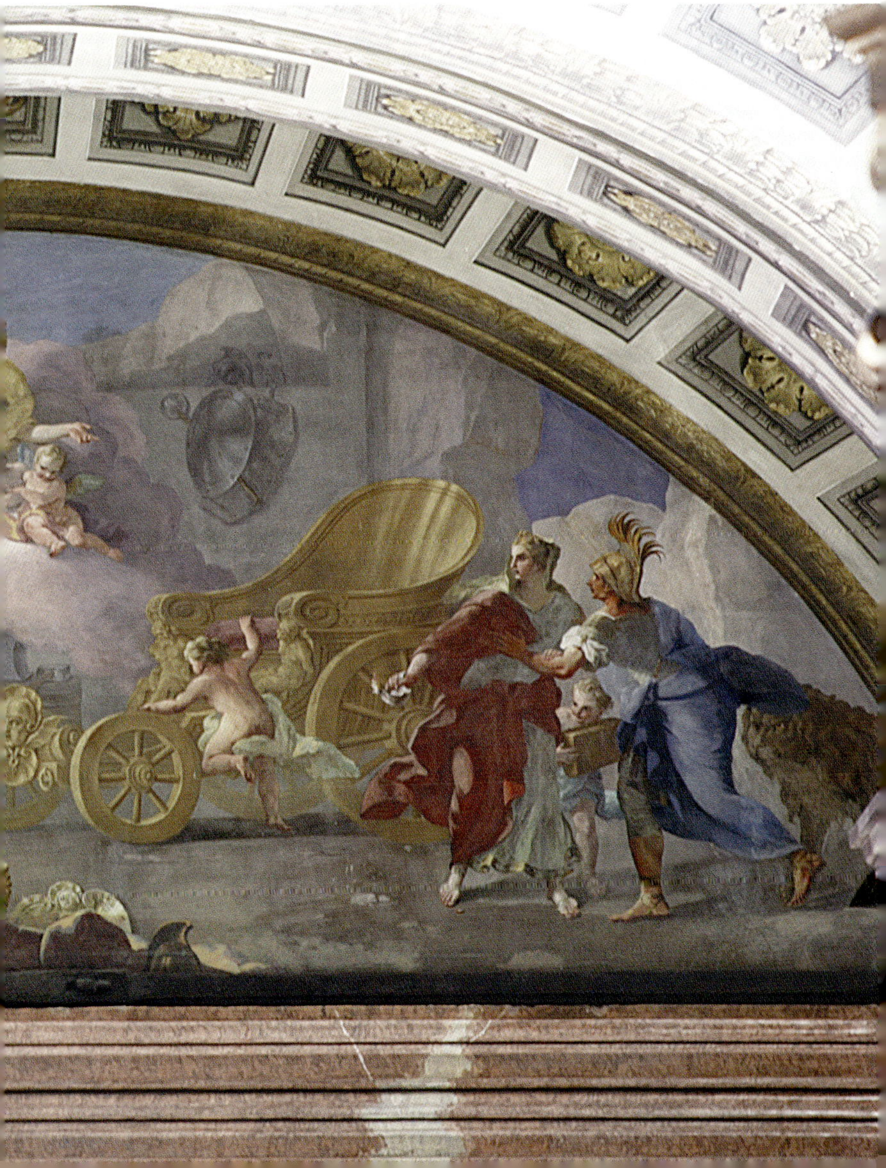

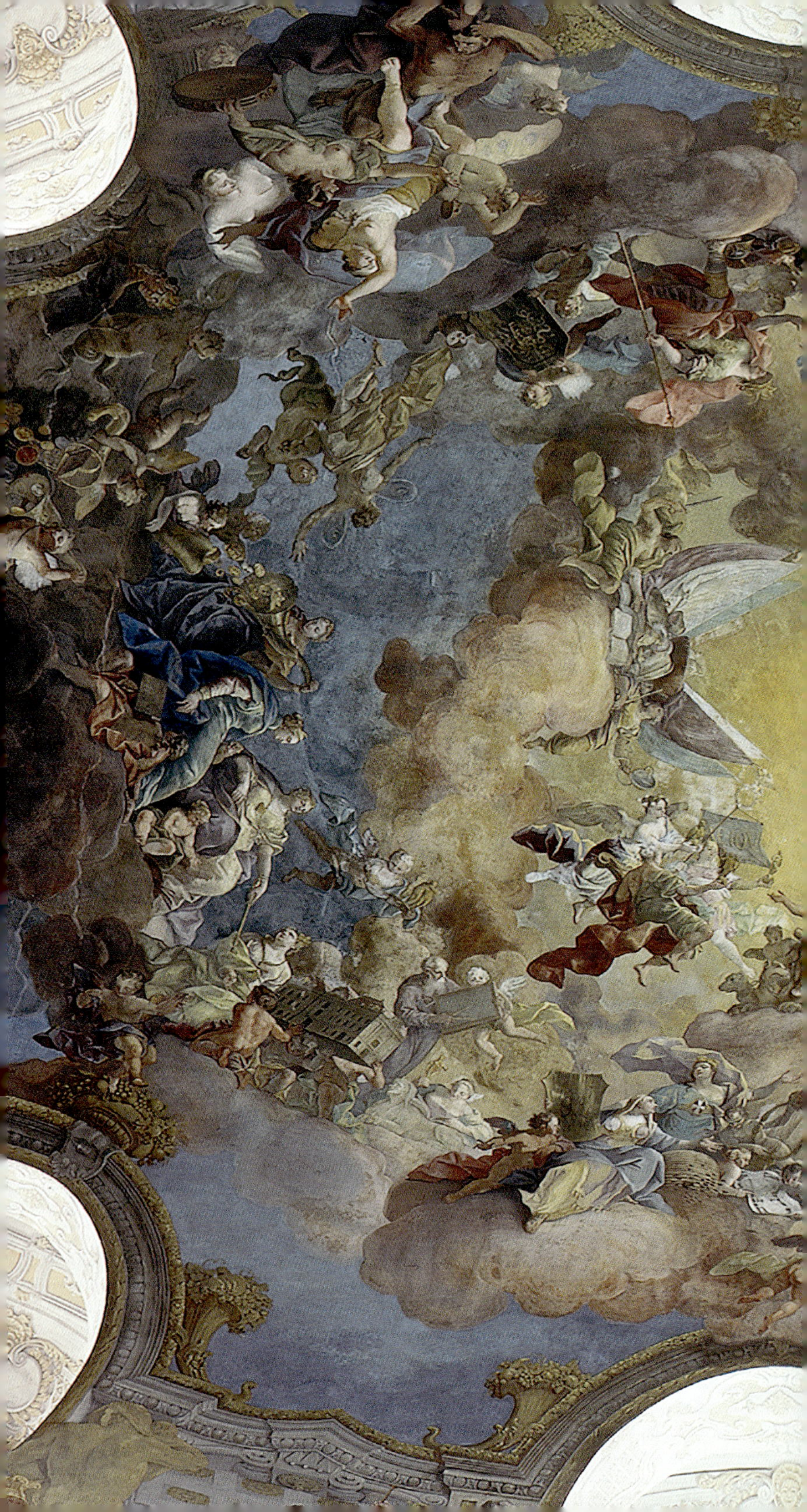

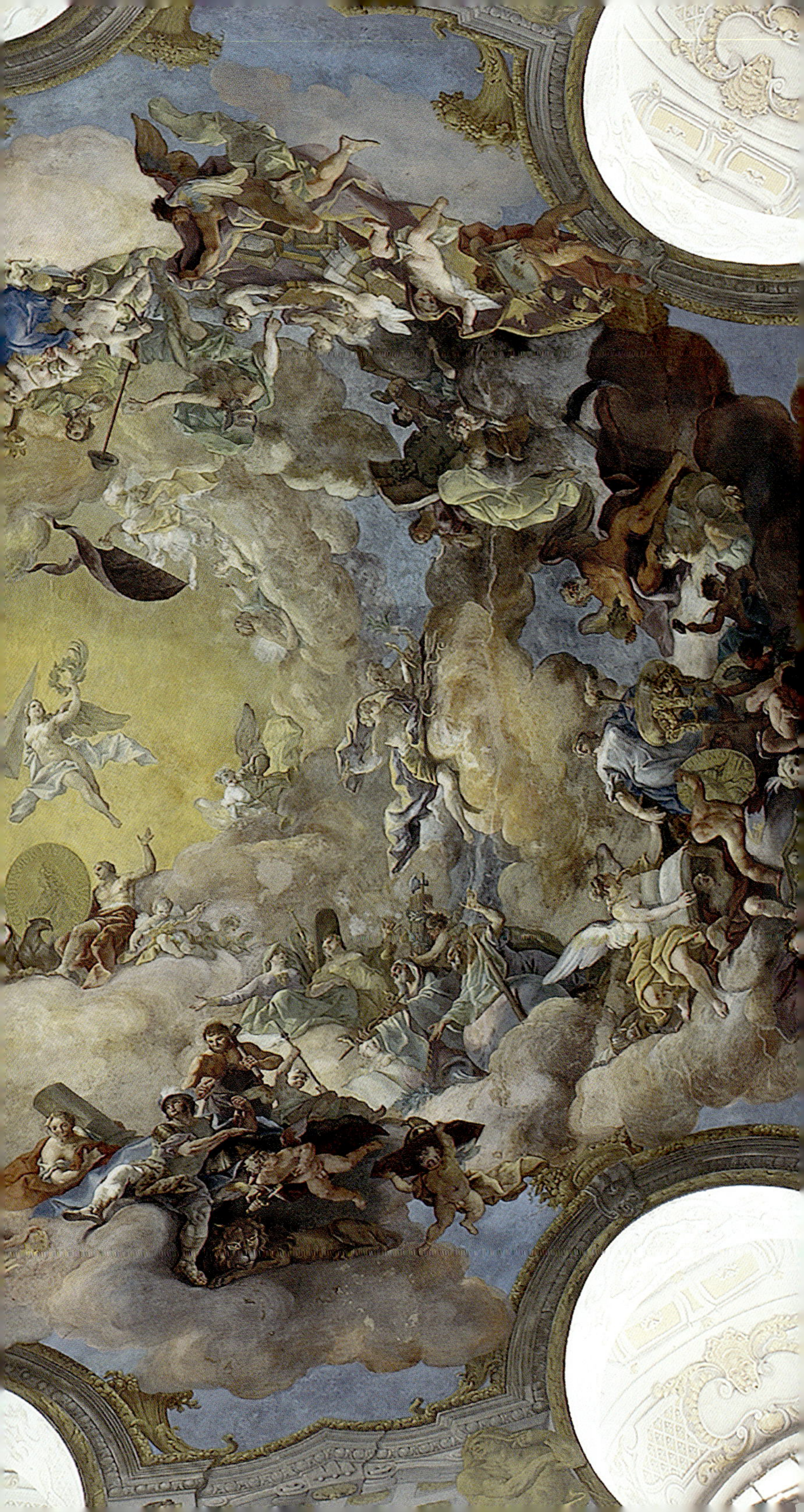

The Frescoes in the Oval Cupola

The frescoed ceiling of the oval cupola offers a sumptuously detailed programme of allegorical representations. A medallion of the emperor ① is held by **Hercules** and **Apollo**, two of the sons of Jupiter, who embody Courage, Strength and Wisdom, qualities that were attributed to Charles VI. The foot of Hercules is placed on the three-headed hound Cerberus, an allusion to the victorious wars against Spain, France and the Turks, only after the end of which it was possible to proceed with the construction of the library.

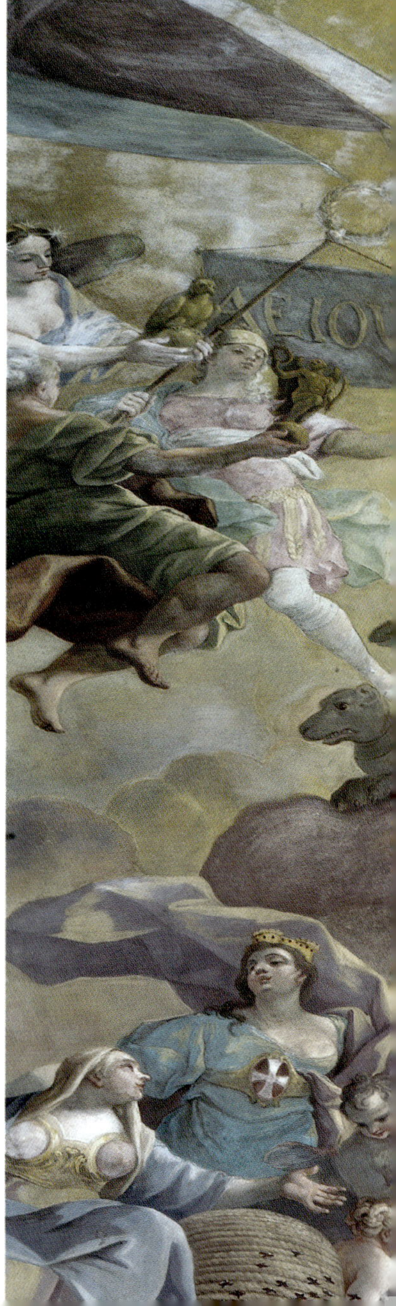

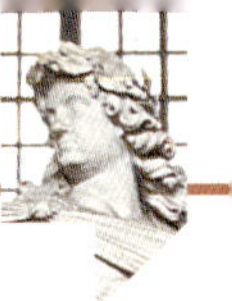

Medallion of Emperor Charles VI held by Hercules and Apollo
detail of the cupola fresco

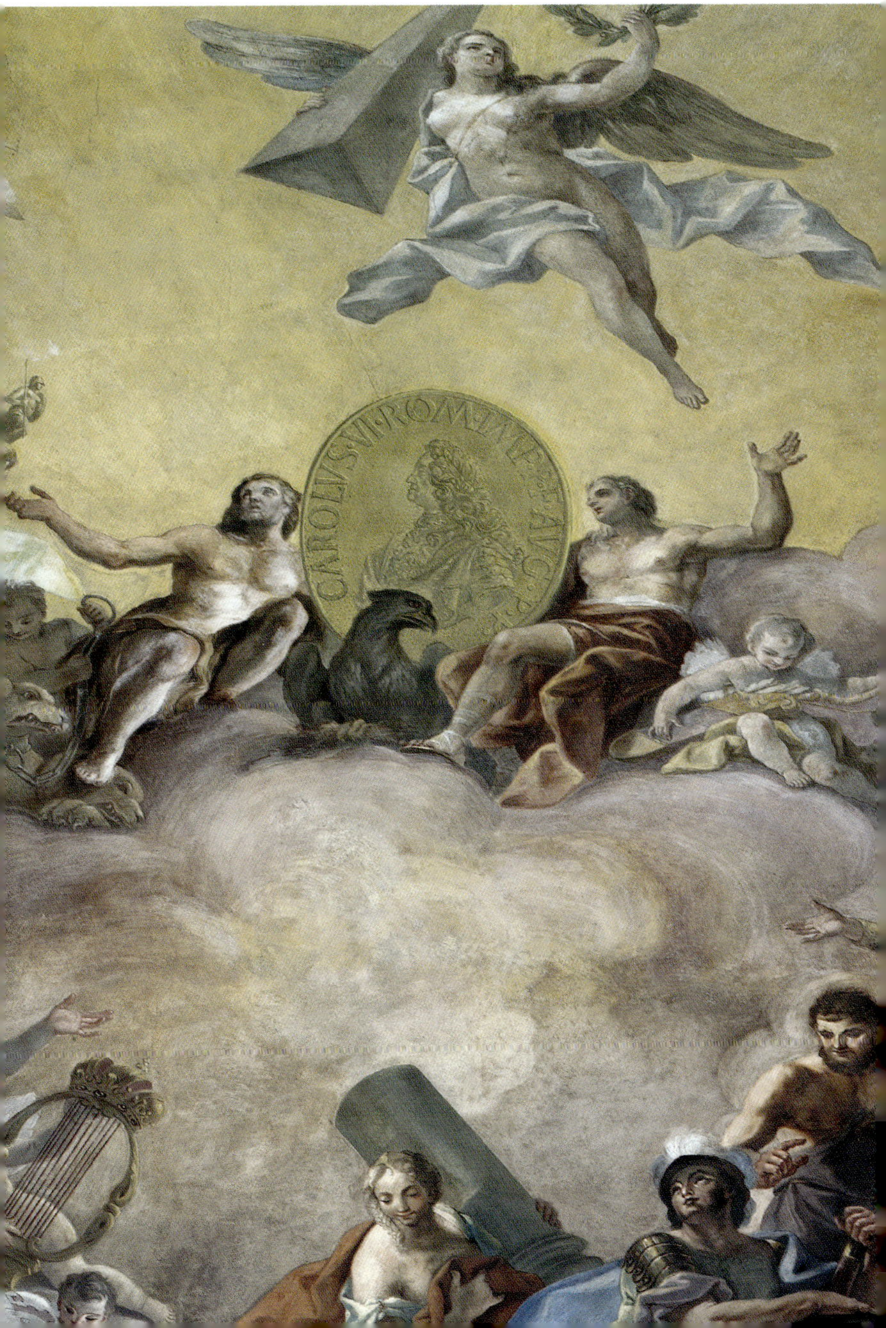

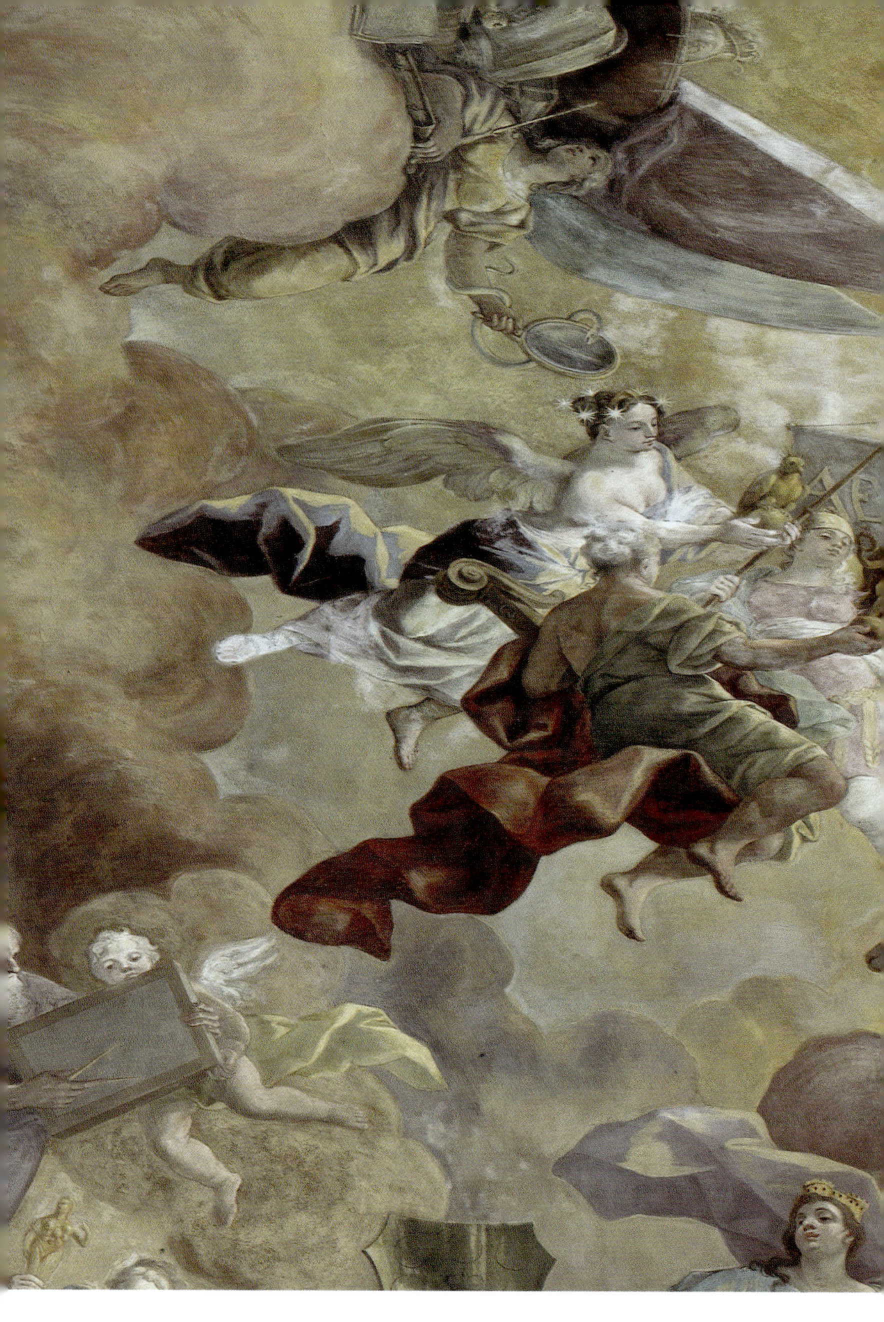

The portrait of the emperor is surrounded by diverse allegorical figures. Visible directly above the emperor is **Glory** ② with a triangular obelisk symbolizing Immortality. To her right is **Fame** ③ with two trumpets, proclaiming the Emperor's repute in both East and West. **Three penates**, or household gods (symbolizing the Happy Reign, the Immortal Memory of Posterity, and the Glory of the House of Habsburg), accompanied by the motto of the Emperor Frederick III, 'A.E.I.O.U.' ④, are

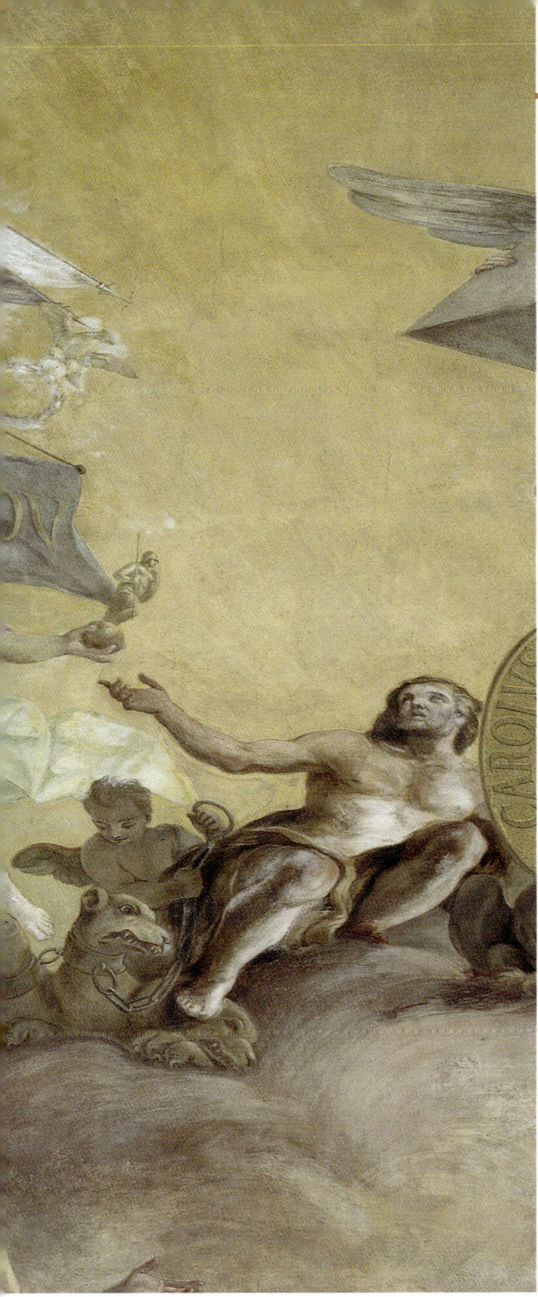

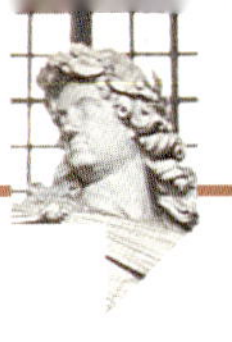

*Three penates present-
ing to Hercules the
golden apples of the
Hesperides*

detail of the cupola
fresco

shown approaching Hercules and presenting him with the golden apples
of the Hesperides.

Also depicted are the **Arts of Rule and of War** ⑤, surrounded by books and trophies. A figure representing the emperor's **Love of Splendour** ⑥ is shown: gesturing with a sceptre to the adjacent, somewhat lower figure of Architecture, whom she orders to commence the construction of the library. Executio ⑦, with a sunflower in his hair, responds to the emperor's command, and two Genii (Albrecht, in his iconographic programme, calls them "little children") display a model of the Court Library.

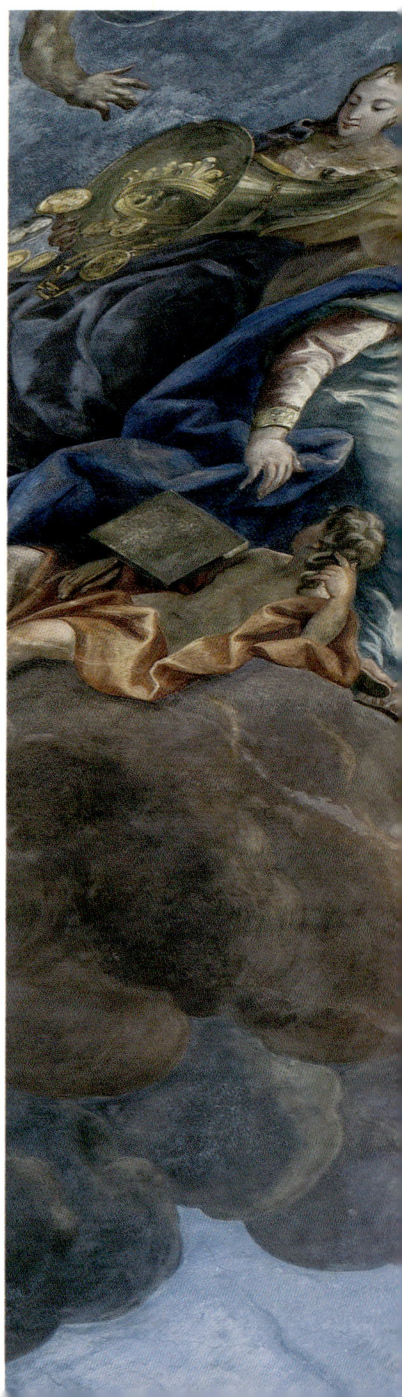

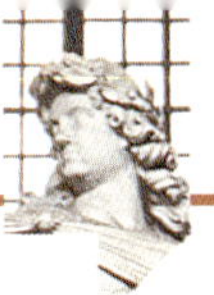

*The emperor's Love of Splendour commands
the construction of the Library*
detail of the cupola fresco

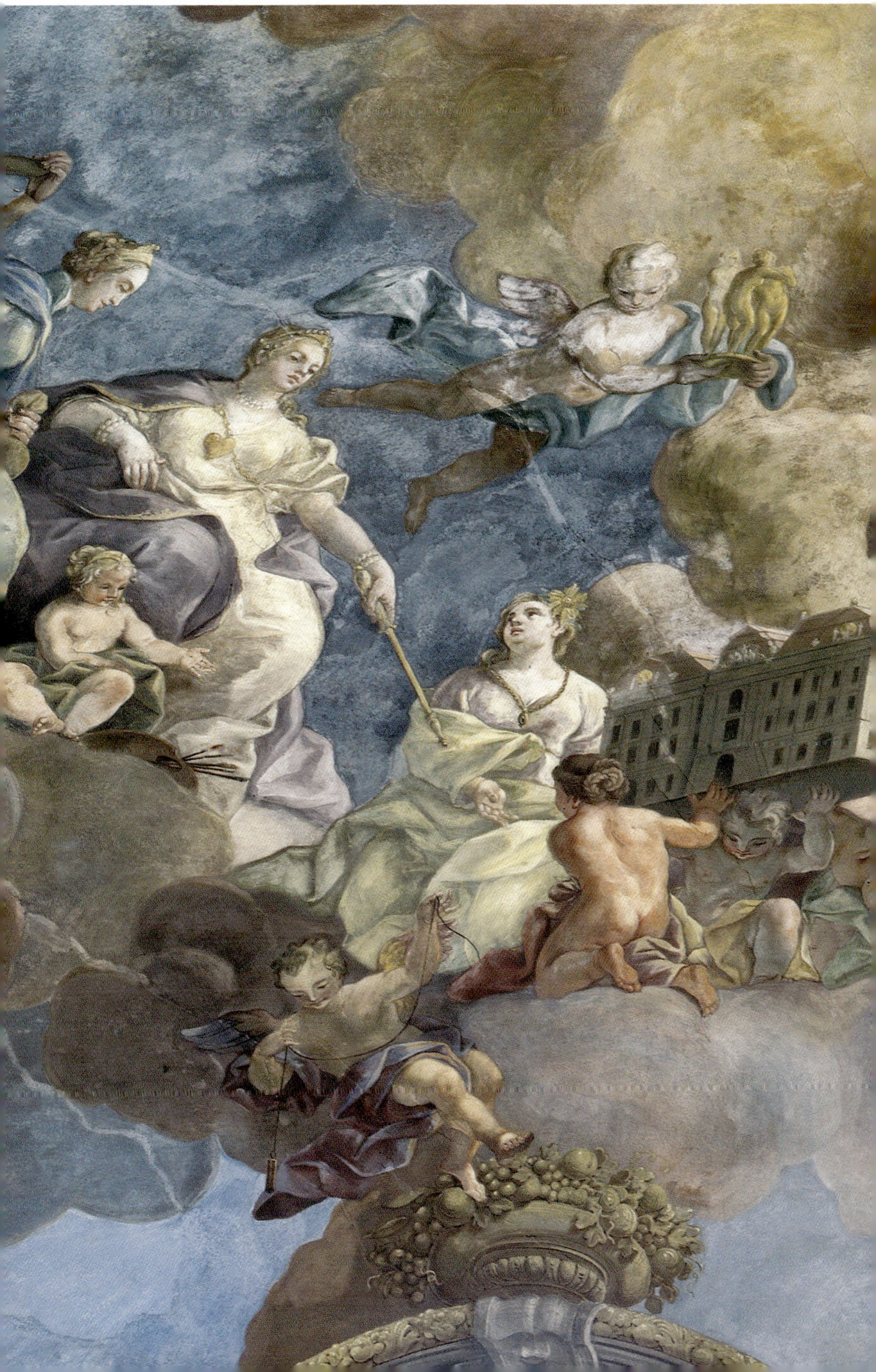

Generosity (8), essential for so large a building, proffers a large purse, while **Austrian Magnanimity** (9), wrapped in a blue cloak, spills from her cornucopia a stream of garlands, gold coins, crowns and badges of honours. Reclining at the feet of **Useful Invention** (10), who holds a picture of Isis in her right hand and an open book in her left, is a sphinx, embodying the difficult task ahead. **Germania** (11) bears a shield with the eagle of the Holy Roman Empire. In front of her two Genii, leaning on a beehive

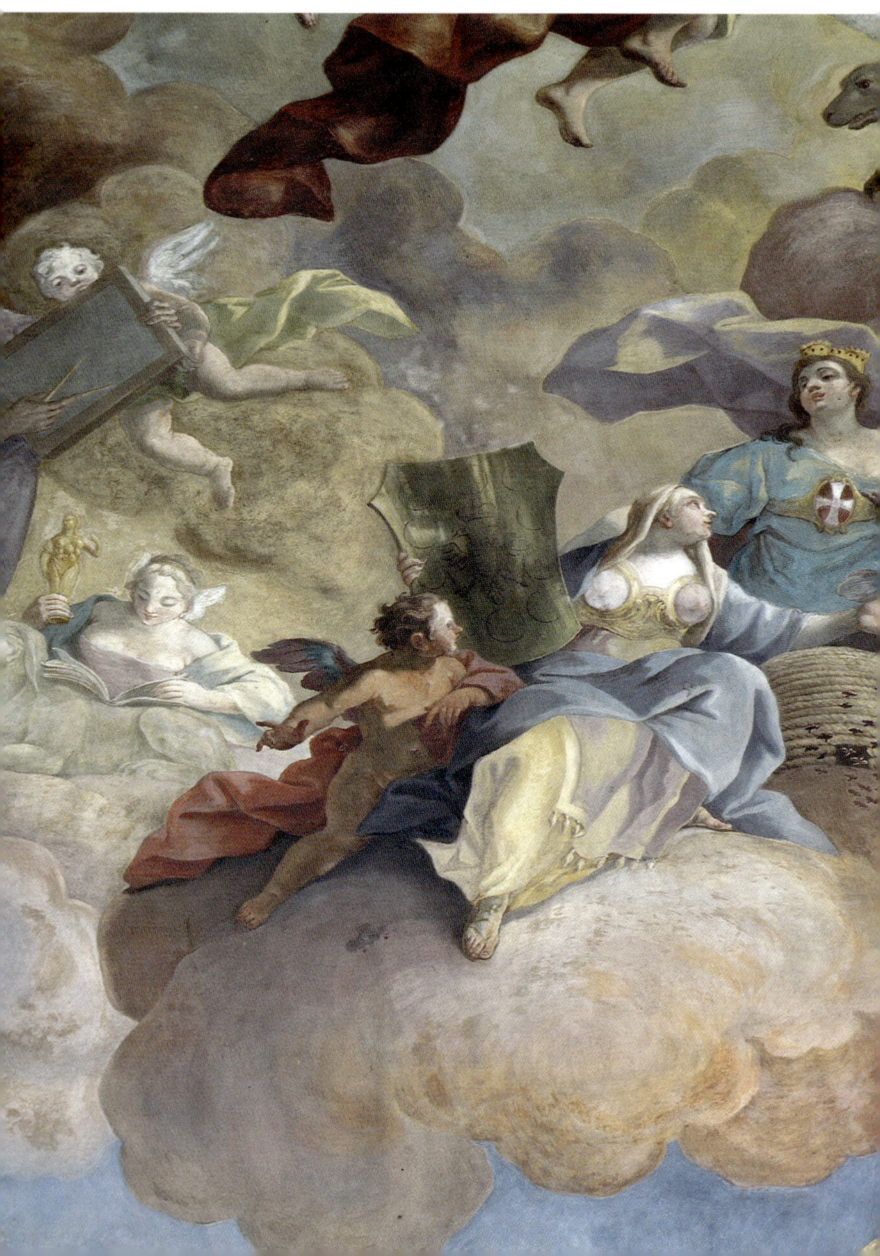

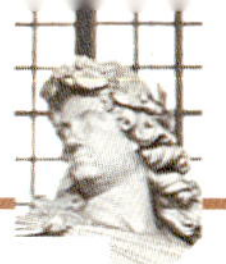

(a symbol of industry) look at a ground plan of the proposed library. The **City of Vienna** ⑫ , bearing her own coat-of-arms on her breast, wears a crown in the form of a wall; next to her a Genius holds a lyre formed out of two Cs (signifying Carolus Caesar).

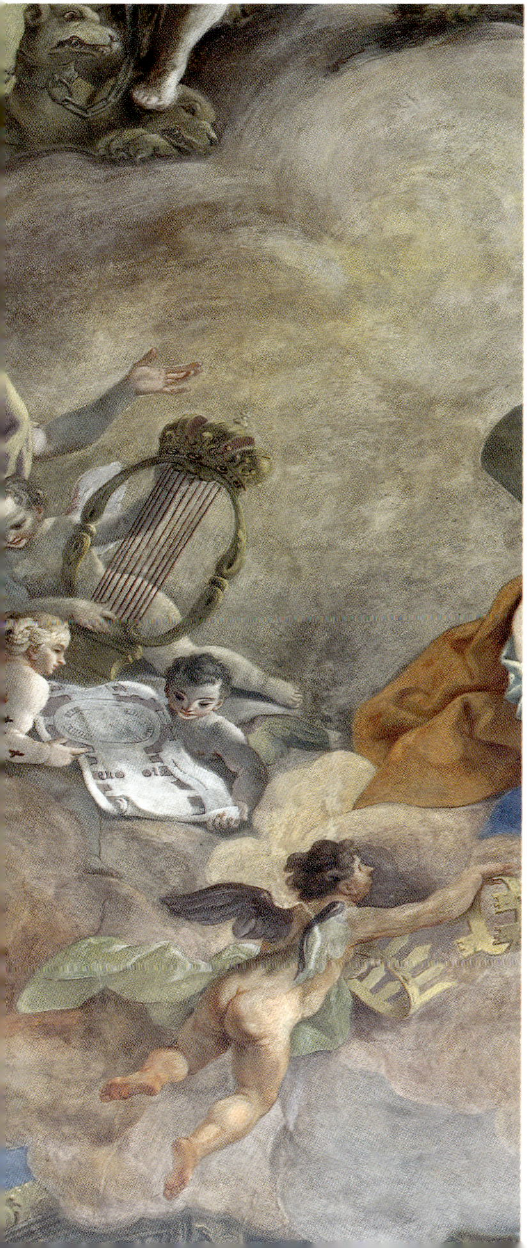

Germania and the City of Vienna

detail of the cupola fresco

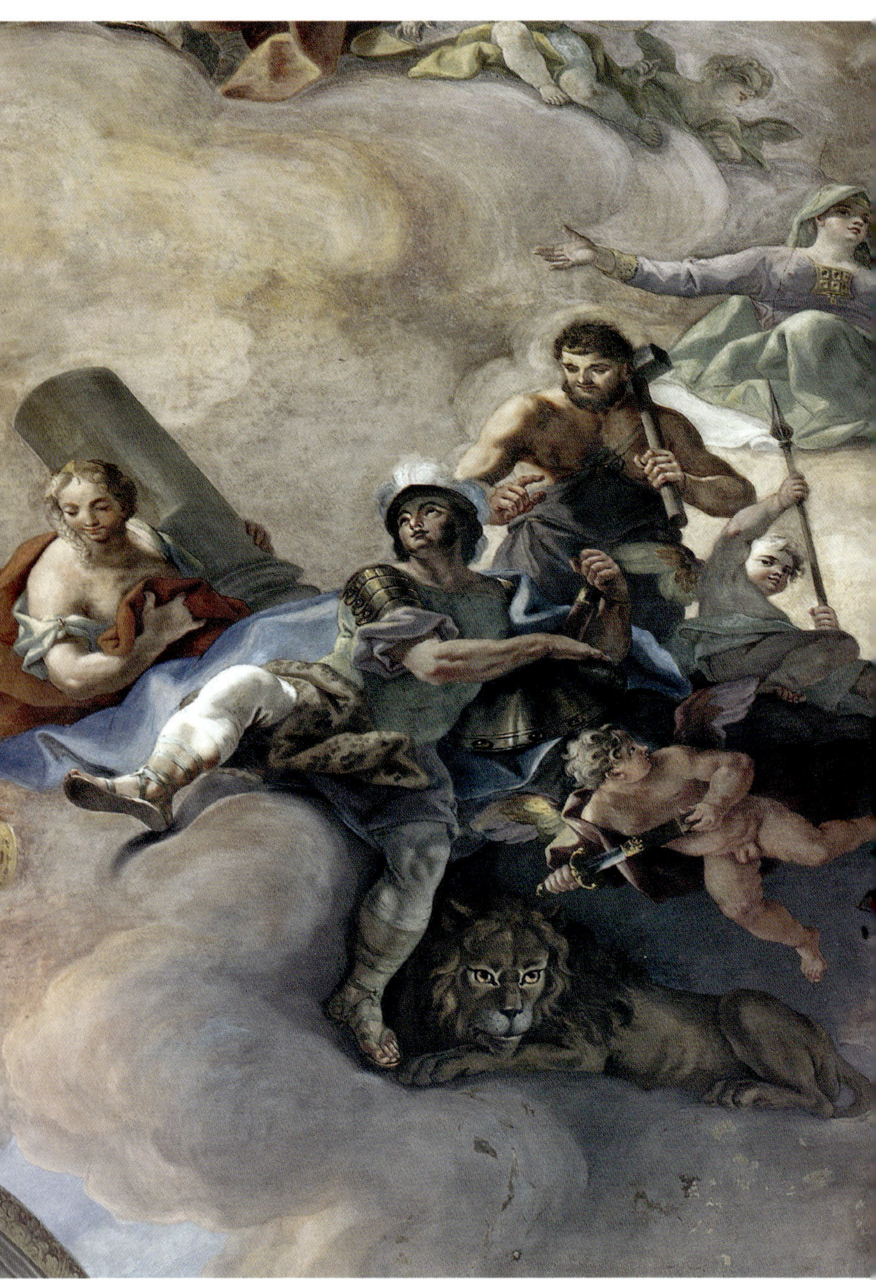

*The Steadfastness of the emperor, Mars and Vulcan
with the four university faculties behind them*
detail of the cupola fresco

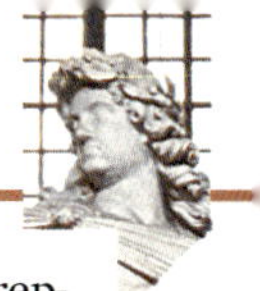

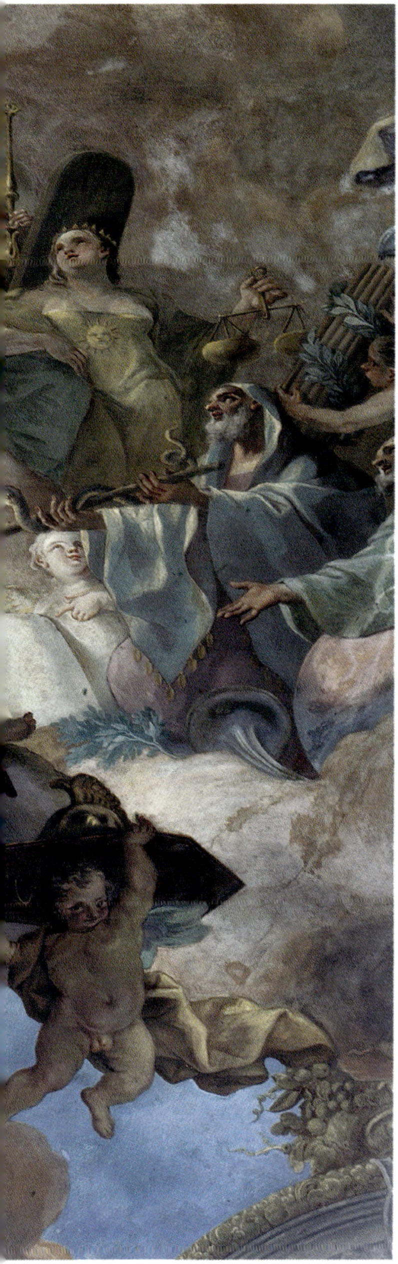

The next group is a symbolic representation of Charles VI's motto, 'constantia et fortitudine'. A figure embodying the **Emperor's steadfastness** ⑬, supports a broken column on her shoulder, while a Genius arrives bearing her victor's crown made up of conquered cities, battles and victories. Close by is **Mars**, the God of War, dressed in a plumed helmet, a cuirass and a tiger skin, and with a lion resting at his feet. Behind Mars stands Vulcan, with his hammer and tongs. There follows a group comprising the **four university** faculties with theit attributes ⑭: **Theology**, **Jurisprudence**, **Medicine** and **Philosophy**.

Gratitude ⑮ is accompanied by the Genius of Study. At the feet of **History** ⑯ – whose allegorical representation reflects a contemporary development, the introduction of a chair of history at Vienna University in 1728–29 – reclines the figure of **Time** ⑰, shown here as a winged, aged man holding a stone bust of Ptolemäus Philadelphus, one of history's greatest book collectors. A **Genius** ⑱ holds a medaillon of **Emperor Maximilian I**, below it a stone relief with a likeness of the Hungarian king **Matthias Corvinus**. Both of these were also celebrated collectors of books. A particularly important allegorical group is that of **Providentia**, who is shown with a torch in her hand and a Janus (or two-faced) head. She is not to be associated with fickleness but with foresight, and so to accommodate, future events – in effect, a human counterpart to Divine Providence.

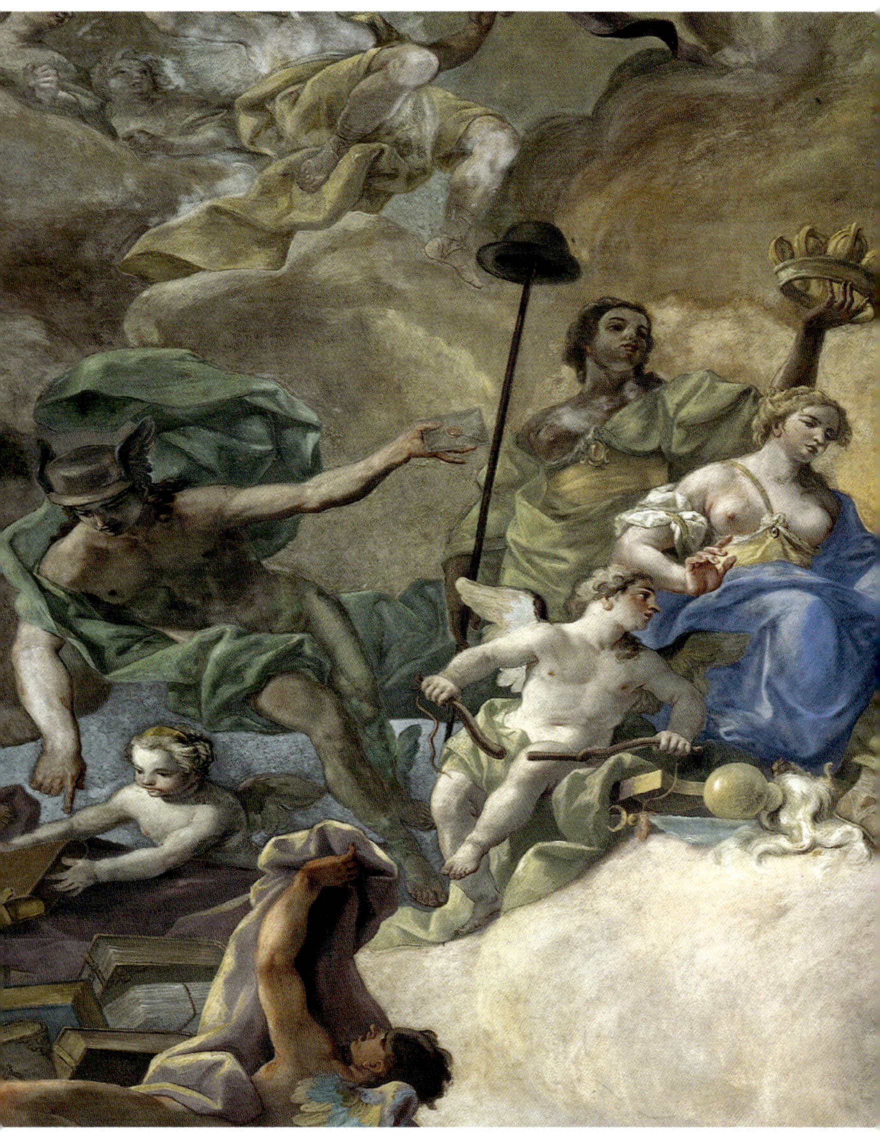

In the next group ⑲ the **Goddess of Peace** presents an olive branch to **Minerva**. Behind her the **Goddess of Commerce**, bearing in one hand the hat of Freedom on a staff, in the other the naval crown *(corona navalis)*.

Beneath this group there is a depiction of Genii unwrapping books from a robe ⑳, which Mercury presents to Minerva. Above the figure of **Mercury** more Genii are seen in flight, puffing air beneath the spread wings of **Fortune** ㉑. Yet another Genius uses the shield of Minerva (which bears a Medusa head) to frighten away the Enemies of Learning ㉒: **Indolence**

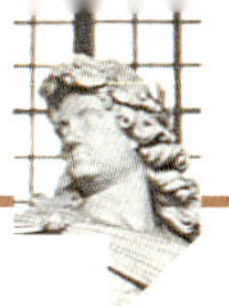

(a corpulent woman with a tambourine), **Misunderstanding** (sporting a mask and long ears), **Ignorance** (with bound eyes), an **Unjustified Reproach** (a horned satyr). Accompanied by Chimeras, Harpies and other fantastical creatures, they are shown fleeing or tumbling into an abyss.

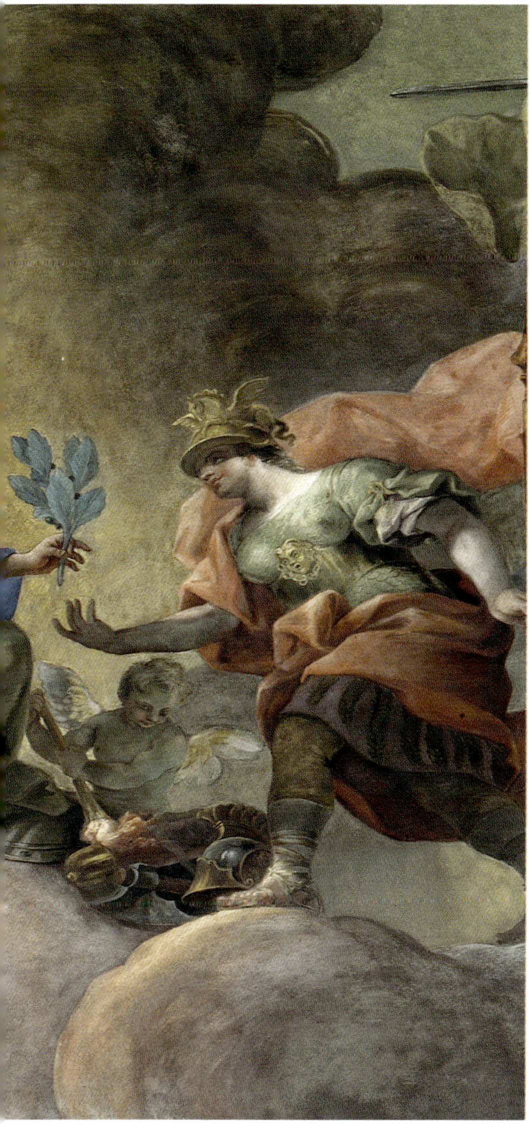

Below his principal fresco decoration, Daniel Gran added an eighteenth-century School of Athens: a painted gallery with eminent exponents of the various arts and the sciences.

THE FRESCOES ON THE THEME OF PEACE

The entrance to the State Hall once used by the emperor and his court was at its western end, opposite the entrance now used by visitors; and it is in fact here that the iconographic programme devised by Conrad Adolph von Albrecht has its intended starting point. The visitor's is first drawn to the lunette above the two massive columns with its celebrated Aurora fresco. This shows the chariot of Apollo, with the god himself ren-

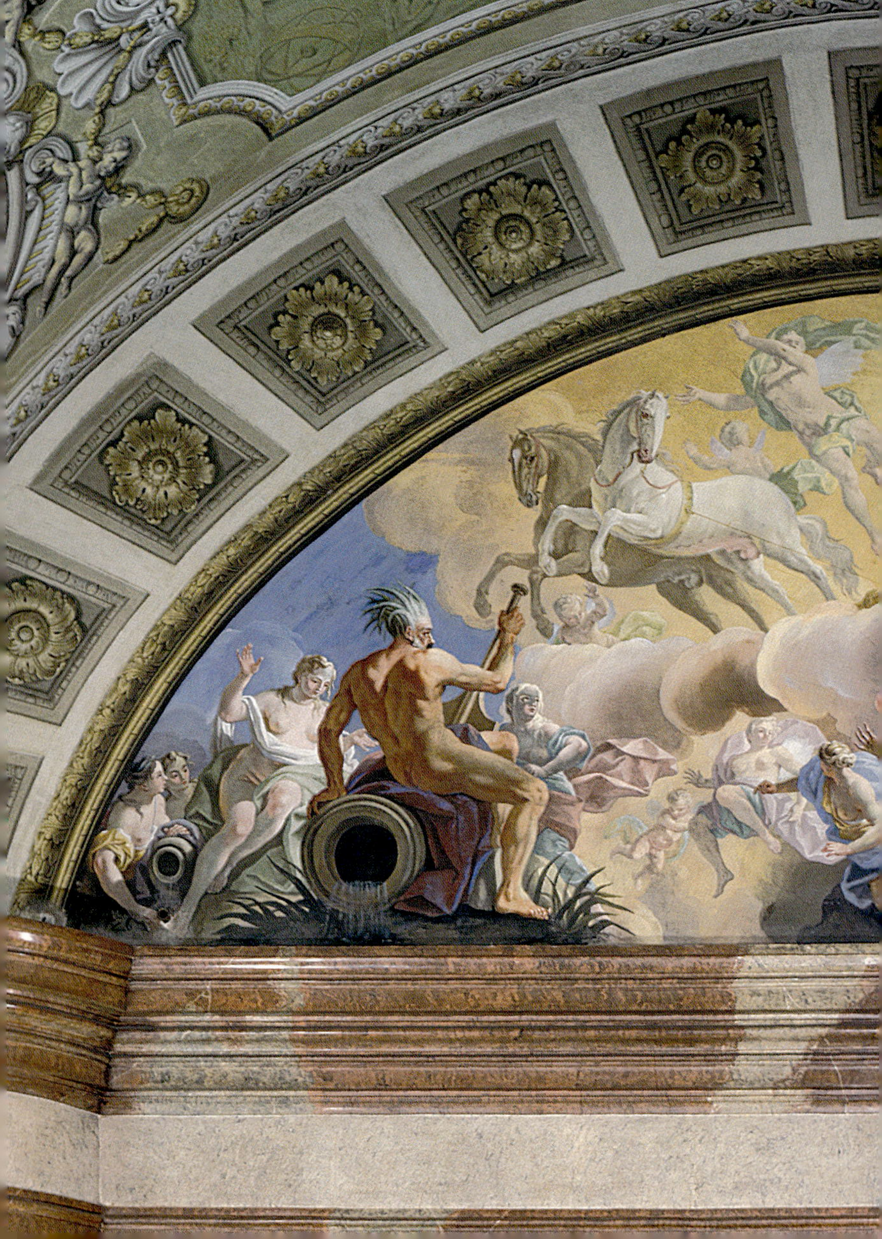

dered as the disc of the sun, while at his side Aurora, the Goddess of Dawn, drives out the demons of the Night. Daniel Gran inscribed this fresco with the date 1726, the year in which he embarked on his work in the State Hall. He completed the work in 1730, as recorded in the inscription to be found in the fresco in the cupola: DANIEL GRAN PINXIT: MDCCXXX.

Aurora
fresco on the theme of peace in the lunette above the first pair of columns

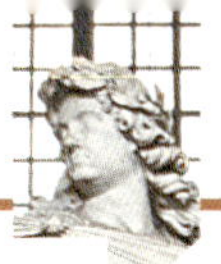

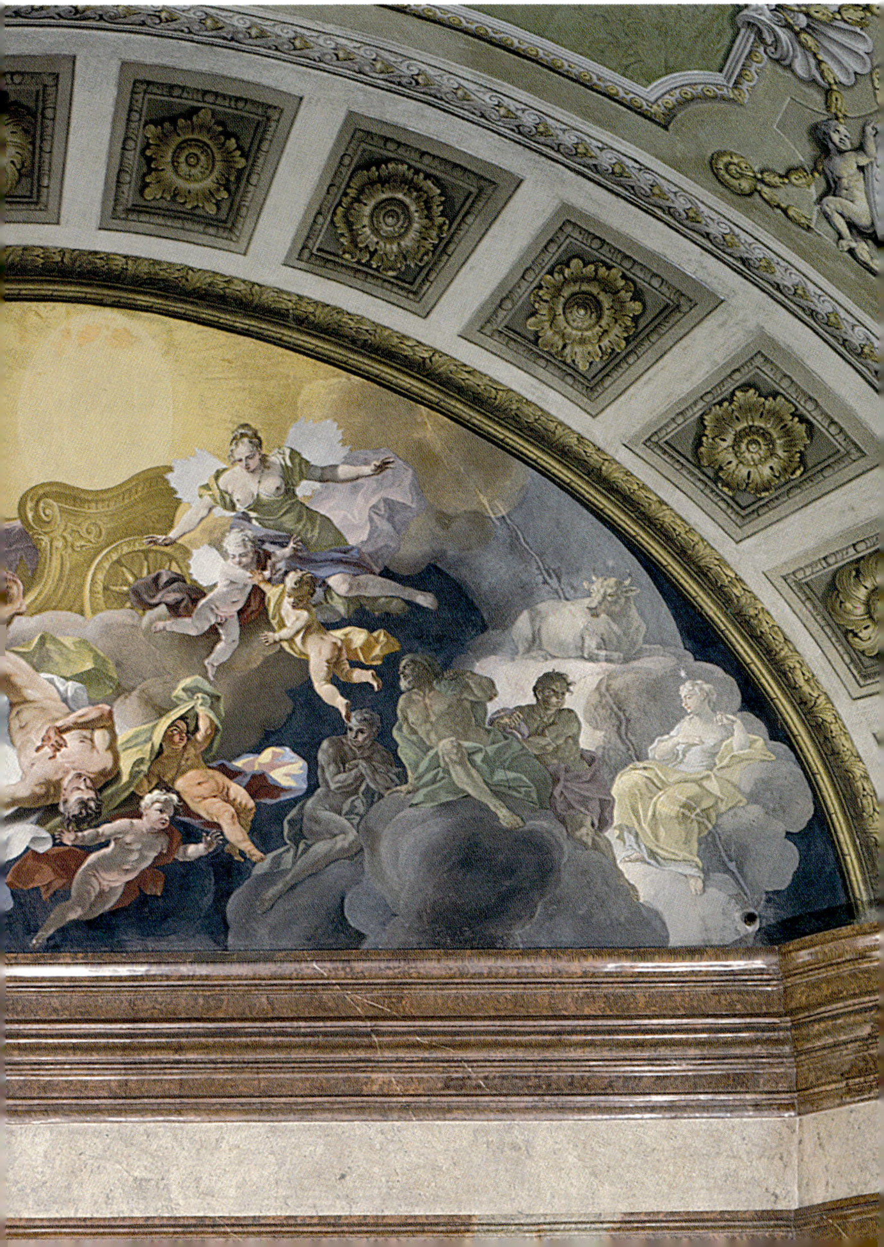

The ceiling fresco celebrates Divina Sapientia and the study of heavenly things and incorporates the allegorical figures of Divine Wisdom (with her all-seeing eye), Theology and Scholarly Endeavour. The allegorical scheme is completed with the representation of Parnassus in the fresco on the cupola side of the Aurora lunette.

Parnassus
fresco on the theme of peace in the lunette above
the first pair of columns on the cupola side

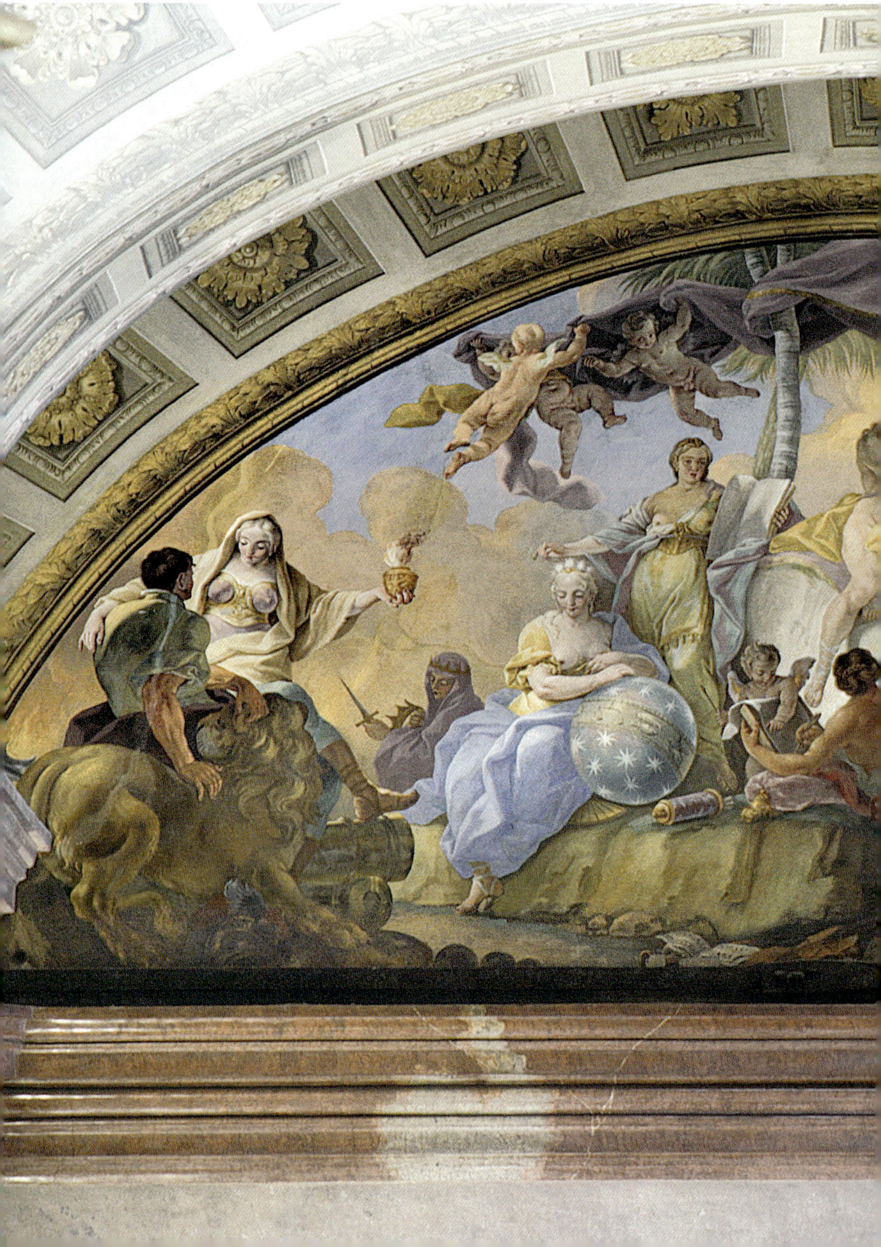

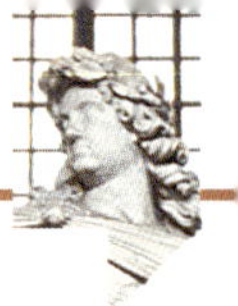

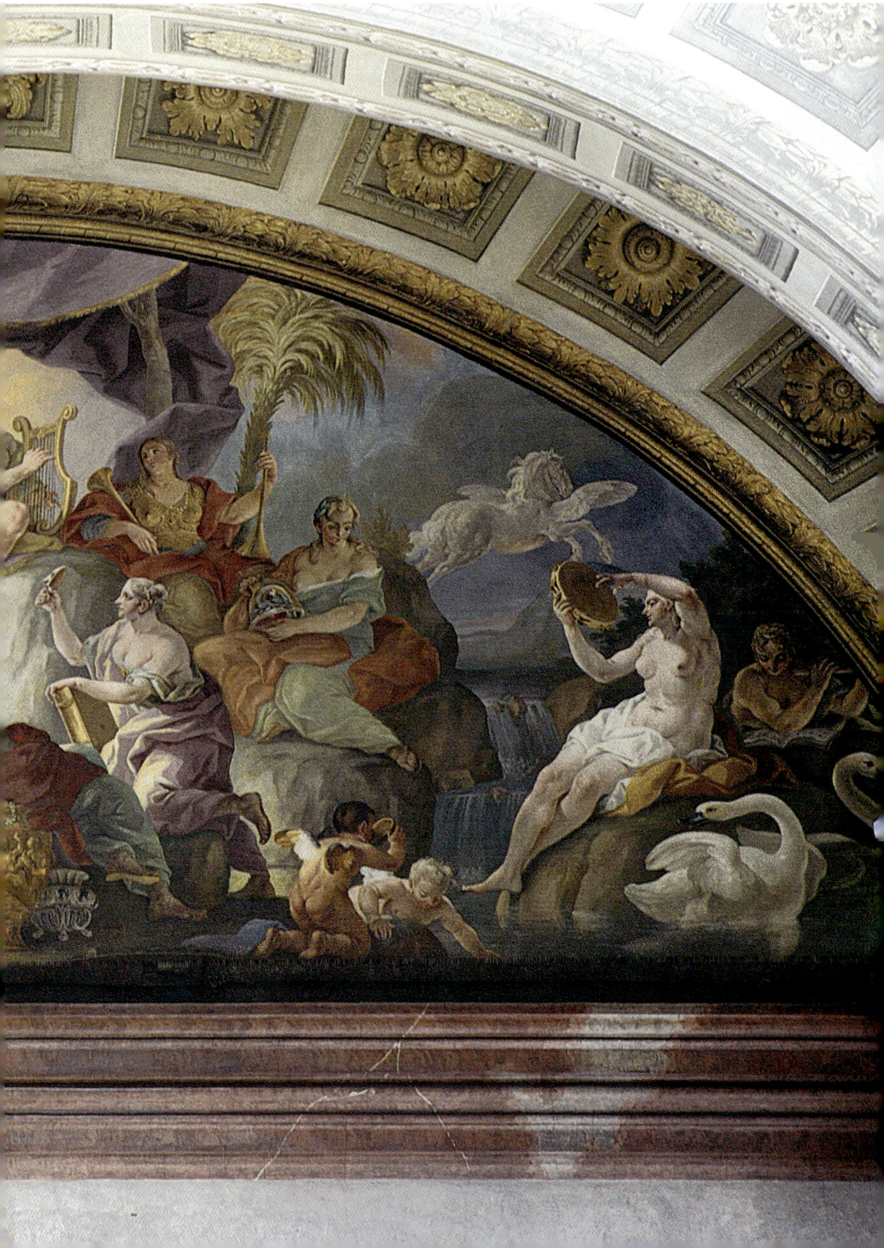

Over the years the foundations of the library building began to settle and several cracks appeared in the cupola wall, especially on its south side. Nikolaus Parcassi, the architect of the lateral wings, evolved a scheme for restoring the building. He introduced two supportive strap arches to help support the weight of the cupola, and around the cupola itself he placed two iron rings. The painter Franz Anton Maulpertsch (1724–1796) was commissioned to restore the frescoes. Maulpertsch completed this work in 1769, as recorded in the cupola opposite the inscription left by Daniel Gran: A. MAULPERTSCH PICTURAM REFECIT MDCCLXIX.

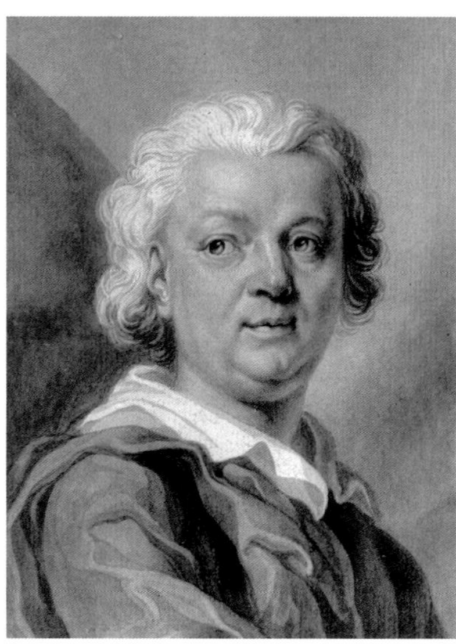

Franz Anton Maulpertsch
1724–96

The painter who carried out the restoration of the State Hall frescoes.

THE LIBRARY HOUSED IN THE STATE HALL

With its architecture, frescoes, marble figures and walnut-wood bookcases, the State Hall epitomizes the eighteenth-century ideal of the Baroque 'universal library'. Originally it also housed the entire holdings of the Court Library. Today some 200,000 books, dating between 1501–1850, are preserved here.

Each bookcase bears a number and each shelf a letter. A specific number identifies each and every book. Also notable are the revolving bookcases, which cover several of the imposing windows visible from outside. These bookcases not only allowed more space for the storage of books within the State Hall, but also permitted the creation of temporary study cabinets, which – unlike the State Hall as a whole – could be heated in winter. They were also known as 'star cabinets' because the identity number of the books located in these bookcases bore an additional star.

Also incorporated within the overall decorative scheme of the State Hall, and placed in the oval at its centre, are four globes: Two pairs of terrestrial and celestial globes made by the Venetian cleric and cosmographer Vincenzo Coronelli (1650–1718). The pair placed towards the east (and the frescoes on the theme of war) is inscribed with dedications to the Venetian Republic and its Doge, Francesco Morosini, and the dates 1692 (in the case of the celestial globe) and 1694 (in that of the terrestrial globe). The pair placed towards the west (and the frescoes on the theme of peace) is similarly dedicated to the Republic of Venice, but also bears a later dedication to the emperor Leopold I.

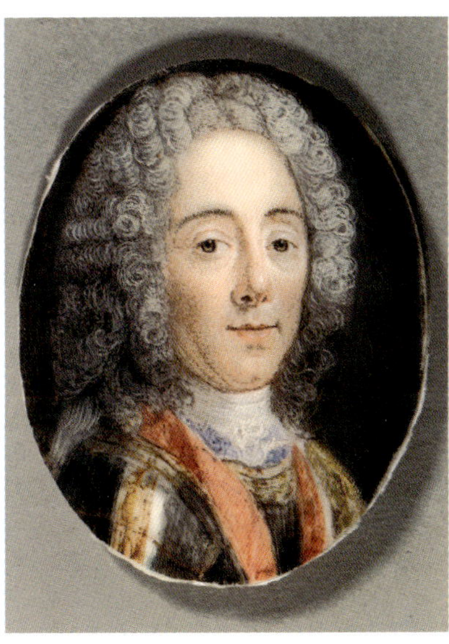

Prince Eugene of Savoy 1663–1736

His celebrated Bibliotheca Eugeniana was installed at the centre of the State Hall.

THE BIBLIOTHECA EUGENIANA

Of particular note are the books forming the library that once belonged to Prince Eugene of Savoy (1663–1736), which was installed in the central oval of the State Hall in 1738. Charles VI acquired this celebrated Bibliotheca Eugeniana from the niece, and heiress, of Prince Eugene, Victoria of Savoy (1684–1763). When Victoria came into her vast inheritance, she was 52 and had already entered a convent. Included within the inheritance were the Belvedere Palace, a Winter Palace in Himmelpfortgasse, a castle and estate in Marchfeld, the library, a collection of paintings and substantial cash assets. Able to offer such a dowry, Victoria swiftly found a husband, albeit one newly twenty years her junior: Prince Josef Friedrich von Sachsen-Hildburghausen. But the marriage ended in divorce in 1744. And when Victoria began to sell off her uncle's estate, the House of Habsburg stepped forward as an eager buyer.

The extremely valuable library was originally housed in Prince Eugene's Winter Palace in Himmelpfortgasse (now the Austrian Ministry of

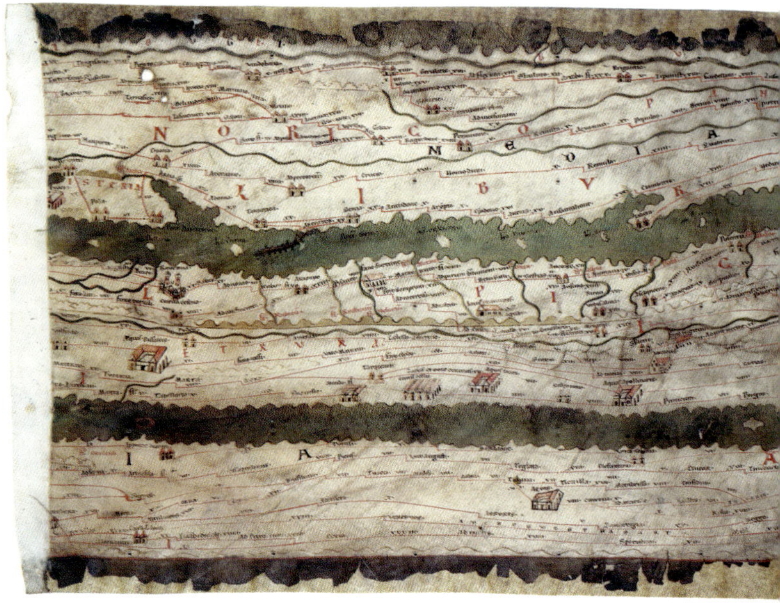

Finances), and at the time of his death had an estimated value of 150,000 gilders. (By comparison, the Belvedere Palace, sold to the empress Maria Theresia in 1752, was valued at 100,000 gilders). At the end of 1737 an agreement was reached whereby Victoria gave up her claim to both the Hungarian island of Ráckeve and the library in return for an annual pension of 10,000 gilders. In 1738 Pius Nicolaus Garelli (1670–1739), who served as prefect of the Imperial Court Library from 1723 to 1739, formally took charge of the library in the name of the emperor.

The Bibliotheca Eugeniana comprises 15,000 choice printed works, 500 volumes and boxes of copper engravings, drawings and miniatures, and 240 valuable manuscripts, which Prince Eugene had collected not merely as status symbols but as a true friend of learning and the sciences, of fine books and art. While certainly reflecting the Prince's particular interests, his library is also a testament to the numerous fields of learning that might be represented in such a collection at this period – from history, to the natural sciences and to the poetry of antiquity.

Prince Eugene was well acquainted with the poet Jean-Baptiste Rousseau (1671–1741) and the philosopher Gottfried Wilhelm Leibniz (1646–1716) and had assembled his library in a relatively short time, between 1712 and 1736. He employed the French librarian and book-binder Etienne Boyer to make a catalogue of the library. This divided its holdings into the following disciplines: theology, jurisprudence, philosophy, natural history, medicine, mathematics, the arts, grammar, rhetoric, poetry, philology, geography and history.

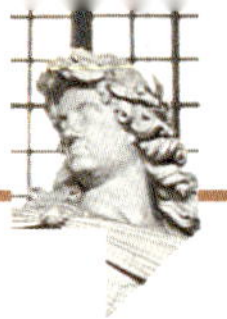

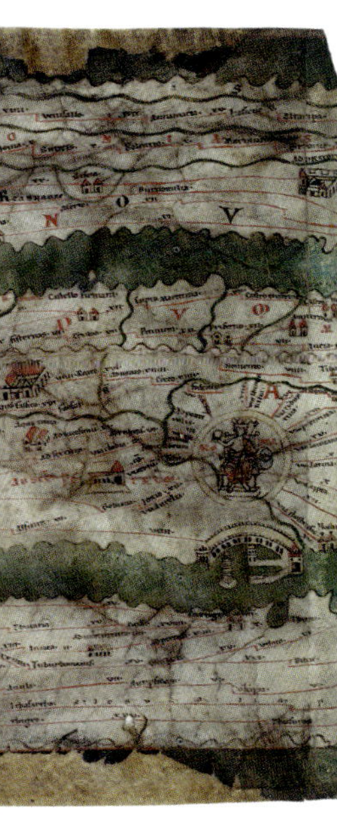

Tabula Peutingeriana
This twelfth-century copy of an ancient Roman street map is regarded as one of the most valuable objects in the Bibliotheca Eugeniana.

The books were all bound in morocco leather and bore their owner's coat-of-arms embossed in gold on both front and back covers. The bound volumes were also colour-coded: history and literature were bound in dark red, theology and law in dark blue, and the sciences in dark yellow. Further colour differentiation served to distinguish between various groups of volumes as arranged on the shelves. Among the most valuable objects in the Bibliotheca Eugeniana was the *Tabula Peutingeriana*, named after its former owner, Conrad Peutinger, a diplomat and personal advisor to Emperor Maximilian I. The Tabula Peutingeriana is a twelfth-century copy of a Roman street map of the second half of the fourth century. It is not a map in the modern sense, however, but a graphic representation of the great highways that traversed the Roman Empire, copied on to a continuous scroll of over six meters in length. This is now to be found in the Department of Manuscripts.

Further famous items in the Bibliotheca Eugeniana are the *Blaeu-Van der Hem Atlas* (now part of the Map Department, and included on the UNESCO register of 'world heritage documents'), as well as exquisitely illuminated manuscripts such as a French thirteenth-century *Bible moralisée* with around 2,000 images, and two volumes dating from the fifteenth century: the *Livre du Cuer d'amours espris du Roi René*, with its beautiful miniatures, and the *Roman de la Rose* of Guillaume de Lorris and Jean de Meung.

The State Hall and the valuable books it houses have twice narrowly escaped destruction when adjacent buildings caught fire: the lateral wing towards the Augustinerkirche on 31 October 1848, and the Redoutensäle on the night of 26/27 November 1992.

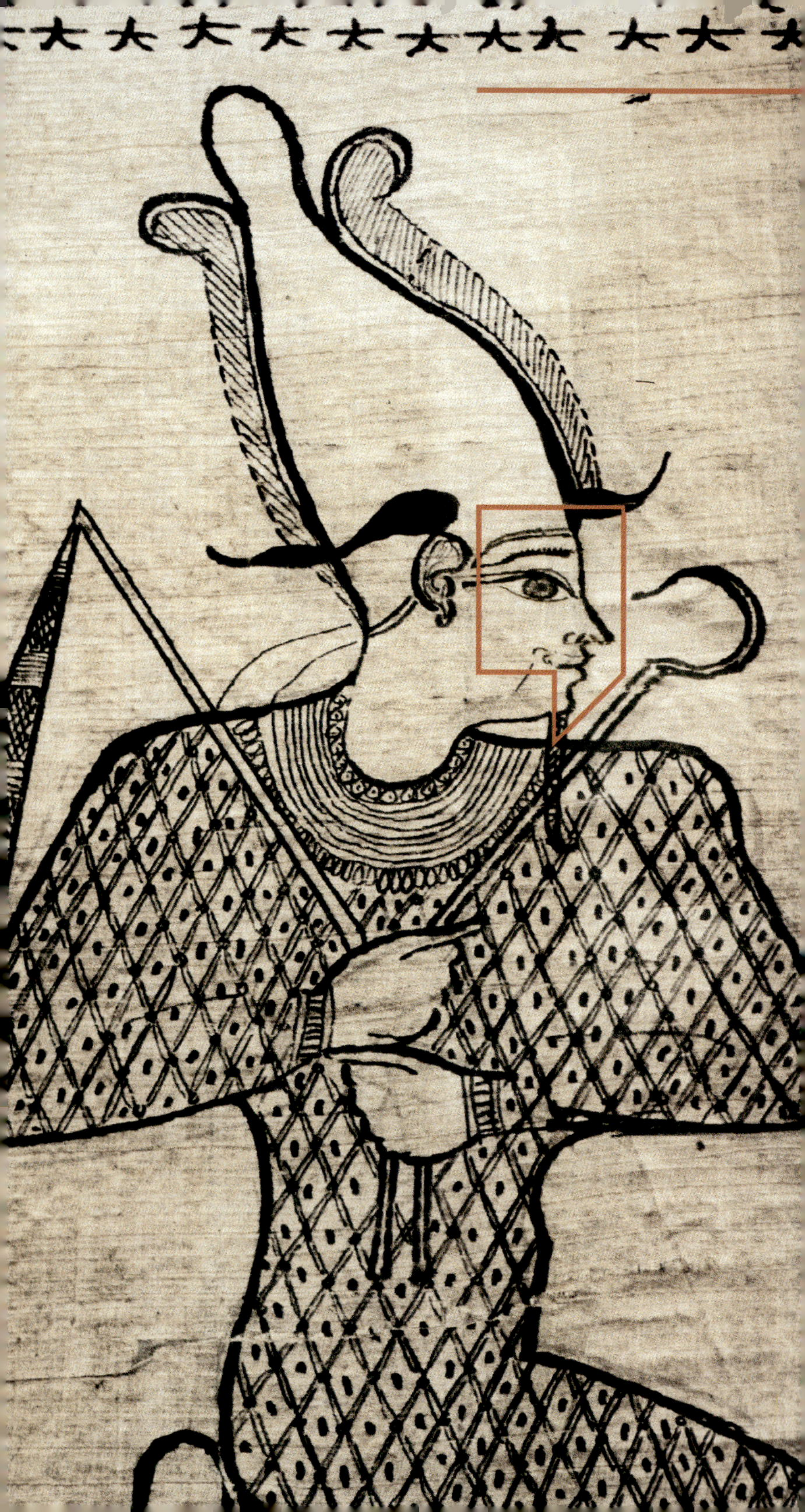

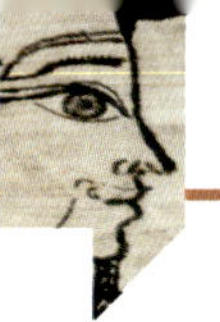

Papyrus Museum and
Department of Papyri

In 1883 the archduke Rainer (1827–1913), a nephew of emper-
or Francis Joseph I, started his own collection of papyri. On 18 August
1899 the archduke presented his collection to the emperor to mark the
latter's birthday. The emperor in turn assigned it to the Court Library as a
special collection. Around 95% of the current holdings of the Library's
papyri derives from the material previously owned by Archduke Rainer.

With 180,000 objects, the Department of Papyri of the Austrian National
Library is the most extensive and most important of its type in the world.
In 2001 it was added to UNESCO's Memory of the World register of 'world
heritage documents'.

Almost every object in the Department of Papyri comes from Egypt. In
1878/79 a group of Egyptian fellaheen (peasant farmers) were hunting for
new stretches of humous soil in Fayum, the largest oasis in Egypt, when
they came, by chance, across the ancient city of Krokodilopolis (Arsinoe;
Medinet el-Fayum), also unearthing its refuge heap, in which numerous
papyri were discovered. By way of the Cairo trade in antiquities, many
papyri made their way to Vienna. The collection eventually acquired by
the archduke was assembled in the late-nineteenth century by the cir-
cumspect Viennese dealer in antiquities, Theodor Graf, who gradually
sold it to the archduke through Josef von Karabaček, professor of Oriental
languages at Vienna University and, from 1899 to 1917, prefect of the
Court Library.

In addition to over 137,000 papyri, the collection embraces a great many
other types of writing support: parchment, diverse types of paper, clay
fragments (ostraca), leather, tablets made of wood and wax, plaquettes in
gold, silver and bronze, textiles, various kinds of stone, animal bones and

Taruma's Book of the Dead second century BC,
detail, see pp. 66/67

fragments of the masks of mummies. Writing was added to some of these surfaces with pen and ink, the pen consisting of a reed (kalamos) and the ink being a mixture of water and gum arabic (the juice of the acacia plant). From the fourth century AD onwards, vitriol ink was also in use. In the case of the wax tablets, the surface was scratched with a stylus.

The samples of writing in the Department of Papyri represent an extraordinarily long historical period, dating from the fifteenth century BC to the fifteenth century AD. There are, accordingly, texts in all of the languages and scripts that were used in Egypt during this period: hieroglyphic, hieratic, demotic, Coptic, Greek, Latin, Aramaic, Hebrew, Syrian, Arabic, even Pahlavi (Middle Persian).

THE PAPYRUS MUSEUM

The earliest and most valuable finds on display in the Papyrus Museum come from Egypt, where in around 3,000 BC the 'paper of antiquity', papyrus, was made from the pulp of the papyrus plant. The resulting sheets were cut into thin strips, superimposed vertically and horizontally, then beaten, pressed, dried and their surfaces smoothed by rubbing with pumice stone or a shell. Stuck together to form a long roll, papyrus could be purchased in the quality and size required, but only at authorized outlets. From the fourth century AD the tougher, albeit also much more expensive, parchment was made from animal skin; but it was never

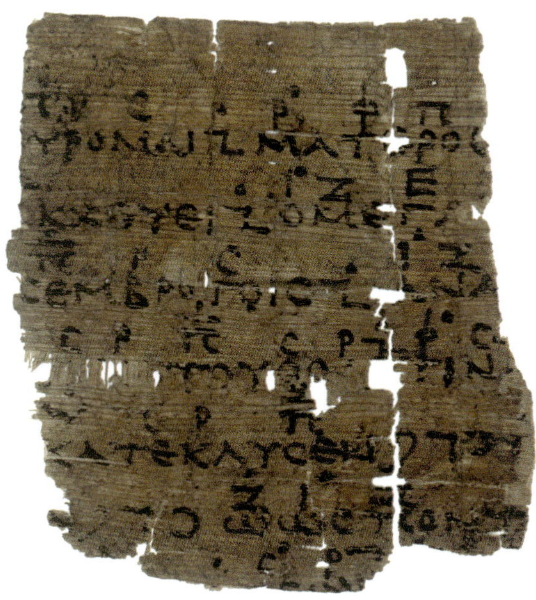

A choral chant from the Oresteia of Euripides with an accompanying vocal and musical score, c. 200–180 BC

a material in everyday use, being reserved on the whole for the production of high-quality books, most notably for Christian literature. In the eight century the Arabs, who had ruled Egypt since 641 AD, introduced paper. This was made from rags and was both much more resilient than papyrus, which had a tendency to become brittle with age, and much cheaper than parchment. By the tenth century paper had altogether replaced papyrus.

In the Viennese Papyrus Museum around 400 objects from the Department of Papyri Collection are on permanent display. Arranged into several thematic groups, these convey a vivid impression of the everyday life and the culture of the inhabitants of Egypt of the time. The display also embraces a series of small temporary exhibitions on specific subjects, which are presented in six glass cases dating from the time of the founding of the collection by Archduke Rainer.

The permanent exhibition at the Papyrus Museum covers the following thematic areas:

| The Study and Conservation of Materials

This section provides information on the production of papyrus, on the state of preservation of papyri, and on the use of papyrus in the wrapping of mummies. It introduces the various writing supports (among them parchment, paper, linen, ostraca) and writing implements. It also exhibits a writing tablet with ink traces and a wax tablet. Diagrams elucidate the stages in the conservation process required by each of these writing materials.

| A School in Antiquity

Displayed here are exercises to test pupils' knowledge of the alphabet and the writing of syllables; the earliest known text for dictation; exercises in essay writing; various mathematical tasks involving numerals, addition, division and tables of fractions; and a book of wax tablets with an ancient form of shorthand (tachygraphy).

| The Literature of Antiquity

Exhibited here are papyri from the twelfth century BC bearing a description of the city of Pi-Ramses; a schematic map of the Fayum region; a novel written in demotic; extracts from the work of Homer, Plato, Isocrates, Hesiod, Herodotus, Xenophon, Cicero, Virgil, Terence and Sallust; a choral chant from the Oresteia of Euripides with an accompanying score; an Arabic novel based on the life of Alexander the Great; the illustrated fragment of another Arabic novel; and a range of Coptic literature, including legends of the martyrs and lives of the saints.

| Administration and Commerce

This display shows legal documents, sales contracts, tax registers, leases, and papyri concerning viticulture and trade with India.

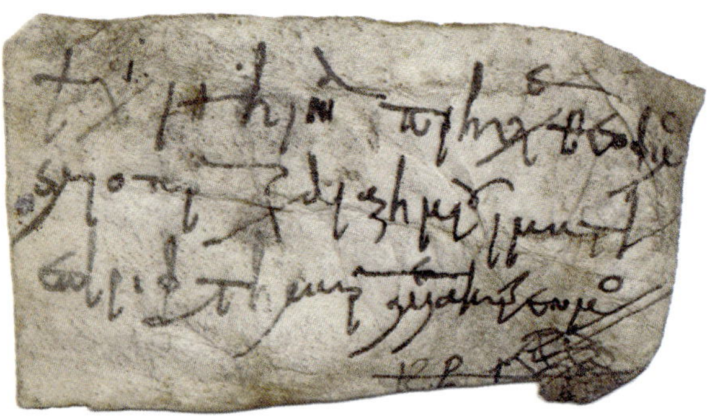

A formal notification of a committed offence seventh century AD

Theophilus, the owner of an oil mill, has discarded his worn-out cloak on the Alexandrine Way and must pay a fine for littering.

| *The Army and the Police*

In this section one can find a loan agreement between two soldiers drawn up in Latin; warrants for interception and arrest; a list of prisoners; and a record of salaries paid to policemen.

| *Everyday Delights, Duties and Perils*

Here one can see examples of private correspondence; an invitation to a party; a musician's work contract; inventories of cutlery and items of clothing; dowry lists; payment made to a hairdresser and a boxer; the formal notification of a committed offence; and the label from an amphora of nutmeg-rose wine.

| *Religion*

The case devoted to this subject contains texts from the Bible (e.g. the Chester-Beatty fragment; Coptic religious literature; a Hebrew parchment with the text of Genesis; a New Testament in Syrian; and a Koran.

| *Magic and medicine*

Exhibited here are amulets (e.g. the Lament of Artemisia); a Sator square (a popular magic formula in antiquity: five words written in a vertical row that reads identicallyfrom left to right, from right to left, from top to bottom, and from bottom to top); amulets to ward off the sting of a scorpion; Aramaic magic bowls; Ethiopian leather rolls and gold lamellae; recipes for cures for eye infections; a form of toothpaste; and a clay fragment with a request for a particular medicine.

| *Textiles*

Exhibited here are a representative selection of Coptic textiles; weavers' articles of apprenticeship; lists of various types of garment; and a weaving manual.

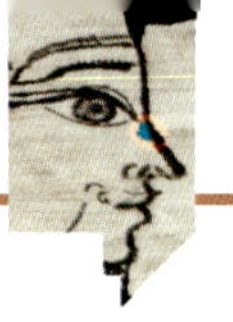

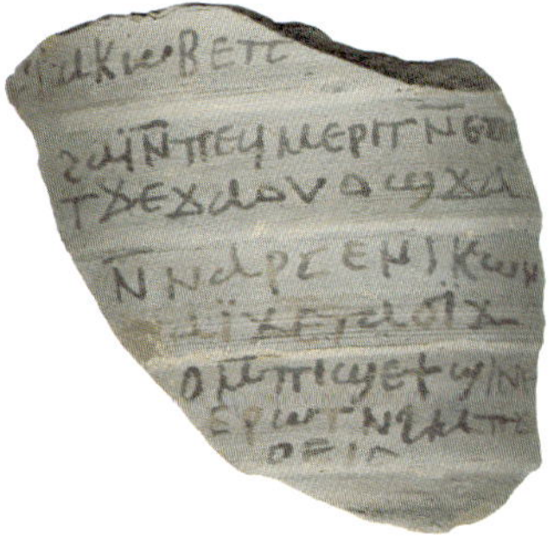

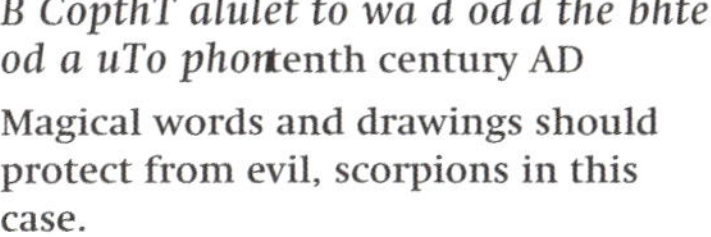

B CopthT alulet to wa d od d the bhte od a uTo phon tenth century AD

Magical words and drawings should protect from evil, scorpions in this case.

CopthT Tlay d aelent bea hne the equeut do a pa thTula ledhTalent eighth century AD:

"Send me a jar of arsenic for my hand, which is covered in pustules."

| Books and book illumination

This section includes illuminated parchment manuscripts; sheets of sketches; parchment and paper bearing 'mirror writing'; and a Coptic book binding.

| The Cult of the Dead

This section displays Books of the Dead and mummy wrappings from Egypt; mummy tablets; the remains of painted shrouds; two portrait heads painted on Roman stucco masks; a Roman mummy mask; mummy portraits; and a list of funeral expenses. Two objects from this section are described here

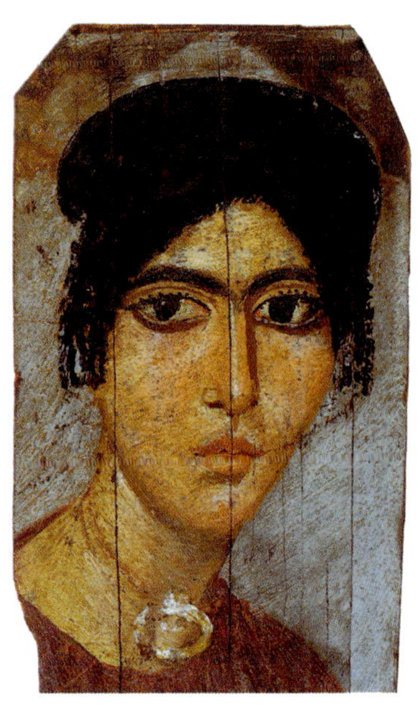

Gully po t aht od a lady second century AD

In this painting technique the colour pigments are fixed with wax. The wax colour is then applied in solid or liquid form and worked with a palette knife.

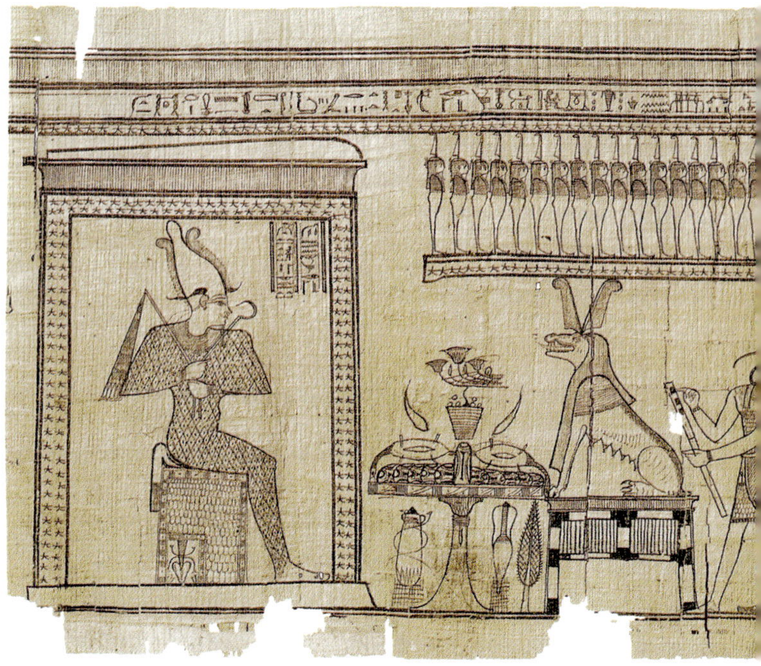

in greater detail: the mummy portrait of a lady from the second century AD and Taruma's Book of the Dead from the second century BC.

From the first century AD developments in ancient Roman portraiture were reflected in the funerary custom of decorating mummies with a portrait of the deceased. By the early fourth century, however, the banning of images encouraged by Early Christianity had already led to a retreat from this custom. In the intervening period mummies had been decorated at their head end with sculpted death masks or with wooden panels bearing a painted portrait. The portrait shown here of a lady from second century AD is executed on a wooden panel with wax colours using the technique known as encaustic.

Taruma's Book of the Dead – a scroll around 8.6 metres in length – is inscribed in hieratic (rapidly written hieroglyphic), with the characters in horizontal rows arranged into generally narrow columns. Outstanding in their artistic quality are the accompanying drawings with a depiction of Taruma being led to the Court of the Dead. In the presence of the hawk-headed god Horus and the jackal-headed god of mummification, Anubis, the heart of the dead woman is placed on a pair of scales in order to weigh it against truth. Meanwhile, the deceased must formally deny, before the highest judge, the god Osiris, and forty-two other judges, that she has committed any of forty-two recognized sins, for example: "I have never injured or killed an animal." A record of the proceedings is kept by the ibis-headed god Toth, who is shown holding a writing tablet and a reed pen. Seated on a pedestal is a monster, a devourer of souls, with a croco-

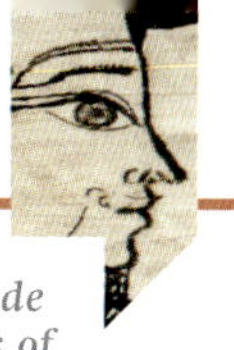

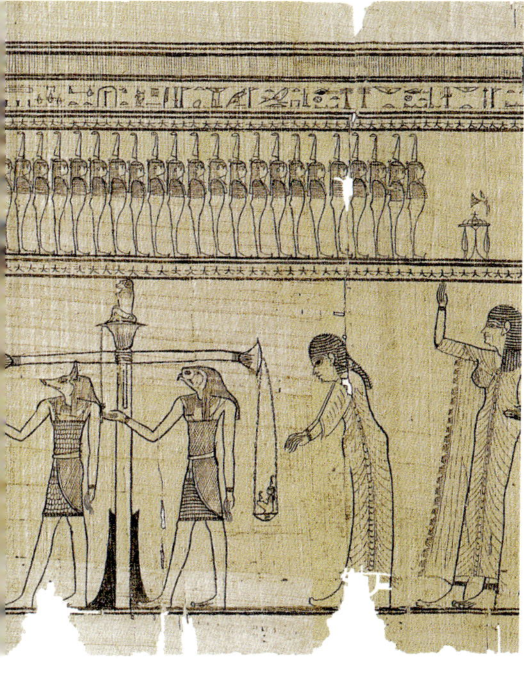

Book of the Dead made for Taruma, priestess of Ptah second century BC

The Book of the Dead depicts in script and drawings a divine judgement before Osiris.

dile head, the body of a lioness and the hind-quarters of a hippopotamus. If the verdict of the Court was negative, this meant the definitive end of the deceased woman's mortal existence.

DEPARTMENT OF PAPYRI

The task of the Department of Papyri is the preservation of writing surfaces of every sort, the ideal being to conserve each item as fully as possible. The best method, now in use for over a century, involves storing the objects (once they have been cleaned and smoothed) on suitable, that is to say pulp- and acid-free, paper under glass, so as to maintain a micro-climate that is as constant as possible with regard to temperature, humidity, etc. Moreover, every opportunity is taken to enlarge the collection and, as far as is possible, to make its holdings accessible to the public.

PAPYROLOGY

Scholarly engagement with the rich legacy of ancient Egypt also embraces the discipline of papyrology, the study of papyri. Owing to the sheer amount of material that has been preserved, the work of papyrologists is much in demand and comprises the initial attempt at deciphering invariably fragmentary texts, followed by their translation and interpretation. There are in fact only around fifty scholars in the entire world who specialize in deciphering papyri; and yet their work supplies scholars in other fields with new and sometimes astonishing source material.

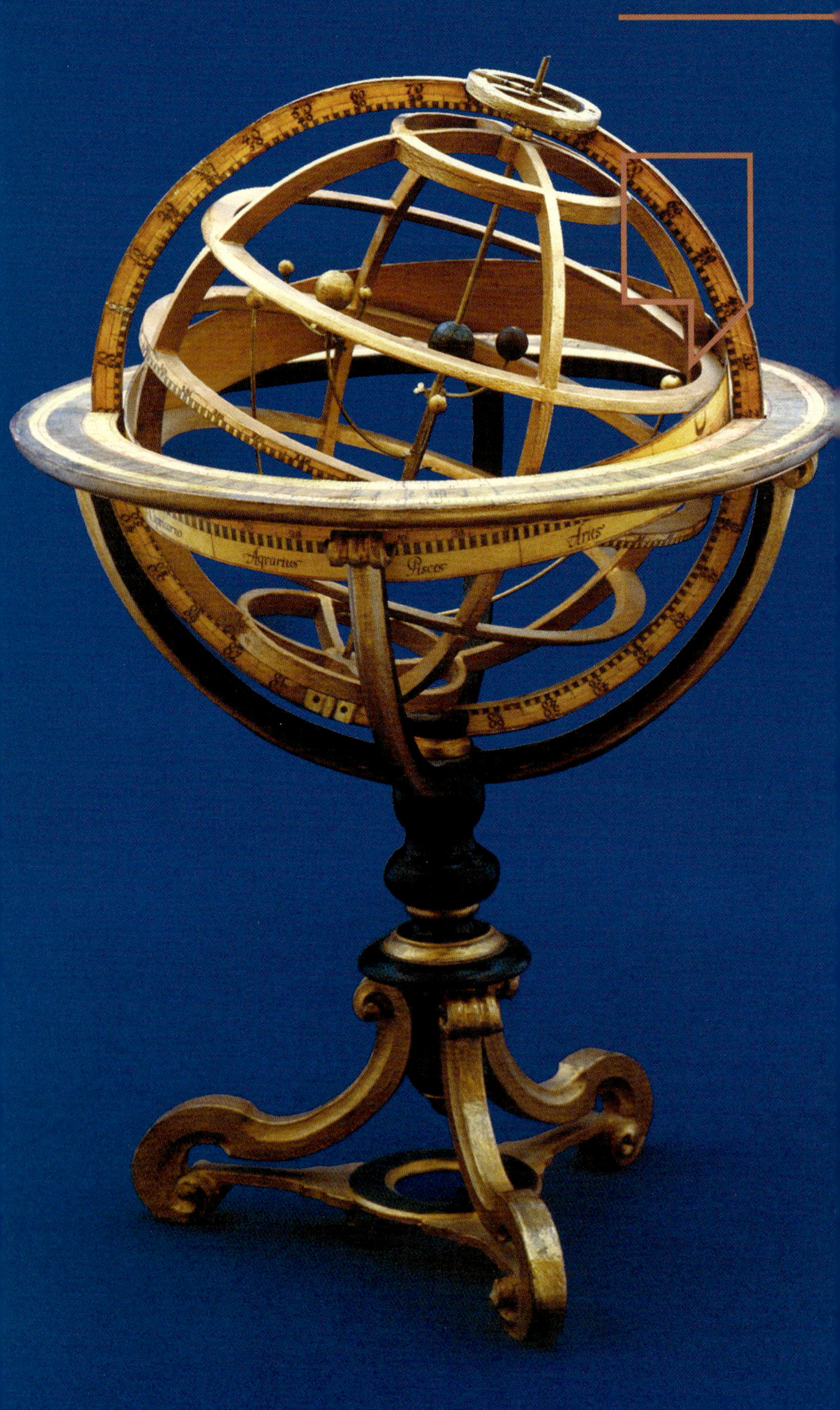

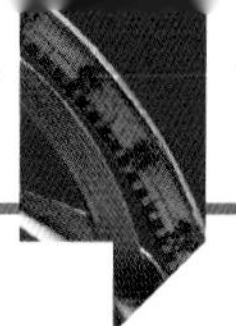

Globe Museum

The Globe Museum is the only collection in the world in which globes and related scientific instruments are not only acquired and researched but are also on open display. Within the Austrian National Library it is affiliated to the Map Department. The globe and map collections are closely connected, be it institutionally, administratively or from the point of view of scholarship and, until 2005, also in terms of their location. Visitors, will, however, discover two very distinct realms.

In the Globe Museum, which is currently still housed on Josefsplatz but which will move, in 2005, to Palais Mollard at 9 Herrengasse in the inner city, objects are prominently displayed and can be examined by any visitor during the opening hours. Guided tours can also be arranged. The objects in the Map Department, are of necessity stored out of sight and, as with the holdings of a specialist library, must be ordered for consultation in a reading room.

In the 1930s globe collectors and enthusiasts in Vienna urged the founding of a state-funded Globe Museum. Before such an institution came into being, a private globe museum (which on occasion also displayed objects from public collections) had already been established in the Viennese home of Robert Haardt (1884–1962), a globe researcher who later became president of the International Coronelli Society for the Study of Globes. In 1953 the Austrian Ministry of Education resolved to establish a state-funded collection of globes to be housed in the Map Department at the Austrian National Library. This new addition to the Library was opened to the public in 1956. In 1986 the Globe Museum was installed in the space it currently occupies, on Josefsplatz. In 2005, however, in expanded form and in a new arrangement, it will be installed in Palais Mollard in Herrengasse. The three principal aims of the Globe Museum in its new home will be to treat the

Andreas Spitzer *Armillary sphere* 1764

The Armillary Sphere is a model of a geocentric world system. Within the skeletal celestial sphere made of wooden rings, the heavenly bodies of the solar system rotate around the earth on moveable brass rods.

full range of themes that may be illustrated and illuminated through the study of globes; to narrate the history of the production of globes; and to provide information on the geographical distribution of globe-making. Visitors will also be able, for the first time in the history of the Globe Museum, to access digitally presented information within the exhibition space.

The holdings of the Globe Museum

The collection of the Globe Museum currently comprises around 380 objects. On exhibition at any given time are over 200 terrestrial and celestial globes, lunar globes and globes representing many of the planets, in addition to scientific instruments connected with globes, such as armillary spheres (three-dimensional models of the celestial sphere constructed out of a set of rings and often incorporating a movable model of the planetary system), planetaria (models of the solar system) and telluria (instruments used to demonstrate the movement of the earth around the sun and of the moon around the earth). The emphasis is on objects made before 1850.

The significance of the Globe Museum resides above all in its capacity to provide the visitor with a comprehensive understanding of the globe as an object, of the historical evolution of cartographic and cosmographic knowledge, and of developments in globe production in past centuries.

Globes are small scale-models of the earth, or of the apparent celestial sphere, or of the moon, or of one of the planets. The advantage of such a three-dimensional form of representation lies in its clarity and in the relative absence of cartographic distortion, be it in the rendering of the continents and the oceans or in the record of the constellations. The disadvantage of globes lies in the fact that, for technical reasons, they can usually only be produced in sizes much smaller than their model in nature and must therefore settle for a considerable degree of generalization.

Globes were made in Greek and Roman antiquity, but only two examples are known to have survived from that period. The ancient science of globe-making was absorbed into Islamic science and scholarship and, with the spread of Islamic influence in Europe, above all in Sicily and in the south of Spain, it was more widely disseminated, especially through emigration to the north and west after the Fall of Constantinople. With the advent of the European Age of Discovery there was a boom in globe production. Globes were now recognized as scientific instruments and as models for use in teaching, and they were eventually mass-produced. Until the mid-nineteenth century it was usual in Europe for globes to be produced in pairs – one terrestrial and one celestial.

Old globes not only testify to the evolution of geographical knowledge and of concepts of the cosmos but are also the fruit of considerable artistic and technical expertise. They have also played a significant role in schemes of domestic decoration and self-representation.

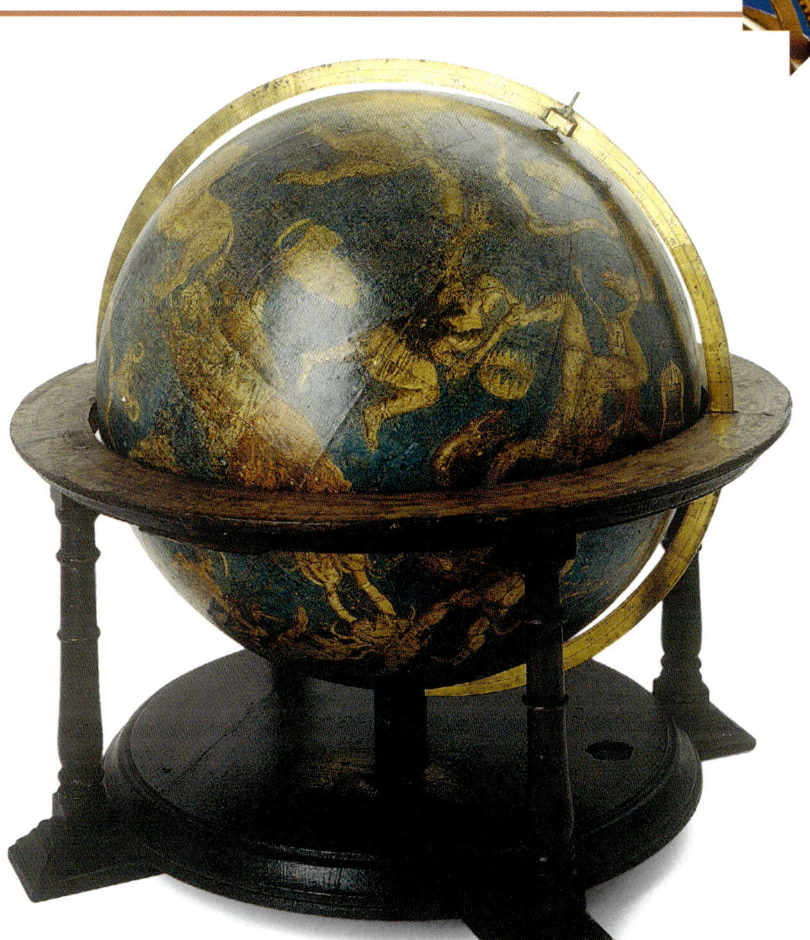

Gerard Mercator *celestial globe* 1551

Highlights of the Collection

Some of the globes on display at the Viennese Globe Museum are exceptional because of their scientific importance and their rarity:

On long-term loan from the private collection of Robert Schmidt, Vienna, is the earliest globe to be found in Austria – a unique piece. This terrestrial globe was made around 1536 by the physician and cosmographer Rainer Gemma Frisius (1508–55) of the University of Louvain. It is astonishingly detailed and provides a record of geographical knowledge in the wake of the great discoveries of the late fifteenth and early sixteenth centuries. At the same time it includes a number of purely speculative geographical features such as a huge southern continent.

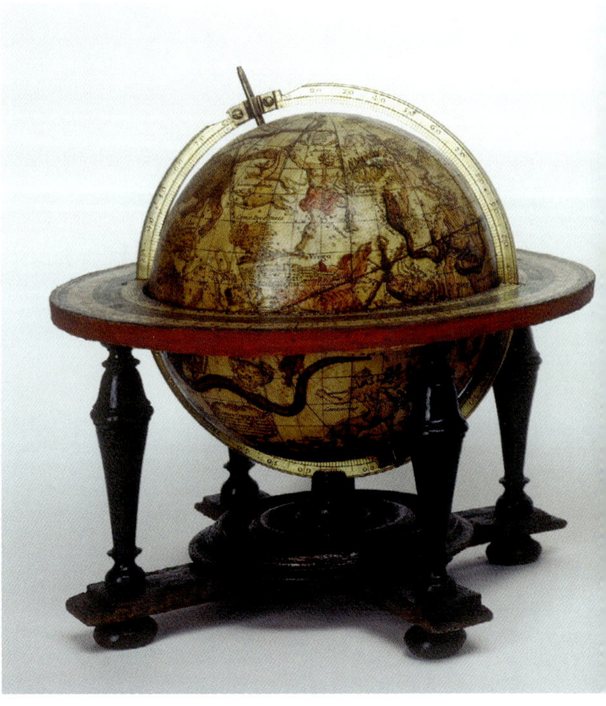

Also especially notable is the pair of globes (terrestrial and celestial) made by Gerard Mercator (1512–94) in 1541 and 1551. This most celebrated of sixteenth-century cartographers was the first to mark the surface of his terrestrial globes with loxodromic spirals (which consistently cut the meridians at the same angle and are of great importance for navigation). In the case of his celestial globes he added two constellations to the 48 that usually appeared: Hair of Berenice and Antinous (see p. 71).

A collection of Dutch globes, among them eleven produced by the publishing family of Blaeu, bears witness to the leading position of Dutch cartography and globe production as well as the high quality in the printing of copper engravings in the first half of the seventeenth century. The cosmos as conceived in the Baroque era is represented by ten globes by the most celebrated globe-maker of this period, Vincenzo Coronelli (1650–1718). This Venetian Minorite cleric, cosmosgrapher and cartographer achieved a milestone in globe-making with his globes measuring 110 cm in diameter. Four globes made by Coronelli have formed part of the Baroque decorative programme of the State Room since its creation in the early eighteenth century (see p. 57).

Globe production in southern Germany was of great importance for the dissemination of globes in Austria in the eighteenth century. The Globe Museum display includes globes made by Johann Gabriel Doppelmayr, Georg Moritz Lowitz, Johann Georg Klinger and a celestial globe by Johann

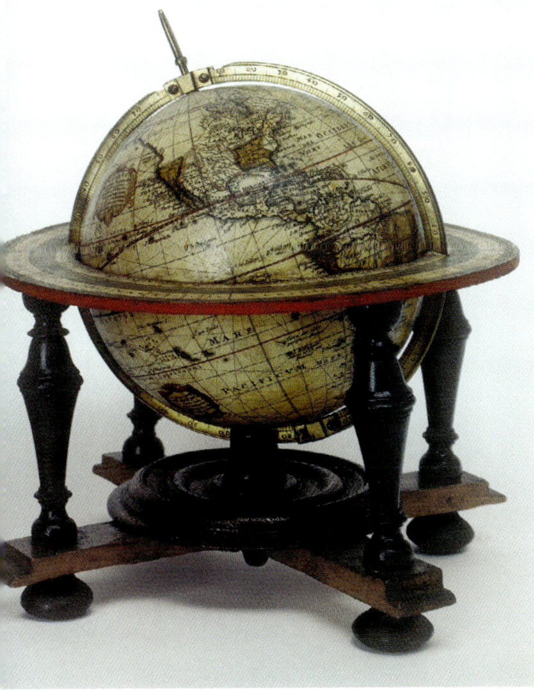

Ludwig Andreae of Nuremberg, in addition to examples of the work of the cartographic publisher and globe-maker Matthäus Seutter of Augsburg.

Austrian globe-making is represented in the display by the work of Joseph Jüttner, who in the early nineteenth century was the first in Austria to engage in the serial production of globes. Also included are the products of the firm of Jan Felkl & Son of Rostok near Prague. Examples of nineteenth-century work from Germany include globes made by Daniel Friedrich Sotzmann of Nuremberg, Carl Friedrich Weiland of Weimar, and the publisher Dietrich Reimer of Berlin. Testimony of the developments in the nineteenth and early twentieth centuries is provided by the collapsible globe made by Anton Sturm and Franz Kaiser; an inflatable terrestrial globe made by Philipp Cella; a globe with a relief surface by Karl Wilhelm Kummer; a geological globe by Wilhelm Dames; and, on long-term loan from the Institute of Geography and Regional Research at Vienna University, two meteorological globes by Carl Kassner.

Globes made in the twentieth century can also be rare, interesting and valuable. A particularly intriguing exhibit is the 'Rollglobus' devised in 1937 by Robert Haardt, in which the absence of the conventional north-south and east-west axes permits an uncompromised approach to each region of the world, while the 'Haardt Earth-gauge' allows the distance between any two locations to be directly measured. Another unusual feature of the display is its collection of lunar and planet globes.

Q'O-GGKALMARL HU

PRECETTI

DI

GRAMMATICA

PER LA

LINGUA FILOSOFICA,

O SIA,

UNIVERSALE,

PROPRIA PER OGNI GENERE DI VITA.

Παυρα μεν, αλλα μαλα λιγεως. HOMERVS.

Quidquid praecipies, esto breuis, ut cito dicta percipiant animi dociles, *teneant que* fideles. HORATIVS.

IN ROMA MDCCLXXIII.
NELLA STAMPERIA DI PAOLO GIUNCHI.

Con Licenza de' Superiori.

Esperanto Museum and
Department of Planned Languages

The Department of Planned Languages houses the world's largest specialist library for interlinguistics and documents a total of around five hundred diverse planned languages, among them Volapük, Ido, Interlingua and Esperanto, the last of which is the most widely used planned language, with several million speakers. Attached to the Department of Planned Languages is the Esperanto Museum, which affords visitors an insight into the history of this language.

In 1927 Hugo Steiner founded the International Esperanto Museum in Vienna, and this was incorporated into the Austrian National Library in 1929. Today, its collection embraces approximately 25,000 books, 2,500 periodicals, 2,000 museum objects, 2,200 autograph texts and manuscripts, 22,000 photographic prints and negatives, 1,100 posters and 40,000 broadsheets. By dint of continuous collecting (interrupted only during the National Socialist period, when the 'Jewish language' was banned), the Austrian National Library can now lay claim to the world's largest library for planned languages and the history and principles of language planning.

Planned languages, that is to say artificial languages, are studied by that branch of learning that has, since the early twentieth century, been known as interlinguistics. There are philosophical planned languages, auxiliary international languages and literary or fictional languages, such as Elvish in Tolkien's trilogy *Lord of the Rings*.

Despite occasional efforts in the medieval period, it was not until the sixteenth century that the first serious schemes for planned languages were developed. The idea of planned languages was an outcome of philosophical speculation on the nature language. It was felt that language should

György Kalmár, title page of *Precetti di Grammatica per la lingua filosofica, osia, universale* Rome 1773

replicate the world as closely as possible and be formed in such a way that only logical thought processes were possible. A series of outstanding individuals in European intellectual history addressed this and related issues, among them Francis Bacon (1561–1626), Jan Ámos Komenský (Comenius) (1592–1670), René Descartes (1596–1650) and Gottfried Wilhelm Leibniz (1646–1716).

By the nineteenth century the situation had altered entirely: owing to the marked increase in international relations, the pragmatic advantages of easier and more direct international communication became increasingly evident as the problem of international understanding became ever more pressing. Alongside French (at that time still the traditional language of diplomacy, of the aristocracy, and of the educated bourgeoisie throughout Europe), Russian, English and German were all gaining in importance as international languages and there was already a degree of conscious competition between them in this respect. Those seeking a solution through

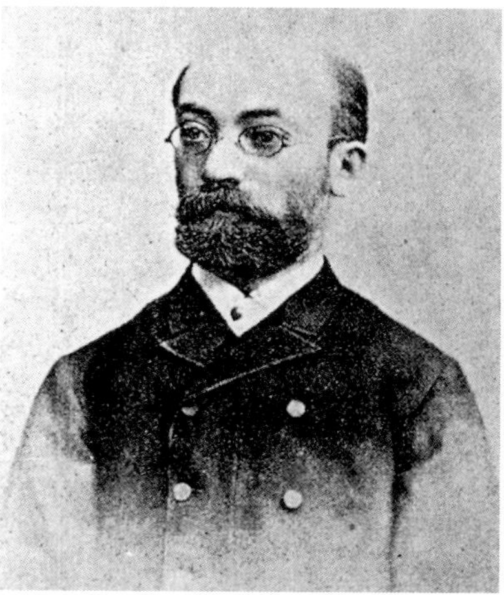

Ludvik L. Zamenhof
1859–1917

First introduced by Zamenhof in 1887, the invented language subsequently named Esperanto gradually evolved into a fully functioning means of verbal expression and communication.

the creation of auxiliary international languages focused above all on the issue of practicality. They recognized that, in order to be broadly adopted, an planned language would have to offer ease of learning and speaking, a truly international character, and the 'feel' of a natural language.

Esperanto

These criteria were finally met to a substantial degree when, in 1887, the Polish ophthalmologist Dr. Ludwik L. Zamenhof (1859–1917) published a slim pamphlet introducing the principles of a new planned language: Esperanto. Over the course of the years this has evolved into one of the world's few fully functional planned languages. There are now over a hundred international Esperanto organizations, the largest being the Universala Esperanto-Asocio (Esperanto World Union), which is based in Rotterdam. Each year an Esperanto World Congress takes place, Vienna having hosted four of these in 1924, 1936, 1970 and 1992

Zamenhof's premise was that the world's various cultures and religions should each retain their distinctive qualities, but must be prepared, to put aside temporarily, the features that divided them. In his view, the fundamental human values were the same in all cultures and all religions; a fundamental unity underlay the diversity of appearances. And this, he argued, was also true in the realm of language. But an international language would only make sense if its potential users were convinced that universal understanding – in spite of persistent differences – was both possible and desirable. The pioneers of Esperanto cultivated the great hope that the peoples of the world might one day meet and deal with each other in just as unprejudiced a fashion as had long been the case with Esperantists. Wars would then soon be a thing of the past. In the early twenty-first century, however, this hope still appears somewhat Utopian.

The development of Esperanto has, however, also proved of relevance to the study of language in general. Interlinguistic research undertaken to

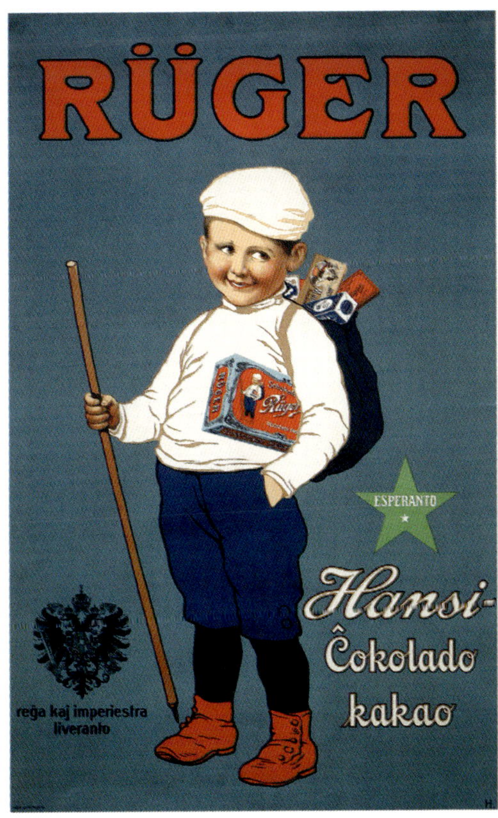

Advertising for children's chocolate in Esperanto

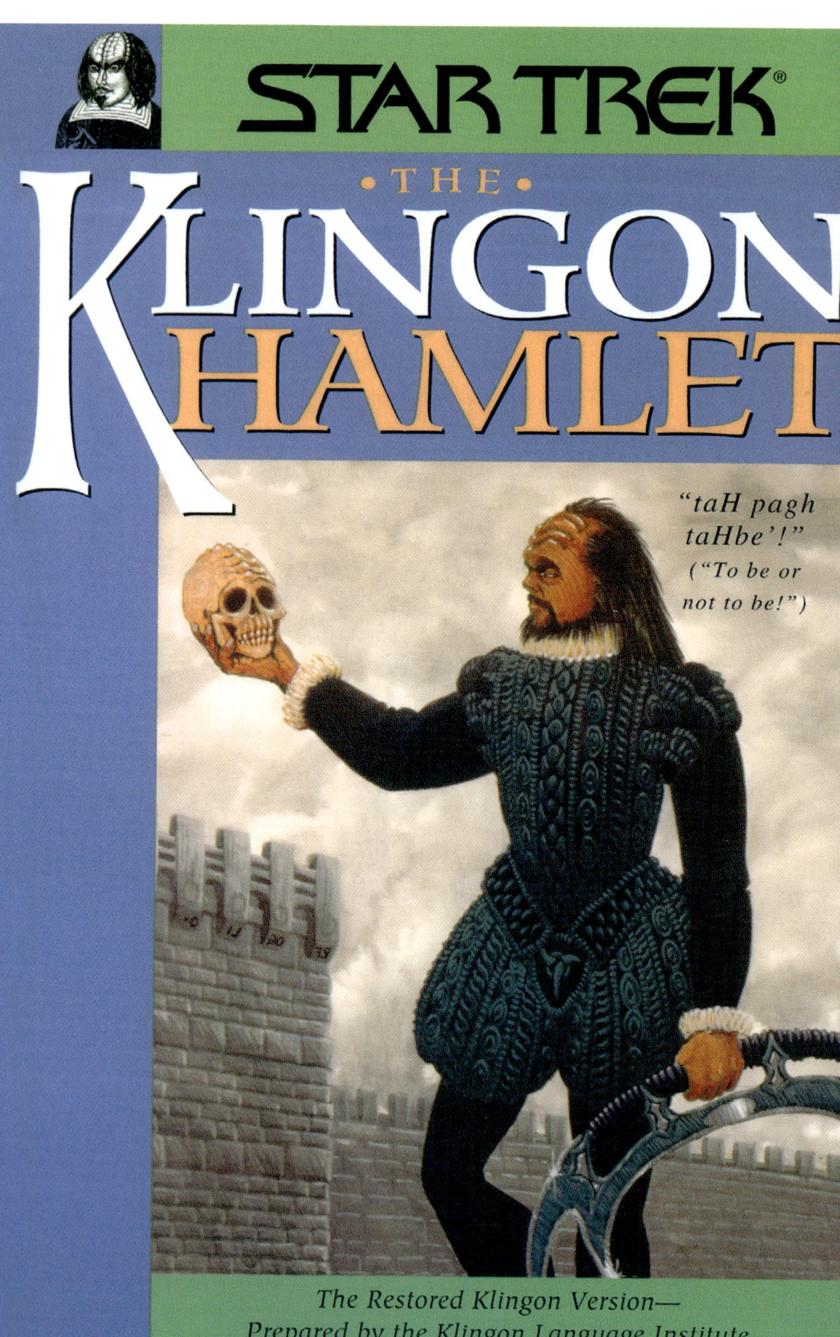

Hamlet in Klingon

Translation of Shakespeares 'Hamlet' in Klingon, the language spoken in outer space in the cult TV series *Star Trek*

counter the prejudice against planned languages had a significant impact on the development of linguistics, with the result that old convictions were overcome and new questions posed, which led, in turn, for example, to the science of applied linguistics. Closely connected with the development of planned languages has been the evolution of related linguistic terminology. Eugen Wüster (1898–1977), a pioneer of the internationalization of linguistic terminology, was able to demonstrate that terminological standardization comes about according to similar principles and patterns as the elaboration of a planned language. The Department of Planned Languages now also houses the literary estate of Eugene Wüster.

The unconventional

The Esperanto Museum also documents some very unconventional attempts to solve the language problem, such as the revival of the languages of classical antiquity. Modern communications technology has in fact come to the aid of this endeavour: both Latin and ancient Greek have found a new popularity as an international means of communication on the Internet. Also included in the museum's exhibits are the latest planned languages, such as Klingon (the language spoken in outer space in the cult TV series *Star Trek*) or the hoax language Starckdeutsch. On a more serious note there are exhibits relating to the efforts to relieve the linguistic chaos that prevailed in the multi-ethnic Danubian Monarchy through the promotion of Neo-Slavic.

Hamlets soliloquy in romanized Klingon:

taH pagh taHbe'. DaH mu'tlheghvam vIqelnIS.

quv'a', yabDaq San vaQ cha, pu' je SIQDI'?

pagh, Seng bIQ'a'Hey SuvmeH nuHmey SuqDI',

'ej, Suvmo', rInmoHDI'? Hegh. Qong – Qong neH –

'ej QongDI', tIq 'oy', wa'SanID Daw"e' je

cho'nISbogh porghDaj rInmoHlaH net Har.

yIn mevbogh mIwvam'e' wIruchqangbej

Hegh. Qong. QongDI' chaq naj. toH, waQlaw' ghu'vam!

HeghDaq maQongtaHvIS, tugh nuq wInajlaH,

volchaHmajvo' jubbe'wI' bep wIwoDDI';

'e' wIqelDI', maHeDnIS. Qugh DISIQnIS,

SIQmoHmo' qechvam. Qugh yIn nI'moH 'oH.

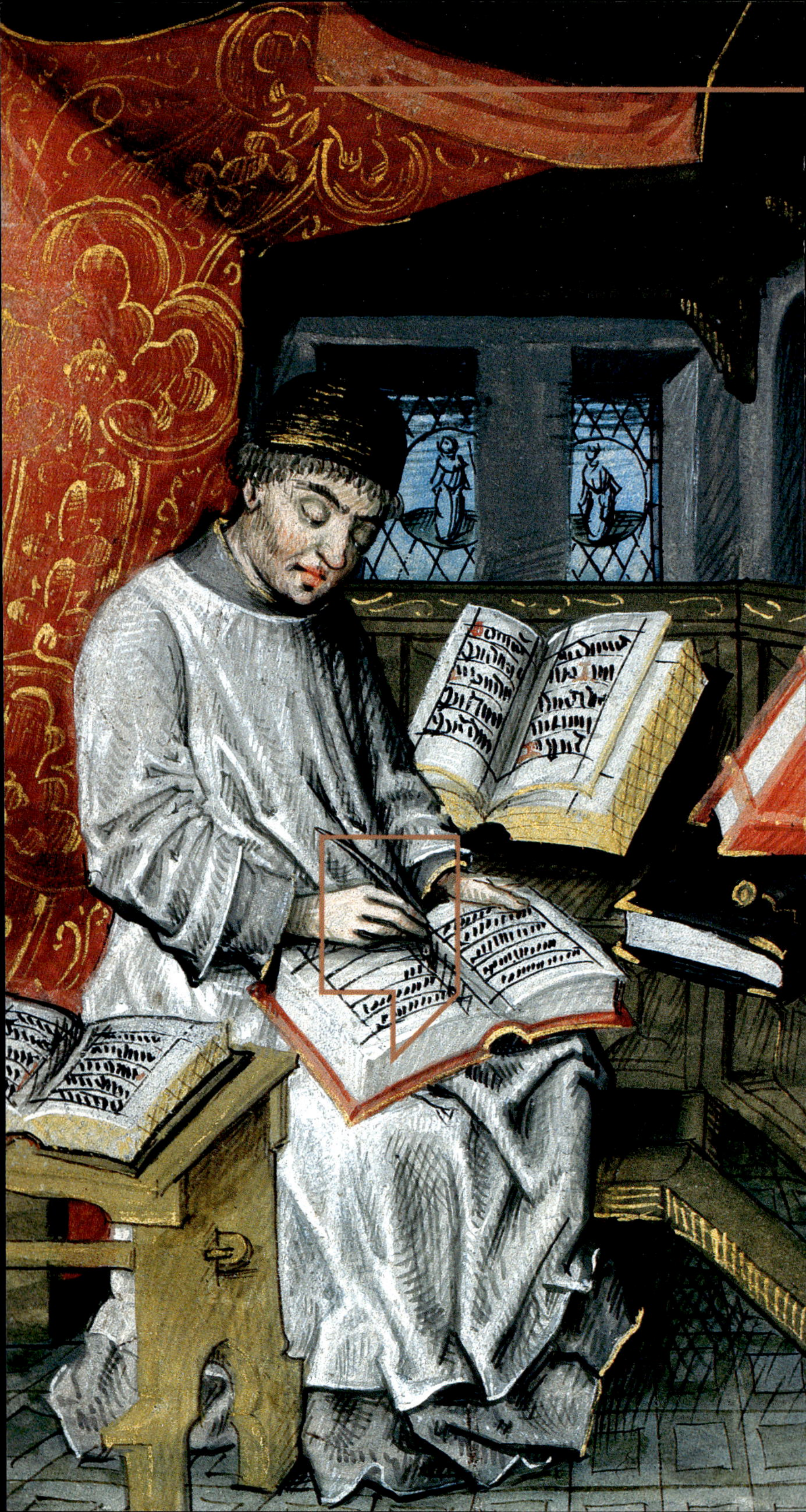

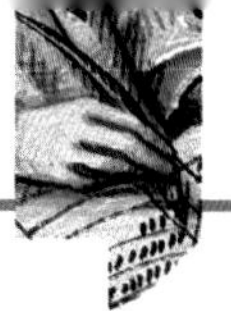

Department of Manuscripts, Autographs and Closed Collections

The beginnings of the largest and most important collection of manuscripts to be found in Austria date from a time even before the first formal appointment of an Imperial Court Librarian, Hugo Blotius (1534–1608), and are traditionally associated with Johannes von Troppau's splendidly decorated Evangelary made in 1368. This oldest recorded surviving Habsburg-Austrian book is regarded as the founding codex of the Austrian National Library and was once in the possession of Archduke Albert III (1350–1395).

Most of the especially valuable items in the Austrian National Library collection are splendid manuscripts of a comparably early date deriving from the collections of princes and members of the nobility, above all the emperors Friedrich III (b. 1415, r. 1452–1493), Maximilian I (b. 1459, r. 1508–19) and Ferdinand I (b. 1503, r. 1558–64).

The Imperial Court Library was greatly enlarged through the absorption of collections of books keenly assembled by scholars such as Wolfgang Lazius (1514–65) and Ghislain von Busbecq (1522–92). Unlike Blotius, neither of these held the position of officially appointed prefect of the Imperial Court Library, but they were both closely connected with this institution.

Further expansion came about by absorbing the Fugger Library; transferring to Vienna in 1665 the collection previously housed at Schloss Ambrus in Innsbruck; acquiring in 1737/38 the library formerly belonging to Prince Eugene of Savoy; and taking over the holdings of the old library of Vienna University in 1756 and those of the Viennese City Library in 1780. The banning of the Jesuit Order from the Habsburg territories in 1773 and the subsequent closing of most of the monasteries by the emperor Joseph II (b. 1741, r. 1765–1790) also brought extensive new holdings to the Court Library.

Thomas à Kempis composing De Imitatione Christi
(Imitation of Christ), Flanders, c. 1500

As the result of a long history of military, political and commercial engagement with the empire of the Ottoman Turks, the accompanying diplomatic interchange with this region, and ultimately of the research trips undertaken by scholars in the nineteenth century, numerous oriental manuscripts came into the possession of the Court Libarary.

Centuries of systematic collecting activity has resulted in a collection that is now markedly universal and international in character. One can find here outstanding examples of the achievement of almost every script culture in existence between the fourth century AD and today. There are manuscripts in Greek and Hebrew as well as numerous languages of the Near, Middle and Far East, including Georgian, Armenian, Coptic, Syrian and Ethiopian, and the languages of India and China.

MANUSCRIPT ILLUMINATION

With the introduction of the codex as a book form, which occurred in the fourth century AD in connection with parchment manuscripts, there was a marked improvement in the way in which text and images might be combined. While it is true that papyrus rolls had been illuminated, parchment bound into a codex opened up significant new possibilities. By the fifteenth century, however, paper had become established as the principal writing support; in the Mediterranean region paper had been in use since the eight century

Manuscript illumination is understood to embrace the arts involved in decorating a text with painted or drawn images, ornaments or elaborate initial letters. Manuscript illumination was an important branch of the fine arts, and in the case of some eras and regions illuminated manuscripts are often the only surviving evidence of the activity of painters. The abundance of images and ornaments served to affirm the value of a manuscript, and often many individuals were engaged in their execution. Simple forms of ornament would often be executed by the scribe or by a calligrapher. The task of the rubricator was to highlight particular parts of the text, such as its beginning. That of the illuminator was to provide the more painterly elements of the decoration. In many cases it is possible to distinguish the work of a master and his assistants within the same illuminated manuscript.

Manuscript illumination was already a highly regarded art in the cultures of antiquity. But it is now above all associated with the Medieval period, its last great efflorescence, in the sixteenth century, overlapping with the invention of printing.

At the Austrian National Library it is possible to trace the historical evolution of manuscript illumination virtually without interruption from late antiquity, through the work of the early medieval, Carolignian, Ottonian and Romanesque periods, to the era of Gothic and finally the Renaissance.

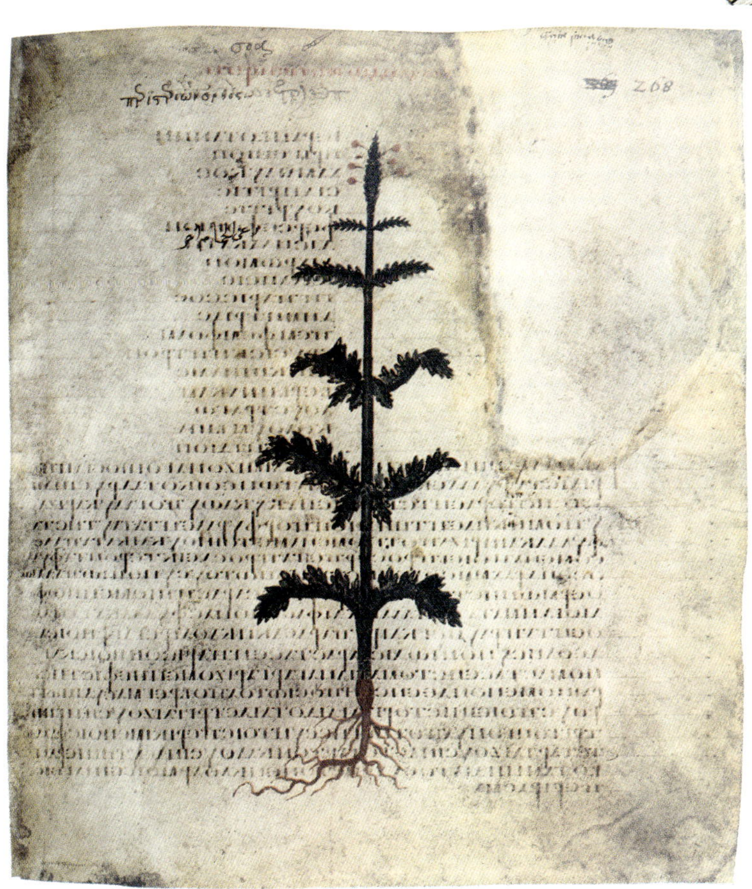

The Viennese Dioscurides Constantinople, around 512
This Byzantine manuscript was for centuries the main source
on which botany drew.

It appears that in the earliest period we now associate with manuscript illumination, works of a scientific character were always illuminated, the combination of text and image proving a great aid to understanding. The Byzantine manuscript known as the *Viennese Dioscurides* – Dioscurides was a Greek physician of the first century AD – was added in 1997, along with all the Greek manuscripts in the Austrian National Library, to the UNESCO register of 'world heritage documents'. It is a collection of botanic-pharmacological texts produced in Constantinople in around 512 for Princess Juliana Anicia, daughter of Flavius Anicius Olybrius (who ruled the western Roman Empire from 472 AD), and was for centuries a source on which other herbals frequently drew. The codex is decorated with images of the physicians of antiquity, of the author himself and of the dedicatee, and of a great many plants. At the beginning there is an alphabetic listing of the plants described in the volume, comparable to the

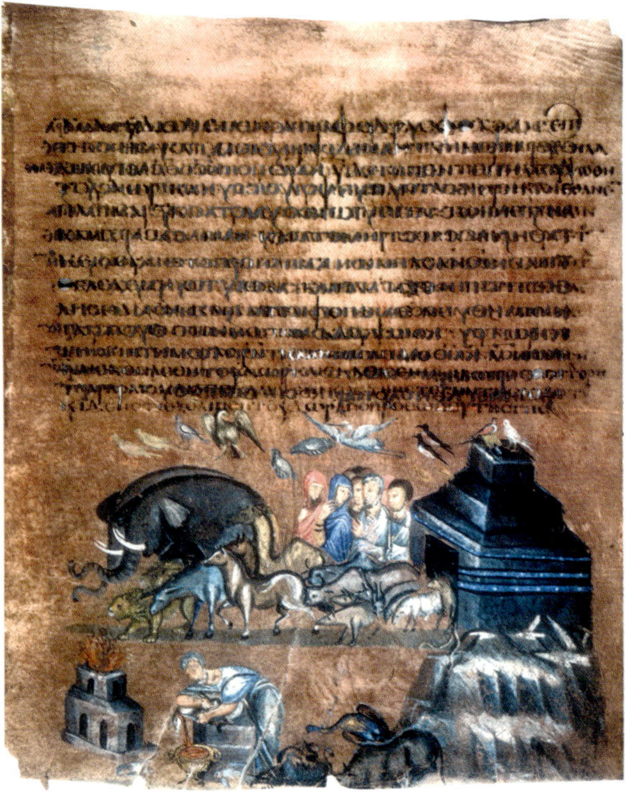

The Viennese Genesis, probably Antioch first half of
the sixth century
Miniature depicting the procession out of the ark and
the sacrifice of Noah

index of a printed book. An appendix contains images of birds, reptiles and insects. An especially sumptuous edition copied in the sixth century was still in use as a work of reference in a hospital in Constantinople in the fourteenth century. By the end of that century the binding was so badly damaged that a new one became necessary.

The *Viennese Genesis* is of particular importance for our knowledge of manuscript illumination in late antiquity. It is assumed to come from Antioch (in Asia Minor) and to date from the first half of the sixth century. The Greek script is written in capitals on purple parchment, a particularly expensive writing support, the use of which is indicative of the significance attached to the transcription of the Bible. The manuscript is illuminated with forty-eight images and was part of one of the earliest surviving illuminated Biblical cycles in the form of a codex.

The evidence of the twenty-four sheets that we still have suggests that they are the remains of a codex that once contained 192 miniatures and

400 to 500 larger scenes. The preserved scenes from the *Viennese Genesis* are arranged in strips and testify to a merging of Jewish manuscript illumination and Hellenistic painting. It is assumed that Crusaders brought the surviving pages to Italy, perhaps to Venice. In 1662 they were bequeathed by Archduke Leopold Wilhelm to Emperor Leopold I and they entered the Court Library in 1664.

Manuscript illumination attained a new high point in the era of Charlemagne (768–814) and his immediate successors An example of the many valuable manuscripts in the Austrian National Library dating from the Carolignian period (780–900) is the Hrabanus Maurus Codex. This contains poems by Hrabanus Maurus (780–856), in which Louis the Pious (778/814–840) is represented as a warrior in the service of Christ.

The Ottonian Renaissance – a term used in analogy to the Carolignian Renaissance – is associated with the rise of literature, art and scientific

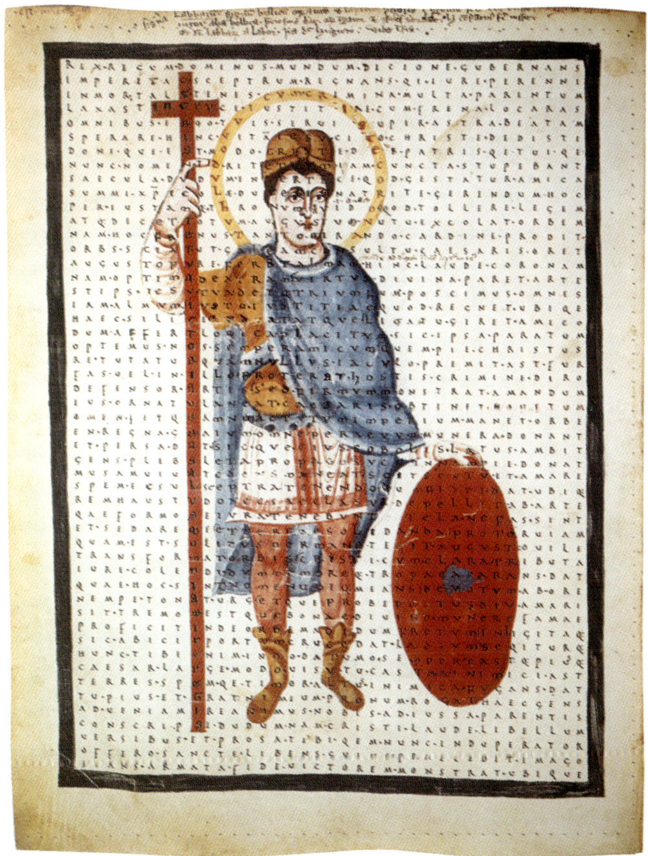

The Hrabanus Maurus Codex: Liber de Laudibus Sanctae Crucis
(Book on the Praise of the Cross)
Pictorial poem showing Louis the Pious as a holy warrior

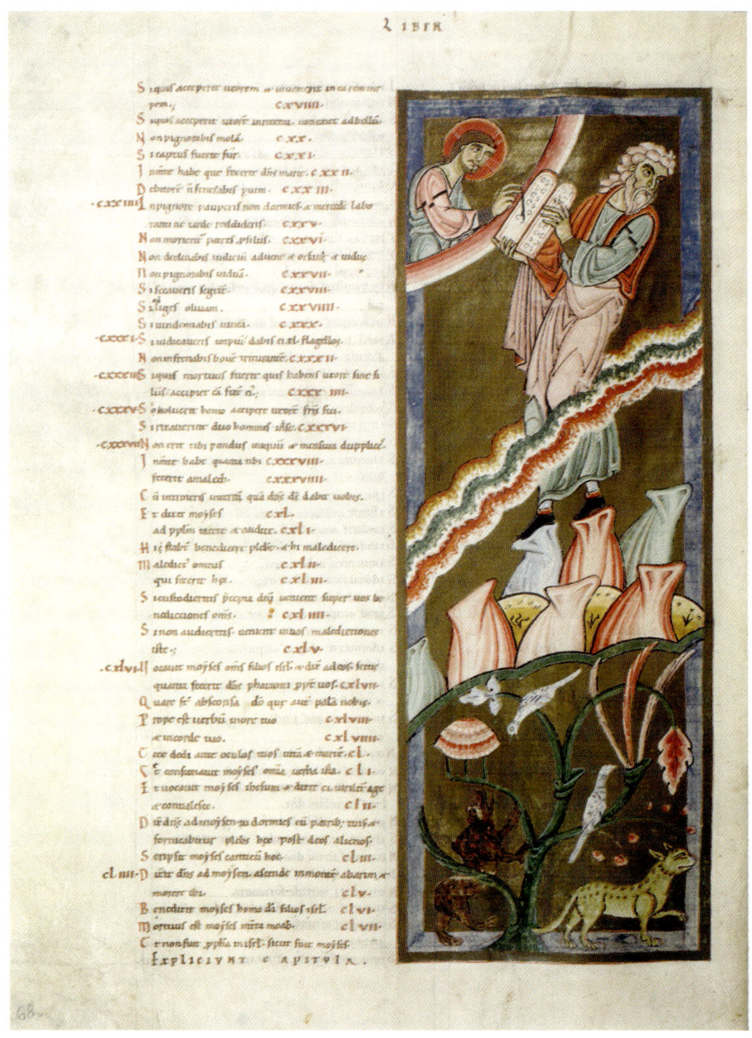

The Admont Bible Salzburg, c. 1150
Entire manuscript page with a miniature of Moses receiving
the tables of the law

learning in the wake of the greater political stability prevailing with the accession of Otto I (936–73). An outstanding example of manuscript illumination in the Ottonian period (which reached its peak in the eleventh century) is the *Life of St. Ulrich*, a work of the School of Reichenau, dating to around 1020/30.

A great many valuable codices have been preserved from the Romanesque period, from the eleventh to the thirteenth century. These include the *Admont Bible* from Salzburg. The Latin manuscript, dating from around

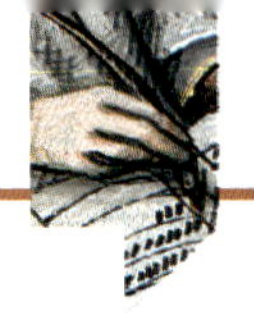

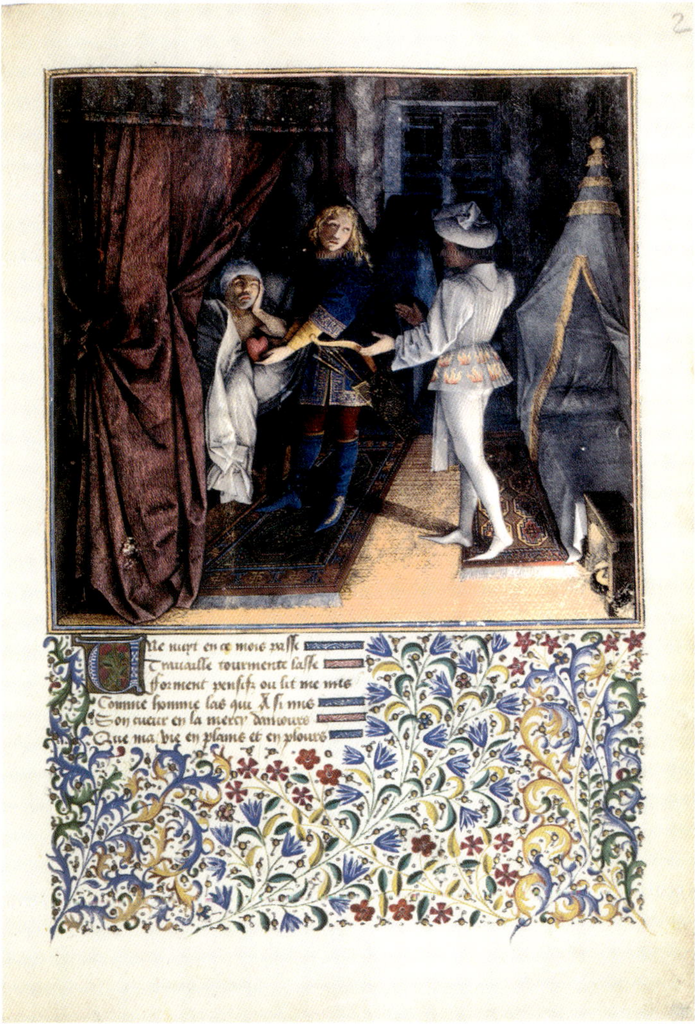

The Master of the Heart *Livre du Cuer d'amours espris* Anjou, after 1460

Entire page containing a short text, ornamentation and a miniature of 'Cupid stealing the heart of the sleeping Duke René of Anjou, which Desire takes into her possession'

1150, came to the Benedictine Monastery of Admont in Styria in the fifteenth century by way of a monastery in western Hungary. In 1937 it was acquired by the Austrian National Library. Apart from its large size, the Bible is especially striking on account of its elaborate decoration with initials and large images incorporating much use of gold and silver.

Among the Austrian National Library's holdings of work from the Gothic period of manuscript illumination, beginning in the thirteenth century, there is a French *Bible moralisée* as well as several of the Books of Hours

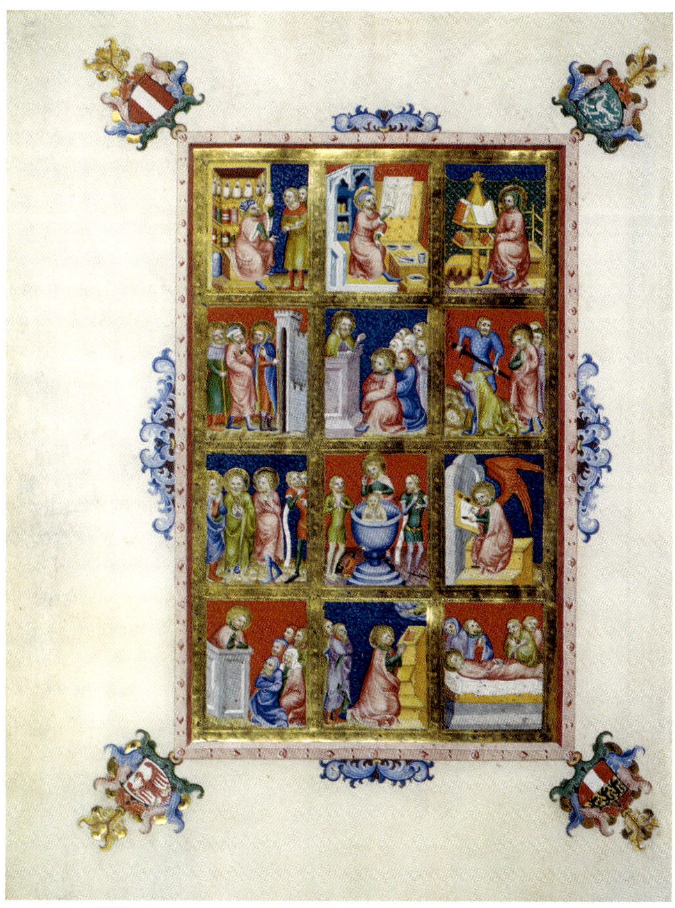

Johannes von Troppau *Evangelary* 1368

This evangelary, written in gold lettering and exquisitely illuminated in the style employed in Bohemia in the fourteenth century, was made for Archduke Albert III.

that came into vogue in the fourteenth and fifteenth centuries. Among these is the *Livre du Cuer d'amours espris* (after 1460), the work of the Master of the Heart (so called after his book), who was attached to the Ducal Court of René of Anjou (r. 1474–80). This is notable for the exceptionally artistic treatment of light in its poetic images.

The Evangelary of Johannes von Troppau, dating from 1368, is another example of Gothic manuscript illumination. As mentioned above, this item derives from the collection of Archduke Albert III. The entire text of the four Gospels is written in gold lettering and is illuminated in the style prevailing in Bohemia in the fourteenth century. Each chapter is decorated with its own ornaments and images. The scenes from the life of

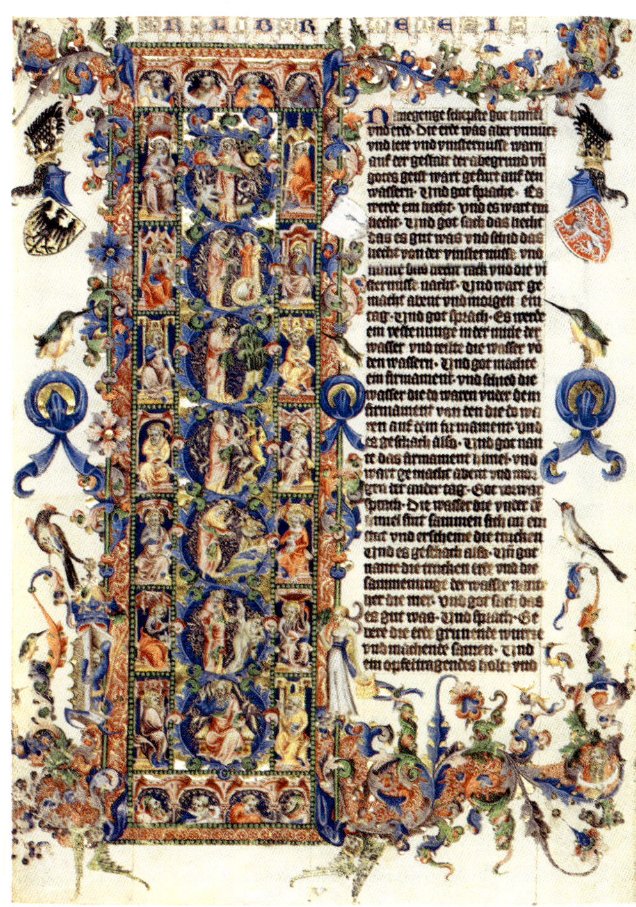

The Wenceslas Bible Prague, c. 1400

Text and the initial I from the Book of Genesis. In the medallions there are depictions of the seven days of creation, framed on either side by figures representing the apostles and prophets. In the borders: the Bohemian coat of arms and the emblems of King Wenceslas, bathing girls and the kingfisher.

Matthew are framed by the coats-of-arms of Austria, Styria, Tyrol and Carinthia – the territories, that Albert III ruled until 1379. The archduke was an outstanding connoisseur of the arts and a patron of Vienna University, who commissioned the translation of works from Latin into locally spoken languages and founded an illumination workshop, in which other valuable manuscripts were produced. The sumptuous silver gilt binding of the Book of the Gospels is contemporary with the manuscript itself. Its lower clasp, however, dates from the time of Frederick III and bears his motto 'A.E.I.O.U.' and the year 1446. The upper clasp is a copy made in 1990. This codex entered the Imperial Court Library at some point between 1721 and 1798.

Manuscript illumination was of considerable importance in Bohemia in the late fourteenth century, during the reign of King Wenceslas IV (Wenzel I as German king), when several masterpieces of the Gothic period were produced. Among the valuable manuscripts to issue from the Wenceslas illumination workshop in Prague around 1400 was the celebrated *Wenceslas Bible*. In contrast to the many manuscript Bibles with Latin texts, for example the *Admont Bible*, the *Wenceslas Bible* was written in German, and this was long before the time of Martin Luther. While extremely impressive with its 2,400 pages, the *Wenceslas Bible* was never finished. The text on each page is arranged in two columns and is illustrated almost throughout, with a total of over 600 images and superb decorative marginalia (see p. 89).

During the Renaissance there was a revival of interest in antiquity, the surviving work was repeatedly copied, and knowledge of the literature of antiquity was encouraged through translations and transcriptions of the original. The Austrian National Library's holdings from this period include a superb edition of the speeches of Cicero (106–43 BC), made between 1480 and 1490 for Ferdinand I of Aragón, King of Naples, (1423/1443–94). The richly illuminated start of the text shows Cicero as an orator in an ecclesiastical interior rendered in perspective. The Austrian National Library today boasts a total of 56,000 *codices manuscripti* representing numerous periods and cultures, and around *codices miniati*, chiefly illuminated manuscripts and diverse 'albums'. These last constitute a unique source for the study of topography and the history of art. The range of the collection spans continents, with examples from the Netherlands to others from as far afield as India, China and Japan. No less diverse is the range of subjects treated in these works: there are architectural drawings, views of cities, images of animals, pattern books, compendia of traditional costumes, miniatures, copies of paintings, coats-of-arms, allegorical figures and so forth. The collection also includes around 300,000 autograph manuscripts. Most of these are letters and short pieces of work, their authors being celebrated individuals from the realms of politics, scholarship, art, literature and other branches of culture. In addition to individual documents, the Library also holds entire literary estates, chiefly of Austrian authors. These embrace material such as typescripts, galley- and page-proofs, and authors' annotated copies of their own books. Such material allows the researcher to trace the evolution of a work or of its successive editions. An example is provided by the manuscripts relating to Ludwig Wittgenstein's (1889–1951) *Tractatus logico-philosophicus*. They reveal the range and the continuity of his engagement with the ideas treated in this text.

Authors represented in the collection of literary estates include Fritz von Herzmanovsky Orlando (1877–1954), Robert Musil (1880–1942) and Ingeborg Bachmann (1926–73). The Department of Manuscripts, Autographs and Closed Collections also conserves, and makes available to users, the literary estates and texts it has acquired from the Austrian Literary Archives (see p. 126).

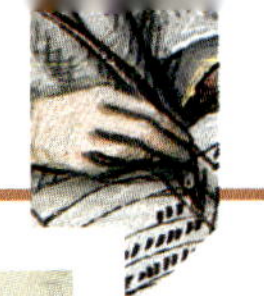

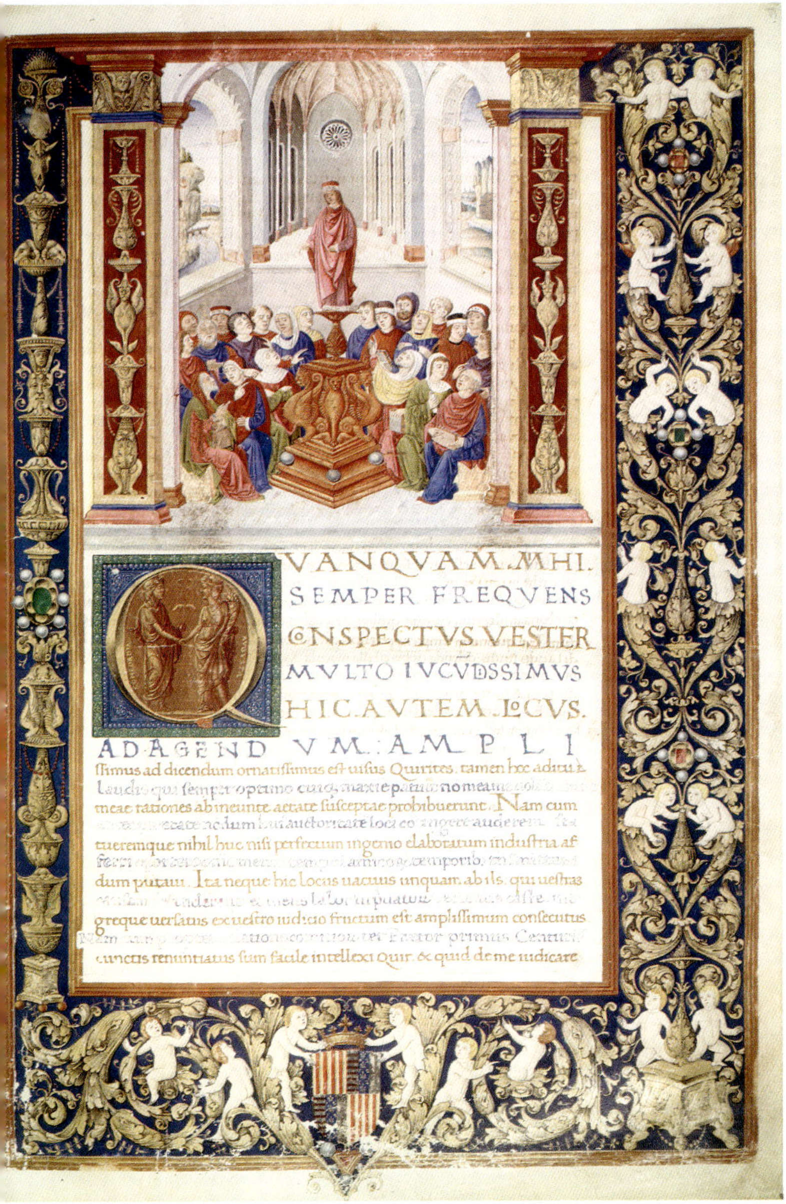

Cicero as orator Naples, between 1480 and 1490

This manuscript shows Cicero as orator in a three-dimensional rendering of a hall-like structure; in the border at the bottom of the page the coat of arms of Ferdinand I of Aragón.

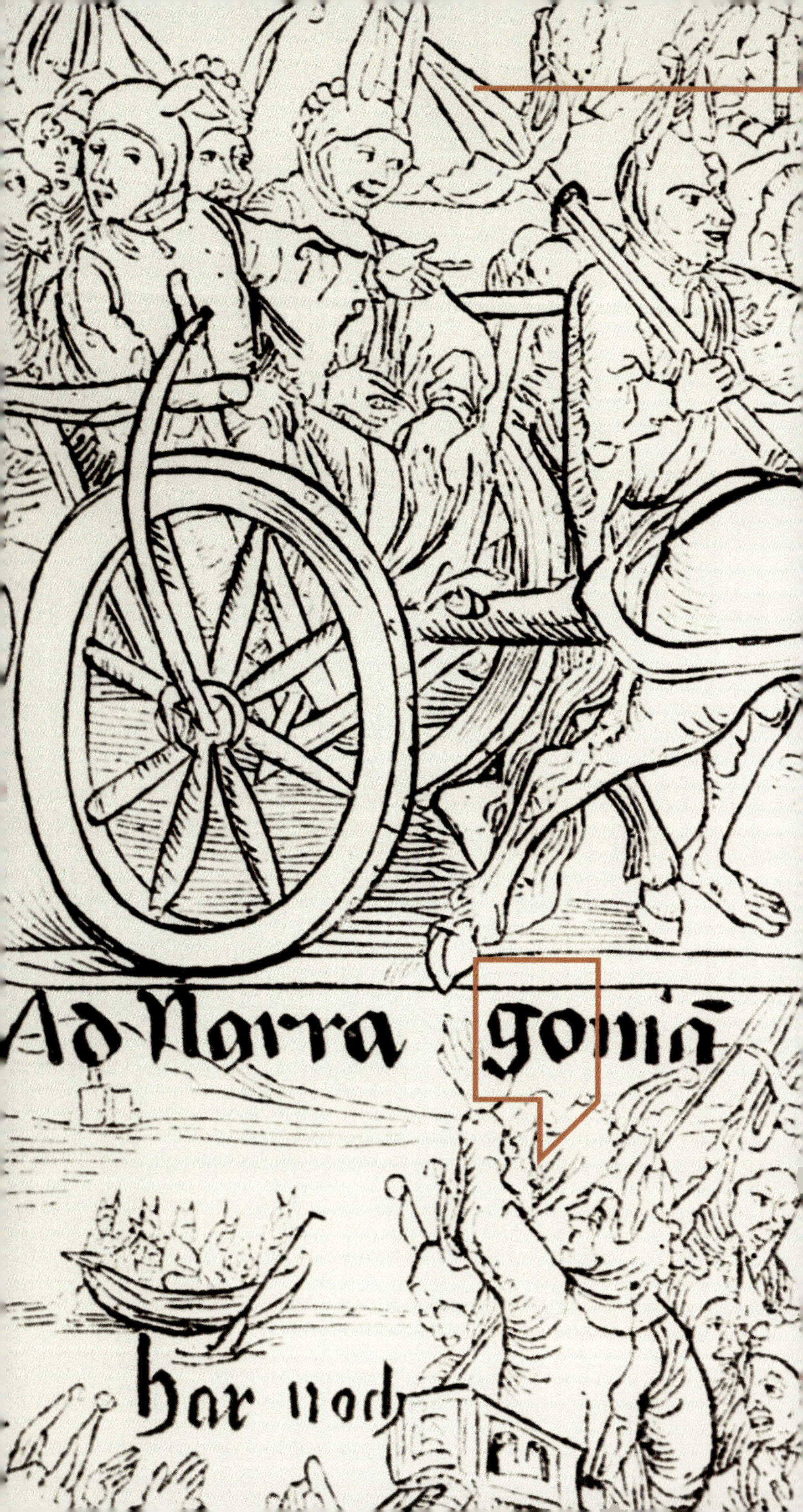

Ad Norra gonū
har noch

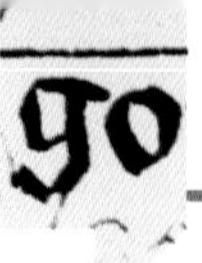

Department of Incunabula,
Old and Precious Books

Manuscripts dating from late antiquity and the medieval period and early examples of printed work were the original core of the former Imperial Court Library. The Department of Incunabula and of Old and Precious Books was, however, founded only in 1995, making it one of the most recently established of the special collections within the Austrian National Library. Its holdings formerly belonged to the Department of Manuscripts and Printed Material. They now comprise incunabula (the term used to describe printed material produced between the invention of printing, in around 1450, and the year 1500), printed material dating between 1501 and 1850, and printed material of any date that is especially rare, valuable or of particular bibliophile interest (specially printed or bound). The department also houses a collection of book bindings and of old Chinese and Japanese books.

INCUNABULA: PRINTED MATERIAL OF
THE FIFTEENTH CENTURY

With approximately 8,000 items, the Austrian National Library's collection of incunabula is one of the most valuable of its type in the world. About a quarter of all the titles printed in the fifteenth century are represented here, among them the only example still to be found in Austria of the 42-line Bible printed by Johannes Gutenberg in Mainz around 1456. It derives from the Dominican Monastery of Maria Steinach near Meran in South Tyrol (now Merano, Italy), which was closed in 1783 (see p. 94).

It is no longer possible to reconstruct in detail the precise history of the acquisition of many incunabula now in the collection of the Austrian National Library. In addition to the early Habsburg acquisitions, there are many incunabula that derive from the circle of Viennese humanists such

Sebastian Brant *The Ship of Fools* detail, see p. 96

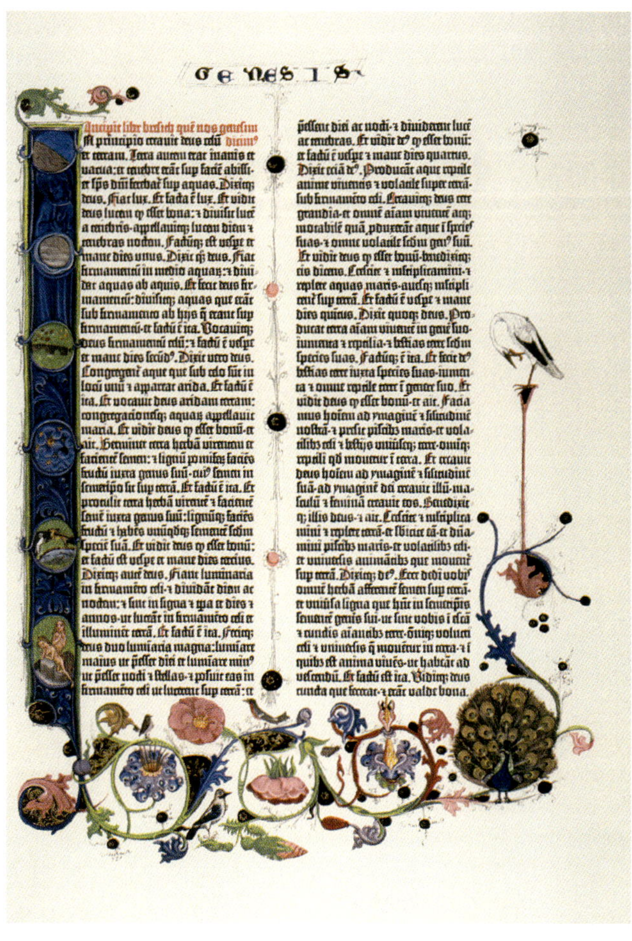

Johannes Gutenberg *Bible* Main, c. 1456
The only example of the 42-line Gutenberg Bible in Austria

as Johann Cuspinian (1473–1529) and from the collection of the Viennese Bishop Johann Fabri (1478–1541). A number of valuable incunabula and other early printed works were to be found in the Habsburg collection that was transferred to Vienna from Schloss Ambras in Innsbruck in 1665: among these were *The Adventure of the Knight Theuerdank* of Maximilian I, of which there were three copies of the version printed in Nuremberg in 1517 and five of that printed in Augsburg in 1519 (see p. 95).

The former library of Prince Eugene of Savoy, acquired by the Imperial Court Library in 1738, contained 200 incunabula. In 1756 364 incunabula were acquired as part of the old collection of the Vienna University Library and 351 in 1780 as part of the Viennese City Library. During the 1770s and 1780s, as most of the monasteries in the Habsburg territories were closed by the emperor Joseph II, around 3,000 incunabula came into the collec-

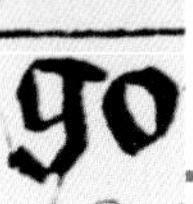

tion of the Imperial Court Library. At that time this institution enjoyed the privilege of receiving information on every work that had been published, and so was in an excellent position to complete its holdings. By the mid-nineteenth century the Imperial Court Library held around 10,000 incunabula. In the early twentieth century, by dint of selling off items of which there were two or more copies in the collection, its overall size was reduced. The last period of substantial enlargement occurred in 1921, when 655 incunabula were transferred to what was now the Austrian National Library from the Fideicommissum Library of the House of Habsburg.

The Austrian National Library's collection of old and precious books, which numbers over half a million volumes, is the fifth largest in the world. It includes a number of self-contained collections as well as valuable individual volumes. Especially notable among the latter is one of only thirteen surviving examples of the 36-line Bible printed in Bamberg in around 1460; a complete edition, printed on parchment, of the Book of Psalms made for use in religious service that was printed by Johann Fust and Peter Schöffer in Mainz in 1457; and examples of almost all of the Bibles printed before 1500. Among other very rare items in the collection is an example of the edition of the *Ship of Fools* by Sebastian Brant (1458–1521) printed by Johann Bergmann in Basel in 1499 and illustrated with 114 woodcuts (see p. 96).

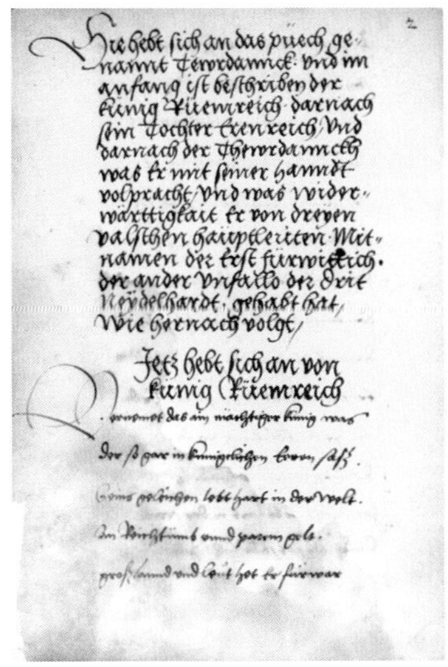

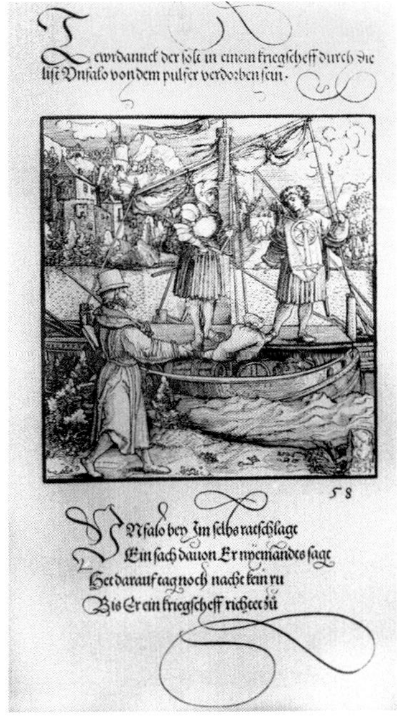

Maximilian I *The Adventures of the Knight Theuerdank* Nuremberg, 1517
Among the most valuable printed works in the collection is the *Theuerdank*. It is a tale of chivalry based on the journey undertaken by Emperor Maximilian I prior to his marriage to Maria of Burgundy.

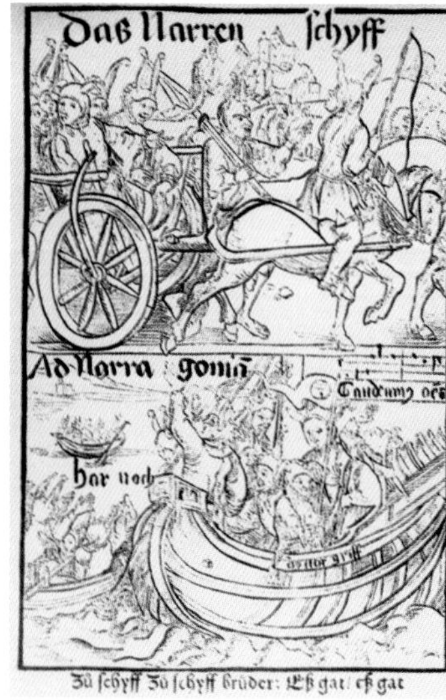
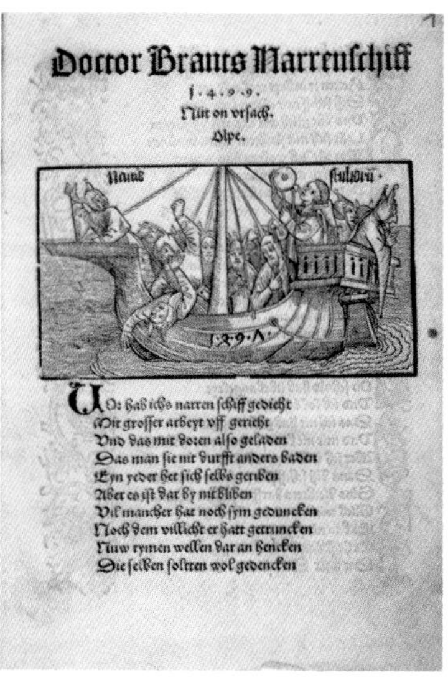

Sebastian Brant *The Ship of Fools* Basle, 1499, title page and first page
of the first edition

PRINTED MATERIAL DATED BETWEEN 1501 AND 1850, AND PRINTED MATERIAL OF PARTICULAR VALUE OR BIBLIOPHILE INTEREST

Of around 55,000 items of printed material dating from the sixteenth century to be found in the Austrian National Library, around 35,000 are in Latin, over 8,000 in German, over 5,000 in French, around 5,000 in Italian, around 1,000 in Spanish, and the rest mainly in Ancient Greek, Hebrew and some of the Slavic languages.

A similar distribution of languages is to be found among the printed works dating from the seventeenth century, a total of around 64,000 volumes, with the exception of the now larger proportion of works in Spanish, these accounting for around 4,000 titles. By comparison with the seventeenth century, the holdings of eighteenth-century printed material, a little over 115,000 works, are notable for a marked increase in German literature, amounting to around five times the size of the earlier one. Works in French exhibit a roughly three-fold increase, and those in Slavic languages an approximately tenfold increase. The remaining eighteenth-century items include around 40,000 works in Latin, around 8,700 in Italian, over 5,000 in English, and around 1,300 in Spanish, the rest being works in Ancient Greek, Hebrew and Magyar (Hungarian).

The 190,000 items of printed material from 1801 to 1850 are notable for a sharp increase in works in the Slavic languages (now around 19,000), in Magyar (around 4,200) and a continuing growth in the number of volumes in German (around 100,000), French (around 20,000), Italian (around

17,000), Spanish (around 2,000) and Ancient Greek (around 900), but a reduction in the number of works in Latin (approximately 16,000).

NEWSPAPERS AND PERIODICALS

Also of particular note is the Austrian National Library's Collection of Newspapers and Periodicals. In Vienna, which by the late fifteenth century had become established as a centre of the book trade, there was a particular tradition of publishing occasional (as opposed to daily or otherwise periodical) newspapers, the so-called 'new newspapers'. Of the 246 issues appearing between 1492 and 1705, no fewer than 195 were published in Vienna.

Only a small proportion of these newspapers has, however, been preserved, and the Austrian National Library's holdings are, accordingly, meagre. The earliest Viennese examples of the periodical publications that began in the seventeenth century are the *Ordinari Zeittungen* published from 1621 by Matthäus Formica (1591–1639). In 1622, as a supplement to this publication, which provided news only from outside Vienna, Formica began publishing the *Ordentliche Postzeittungen*, devoted to news about Vienna (above all the Imperial Court) and news from eastern and south-eastern Europe. The Austrian National Library also holds issues of the *Wiennerisches Diarium*, which first appeared in 1703 and continues to this day, as the *Wiener Zeitung*, making it one of the longest surviving daily newspapers in the world.

The Austrian National Library's holdings of eighteenth- and nineteenth-century newspapers and periodicals are especially notable for publications from across the Danubian Monarchy and embrace material in the

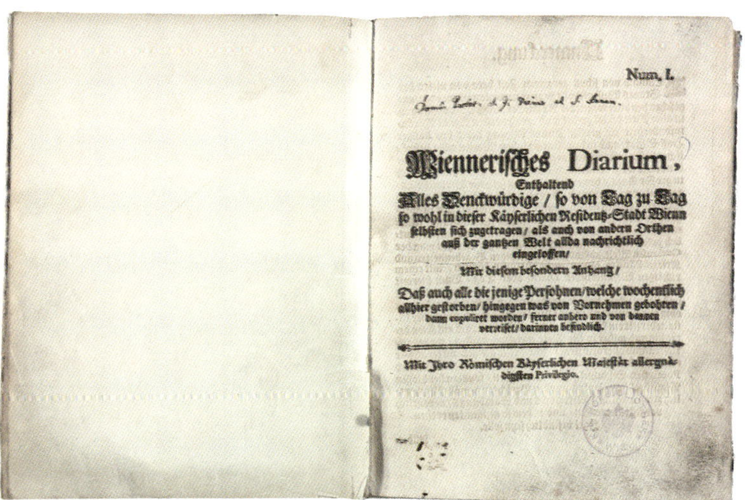

Wiennerisches Diarium
First published in 1703, the *Wiennerisches Diarium* is one of the longest surviving daily newspapers in the world.

Augustinerlesesaal (Augustinian Reading Room)
The frescoes by Johann Wenzel Bergl depict an allegory of
Parnassus and the four university faculties.

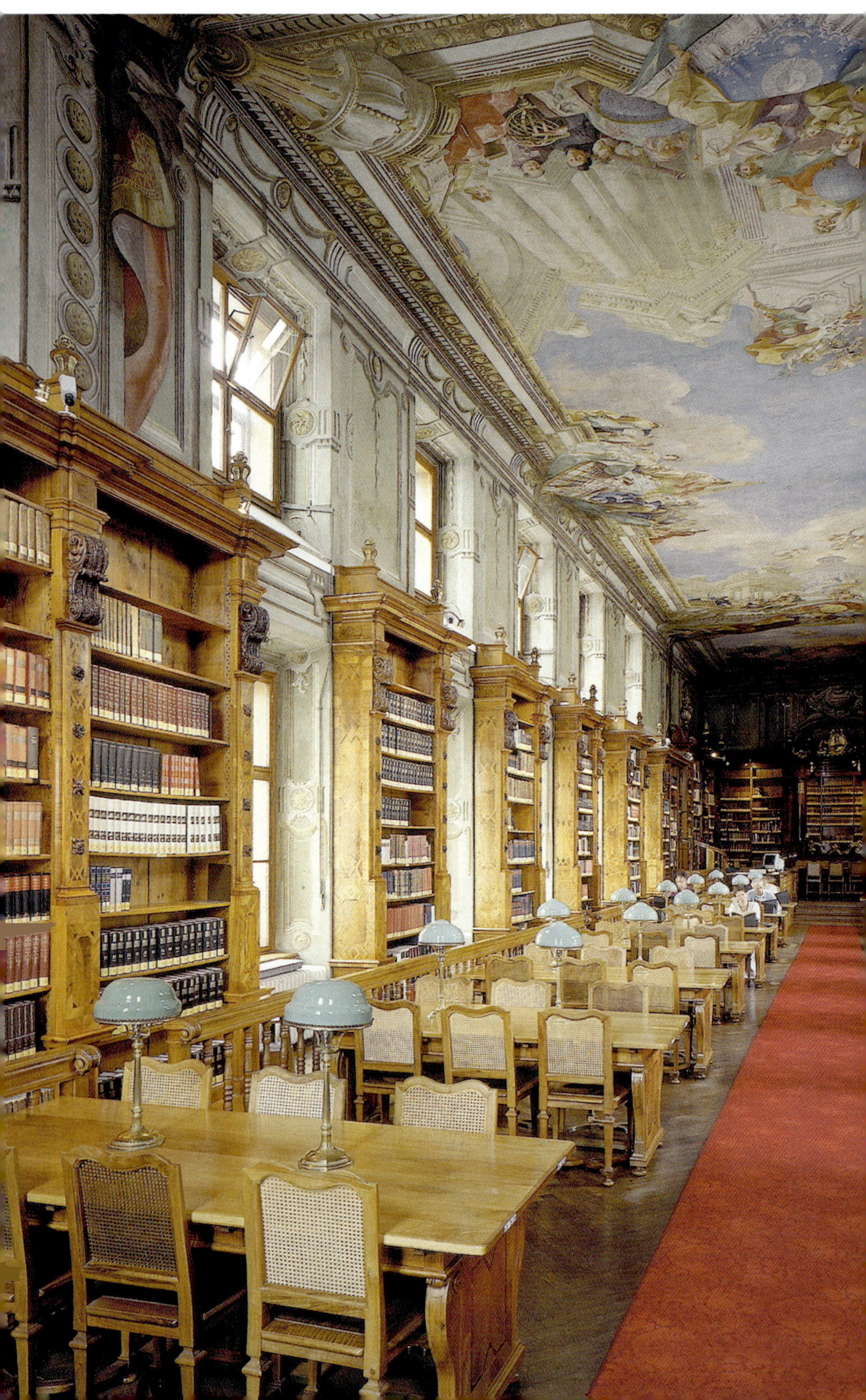

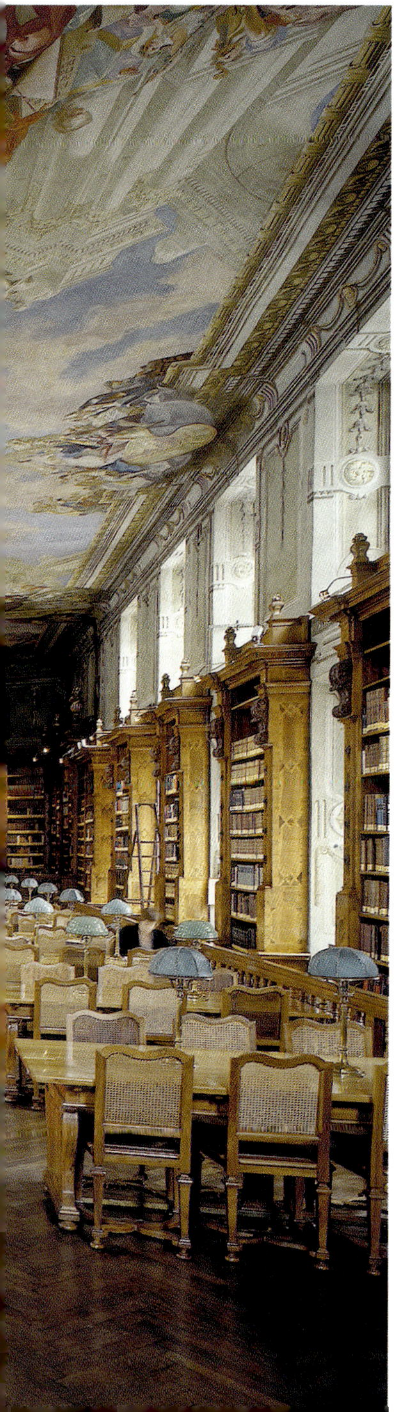

numerous languages that were in use there, including German, Italian, Czech, Polish, Magyar, Serbian and Croatian, but also Latin.

The Collection of Book Bindings

Complementing the Austrian National Library's holdings of incunabula, old and precious books is a collection of valuable book bindings. The binding of a book always had a more than merely practical function: it was an important element in its decorative presentation. This collection offers an insight into the evolution of book binding from the medieval period to the present day.

Using the Collection

The Augustinerlesesaal – the Baroque reading room that houses the Austrian National Library's Department of Incunabula, Old and Precious Books – is so called because it was formerly the Library of the Augustinian Monastery adjacent to the Imperial Court Library. In 1831 this was incorporated into the Imperial Court Library and since 1906 has been accessible as a reading room to the Library's users. Its ceiling frescoes were painted between 1773 and 1775 by Johann Wenzel Bergl and depict an allegory of Parnassus and the Four University Faculties. The Augustinerlesesaal is reserved exclusively for those using the Library and is not otherwise open to visitors.

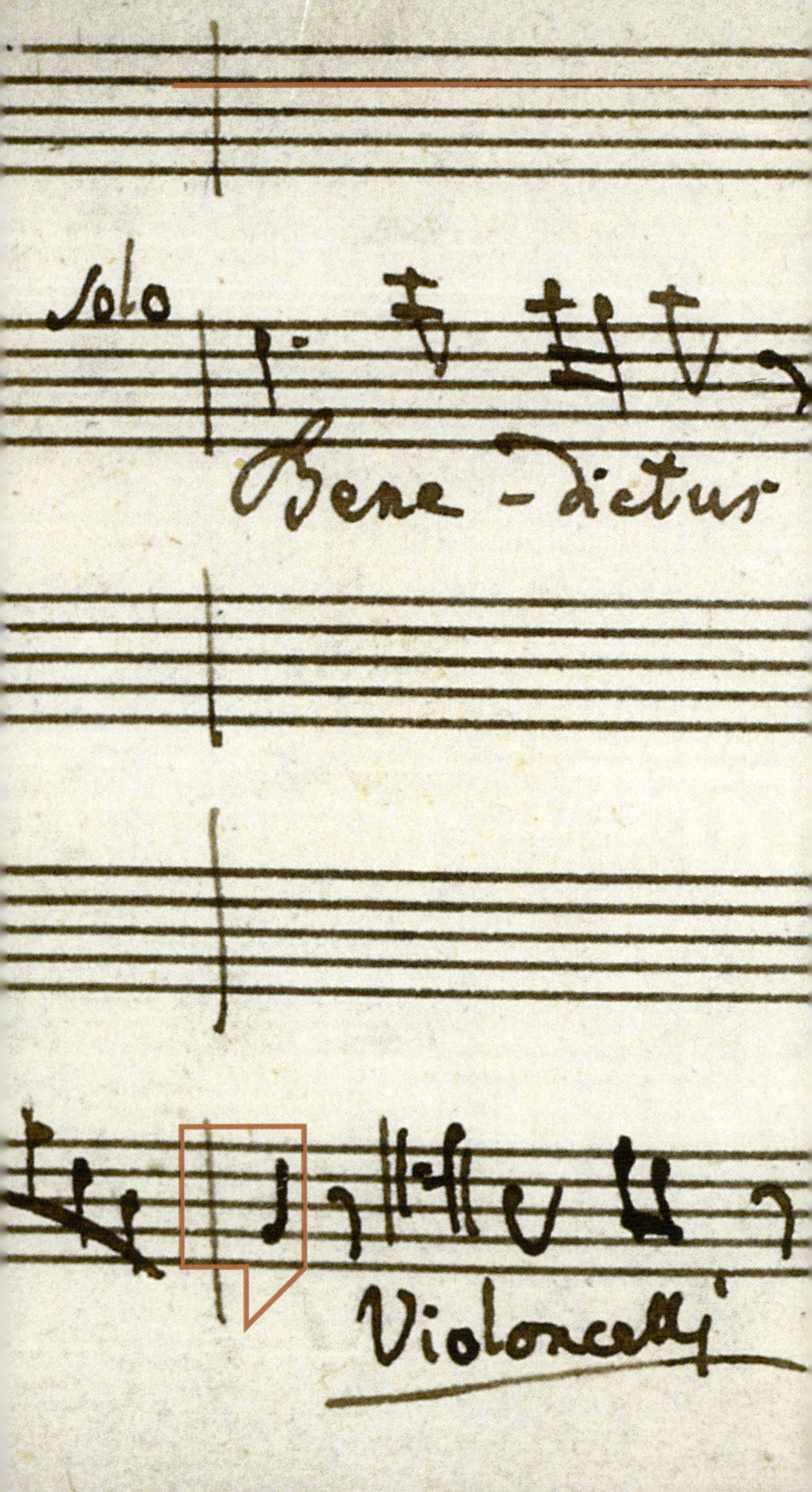

Solo
Bene - dictus
Violoncelli

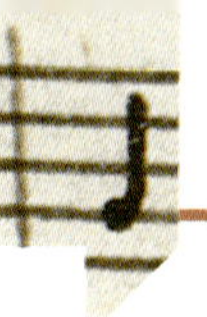

Department of Music

The Austrian National Library's Department of Music is a modern specialist library intended for everyday use by scholars and other interested individuals, and simultaneously Austria's largest music archive. Its holdings comprise manuscript and printed scores, vocal scores for opera (libretti) and other forms of vocal music, musicological literature, recordings on disc, tape and CD, and the estates of important Austrian composers. In principle, users of the music collection have access to all these categories of its holdings.

THE HOLDINGS

Historically, the most important part of the Austrian National Library's Department of Music consists of around 50,000 manuscript scores, including extremely valuable autograph manuscripts of the work of composers such as Joseph Haydn, Wolfgang Amadeus Mozart, Ludwig van Beethoven, Franz Schubert, Anton Bruckner and others. The liturgical practice of the late medieval period is documented in the form of large choral books, while the history of Austrian music of the last four or five centuries is recorded in the manuscripts made by numerous copyists, in particular material formerly belonging to the Viennese Imperial Court Orchestra and that derived from old theatre and church archives.

The collection of around 120,000 printed scores supplies an outstanding record of the history of Western music in its entirety. Owing, however, to the obligation placed on Austrian publishers to supply the Imperial Court Library with a copy of every item published, the coverage of the history of Austrian music is especially thorough. And it is in this respect that the Department of Music serves as the central music archive for Austria.

Around 8,000 libretti constitute a valuable source of information on the history and continuing evolution of music in the context of theatre, and in

Wolfgang Amadeus Mozart *Requiem (K 626)* detail, see p.103

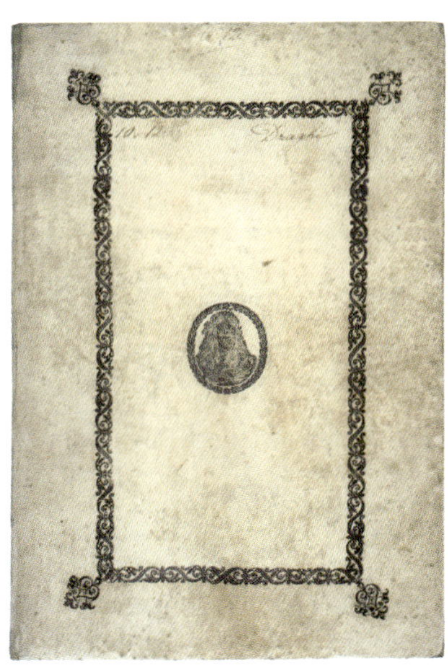

The 'bedroom library'
All the volumes of the 'bedroom library' of Emperor Leopold I are bound in white parchment, their covers bearing a gilt-embossed portrait of the emperor or a double-headed imperial eagle and the emperor's motto, 'consilio et industria' (With Prudence and Diligence).

particular on opera of the Baroque era. The archive of photographic facsimiles, a collection of around 60,000 items initially assembled by Anthony van Hoboken (1887–1983), offers users the possibility of studying manuscript scores that are not to be found in the Austrian National Library collection.

The Department of Music also houses the estates of many composers and performers, notable among them being Anton Bruckner, Alban Berg, Hans Pfitzner and numerous Austrian composers of the twentieth century. Over 15,000 items of recorded music (on disc, tape and CD) provide thorough aural documentation, above all, of the history of music in Austria.

THE HISTORY OF THE MUSIC COLLECTION

There is evidence that both manuscript and early printed scores were already being collected during the reign of Emperor Ferdinand I (b. 1503, r. 1556–64). Between the mid-seventeenth and the mid-eighteenth centuries, the Habsburg emperors, who were great music enthusiasts and often dabbled in composition themselves, contributed to a flourishing musical culture at the Imperial Court. The real beginnings of the Austrian National Library's music collection were provided by the music-related segments of the library compiled by members of the great banking family of Fugger, initiated by Raymund Fugger (1489–1535). In 1654, in the reign of Emperor Ferdinand II (b. 1608, r. 1637–57), the Fugger Library was acquired by the Imperial Court Library from Albert Fugger (1624–92), who was forced by debt into making this sale. However, not all of the musical items deriving from the Fugger Library have survived. Among the notable imperial contributions to the future music collection are the manuscript scores produced by Emperor Leopold I (b. 1640,

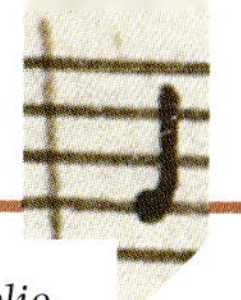

r. 1658–1705), and bound in white parchment, which comprise the *biblio-theca cubicularis*, or 'bedroom library'. Among their successors is a collection of manuscript scores dating from the reign of Charles VI (b. 1685, r. 1711–40) and bound in brown leather. These collections reveal the broad range of music that was enjoyed at the Viennese court, but also the particular interest there in Italian opera and in oratorio.

Gottfried van Swieten, who served as prefect of the Imperial Court Library from 1777 to 1803, did a great deal to promote its musical collection. Further expansion occurred in 1826 thanks to the prefect Moritz Graf von Dietrichstein (1775–1864), who had the older material belonging to the Imperial Court Orchestra transferred to the Imperial Court Library. Dietrichstein also commissioned Anton Schmid (1787–1857) to make a new catalogue of all the holdings of the Imperial Court Library related to music, and to shelve these separately. Schmid completed this task in three years; and from 1829 the Department of Music constituted a separate section within the Imperial Court Library.

Dietrichstein appointed Ignaz von Mosel (1772–1844) as the first curator of the music collection. And it was thanks to Mosel that, in the period between 1831 and 1838, the Department of Music acquired the autograph manuscript that remains its most valuable: the last work by Wolfgang Amadeus Mozart (1756–91), his Requiem (K 626). In 1791 Mozart received an anonymous commission for a Mass for the Dead, but he himself died before he was able to finish the work. His widow, Constanze (1762–1842), had it completed by Mozart's pupil Franz Xaver Süssmayr (1766–1803) and sent to the individual who had originally commissioned it, Franz Graf Walsegg-Stuppach (1763–1827). In addition to Mozart's autograph manu-

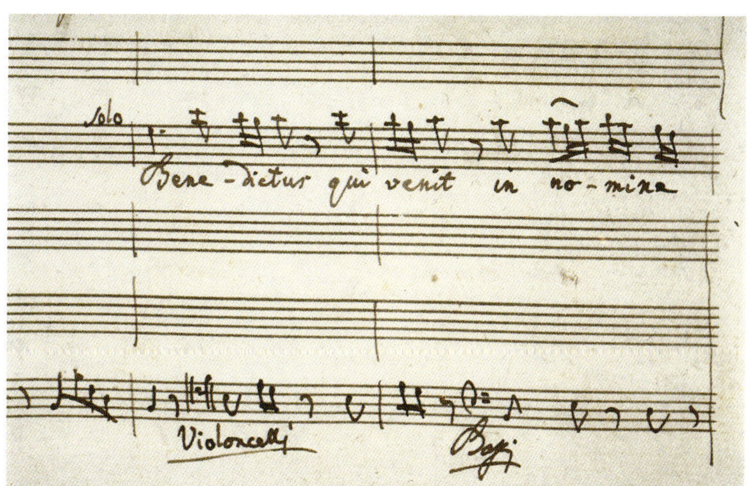

Wolfgang Amadeus Mozart *Requiem (K 626)*
Detail from his so-called working score, 1791

script of the Requiem, known as the working score, the Department of Music also houses the score Süssmayr delivered.

In 1897 the music collection acquired virtually the entire estate of Anton Bruckner (1824–96) in accordance with stipulations made in the composer's will. Comprising not only manuscript and printed scores of all his chief works, but also extensive biographical material, this collection constitutes a unique Bruckner Archive, and a crucial addition to the music collection. Another nineteenth-century composer exceptionally well represented within the music collection, especially as regards autograph scores, is Hugo Wolf (1860–1903).

In 1920 the Department of Music moved into the building of the Albertina. And it was here that it finally established the two-fold function that it retains to this day: as a valued archive of the musical heritage and as a modern scholarly library.

In 1974 the Department of Music acquired the estate of another composer of no less importance than Anton Bruckner when Helene Berg, the widow of Alban Berg (1885–1935), bequeathed to the Austrian National Library

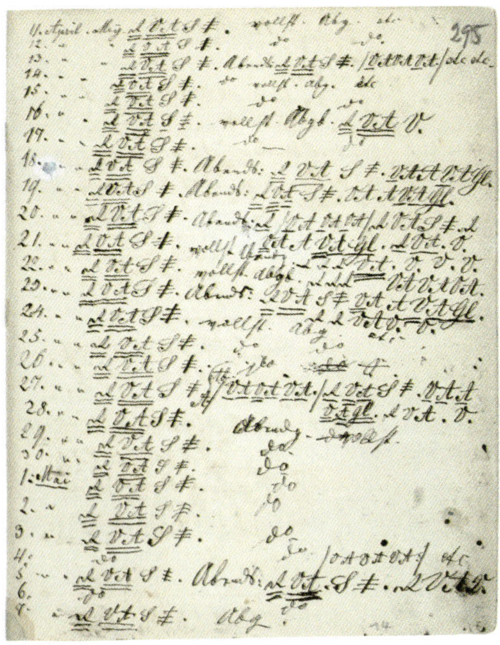

Anton Bruckner *devotional notes*

The notes made in a pocket calendar for the academic year 1894/95 testify to Anton Bruckner's deep Catholic faith. The letters V, for 'Vater Unser' (Our Father), and A, for 'Ave Maria', identify the prayers, and the underlining in each case indicates how often Bruckner said these particular prayers on the date in question.

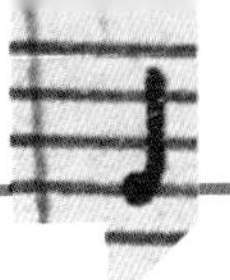

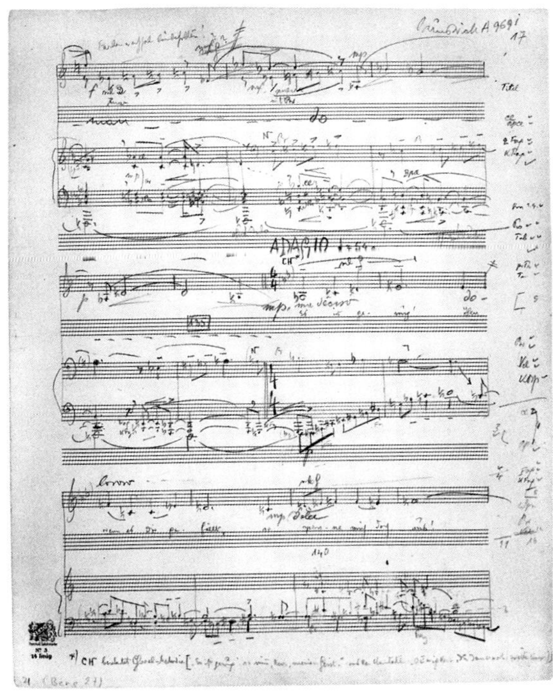

Alban Berg from the Violin Concerto Particell *autograph*

the extensive material left to her by her late husband. Manuscript scores, numerous musical sketches, notes and thousands of letters belonging to this key member of the Second Viennese School bear outstanding witness to the intellectual life of Vienna in the first thirty-five years of the twentieth century. 1974 was also the year in which the Austrian National Library was able to acquire Anthony van Hoboken's collection of around 8,000 first and early printed editions of works by all the great composers from Bach to Brahms.

The Department of Music will soon confront exciting new challenges. In mid-2005, in addition to its move into the Palais Mollard, at 9 Herrengasse in the inner city, it will embark on the digitalization of all its card catalogues. By 2006 it will be possible to access its entire catalogue on the Internet.

USING THE MUSIC COLLECTION

An Austrian National Library User's Card (*Benützungskarte*) provides access to the Department of Music (which does, of course, have its own user guidelines and regulations). The Department of Music is a reference library with much of its holdings on open-shelf access. Access to autograph and other manuscript scores is, however, limited and must be formally requested in advance.

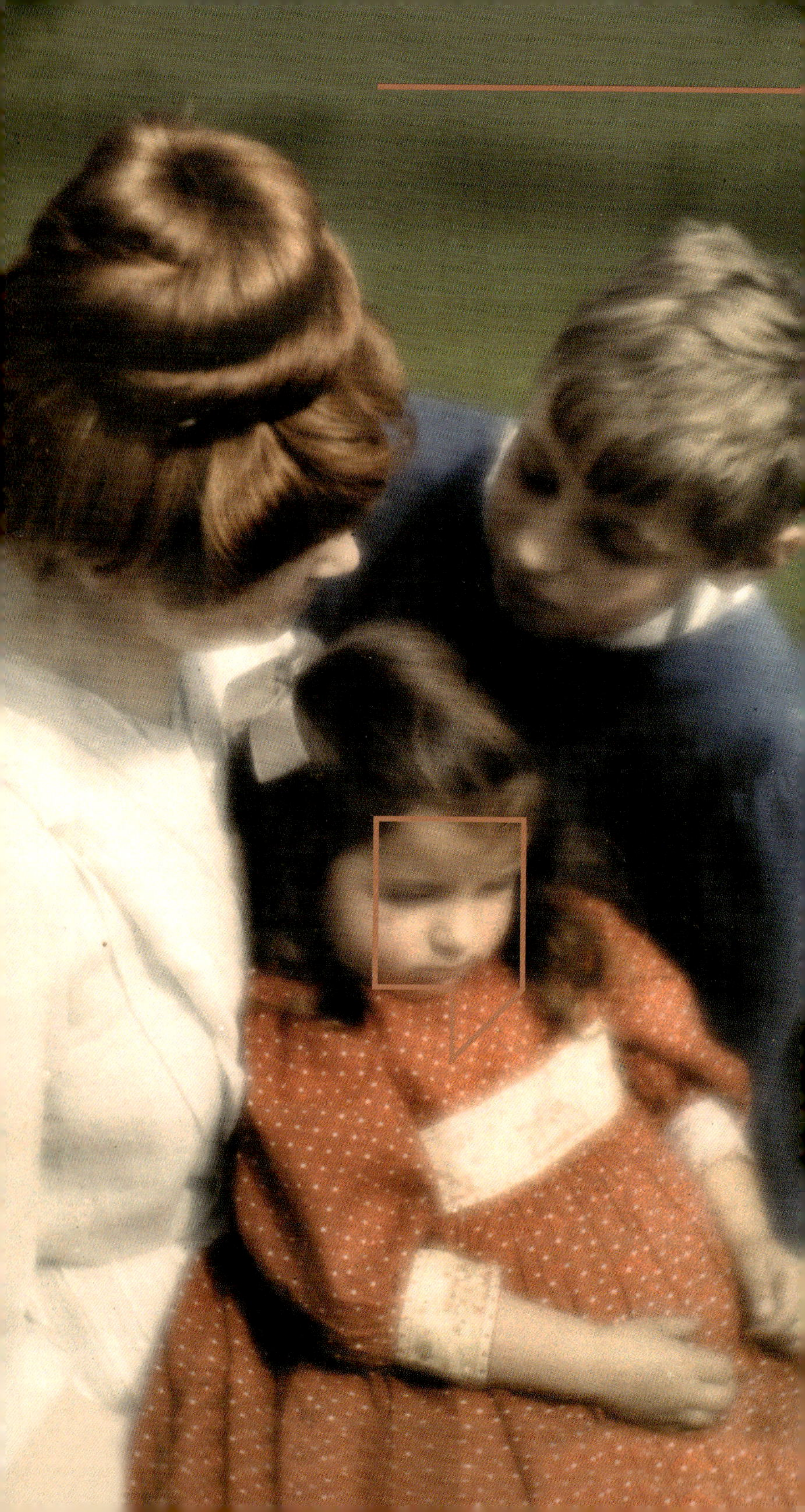

Picture Archive

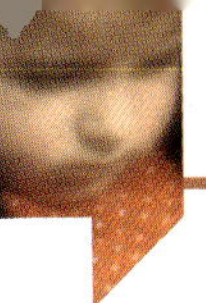

The Austrian National Library's Picture Archive is the largest collection of visual documentation to be found in Austria. It in fact combines the functions of an archive, an extensive specialist picture agency, and photographic reproduction service. The Picture Archive serves the Austrian National Library as the central point through which images relating to all its collections may be ordered.

The origins of the Picture Archive lie in the former family library of the House of Habsburg, an impressive collection of prints and drawings and extensive holdings of photographic documentation with material dating back to the early years of photography.

Both the Habsburg collection of portraits and the Habsburg family library originated in the enthusiastic collecting activity of the archduke Francis (b. 1768) who served as the last Habsburg Holy Roman emperor and then, as Francis I, as the first emperor of Austria (r. 1804–35). Even as a child, he had taken a great interest in books and copper engravings – above all, engraved portraits. During his relatively long lifetime his collection continued to grow, eventually numbering around 100,000 items. In his will he stipulated that his library and his collections of art should be united into a Fideicommissum (indivisible inheritance), to be entrusted to his oldest living male descendant. This tradition was maintained until the very end of Habsburg rule, in 1918; during this period of nearly eighty years the libraries and other collections of family members were added to the holdings of the Fideicommissum.

In 1921 the collection formerly known as the Imperial and Royal Family Fideicommissum of the House of Habsburg-Lorraine became the Portrait Collection, one of the special collections within the Austrian National Library. In 1939 came the first moves towards the establishment of a section of the Austrian National Library specializing in photography with the founding of the Picture Archive as the central source of visual documen-

Heinrich Kühn photograph of Mary Warner, Lotte and Walter Kühn
1907/8, detail, see p. 110

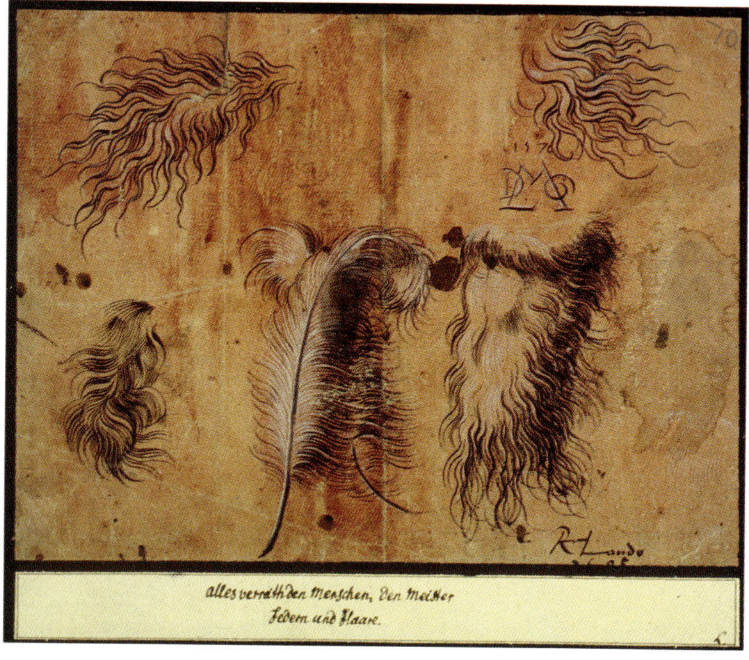

Daniel Lindtmayer *Feathers, Hairs and Beards* 1570
Drawing (Collection Johann Caspar Lavater)

tation in the form of photographic negatives. With the simultaneous incorporation of the Austrian Photograph and Transparency Archive and the Austrian Photograph, Transparency and Film Service, the new Picture Archive was immediately established as one of the largest state collections of photographic negatives to be found in German-speaking Europe. The decisive turning point occurred in 1947 with the fusion of the Portrait Collection and the Picture Archive.

The Collection of Prints and Drawings and the Portrait Collection

The Collection of Prints and Drawings now comprises over 500,000 items: drawings, watercolours and printed works in a wide range of media and techniques. It embraces records of historical events, landscapes and city views, architectural images, records of plants and animals, and a great deal more. Its outstanding strength, however, is its collection of portraits: around 200,000 printed images of notable individuals. The arrangement of portraits into family groups, especially in the case of ruling and aristocratic dynasties, and also according to profession, derives from the system employed by Francis I.

Also of note in the Collection of Prints and Drawings are the holdings of botanical and zoological images, the group of over 600 portrait miniatures (mostly of members of the House of Habsburg), and the collection of around 22,000 prints works on paper assembled by the celebrated Swiss physiognomist Johann Caspar Lavater (1741–1801), which Francis I acquired in 1828 from the bankrupt's assets of the banker Moritz Graf Fries (1777–1826). During his lifetime Lavater established a pan-European reputation: he corresponded with the philosopher Immanuel Kant (1724–1804), and collaborated with Johann Wolfgang von Goethe (1749–1832) on a number of texts.

THE PHOTOGRAPHIC COLLECTION

The Picture Archive is the largest collection in Austria of earlier and contemporary photographic documentation. With around 2,000,000 items its thematic range is enormous, although its greatest strength lies in its holdings of material related to Austria. Daguerrotypes, the earliest form of photography as we understand it today, were already being added to the portrait collection within the Fideicommissum by around 1850.

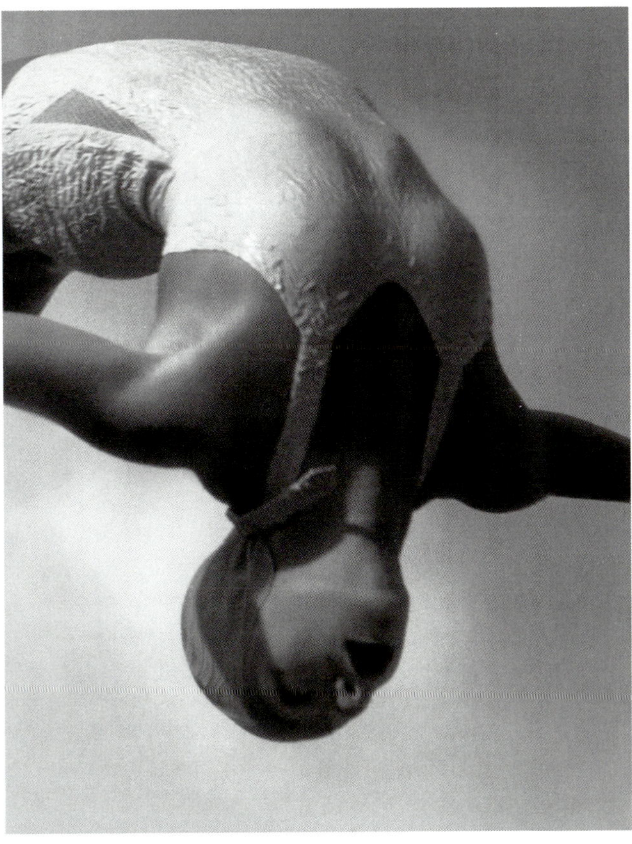

Lothar Rübelt *photograph of Dorothy Poynton*
Olympic winner in diving 1930s

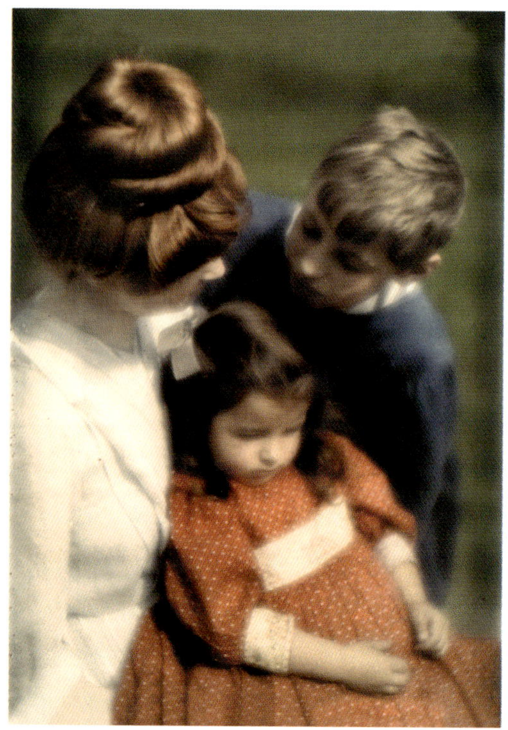

Heinrich Kühn *photograph of Mary Warner,
Lotte and Walter Kühn* 1907/8, autochrome

The core of the Photographic Collection is the material that has been systematically collected since 1945: the photo series, complete archives and estates of important Austrian photographers. Thematically, the emphasis is on portrait photography; the famous Viennese photographic studio Atelier d'Ora (especially significant with regard to the theatre and the world of fashion); documentary photography and reportage, above all between 1850 and 1990, including the estate of Joe Heydecker (1916–97) and material already bequeathed by Harry Weber (b. 1921); early examples of travel photography and photography recording expeditions; nineteenth-century topographical and industrial photography; the estate of Heinrich Kühn (1866–1944), most notable for its pictorialist autochromes; the collection of around 33,000 negatives belonging to the Austrian war propaganda office of 1914–18, the Kriegspressequartier; and the photographic record of post-war Modernist architecture created by Lucca Chmel (1911–99).

In 2003 the Austrian National Library received the long-term loan of a collection of early sports photography by Lothar Rübelt (1901–91), and in 2004 it was able to acquire a collection of photographic portraits by Ferdinand Schmutzer (1870–1929) and valuable collections of documentary photography by Otto Croÿ (1902–77) and Erich Lessing (b. 1923).

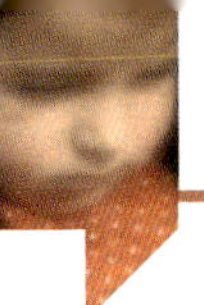

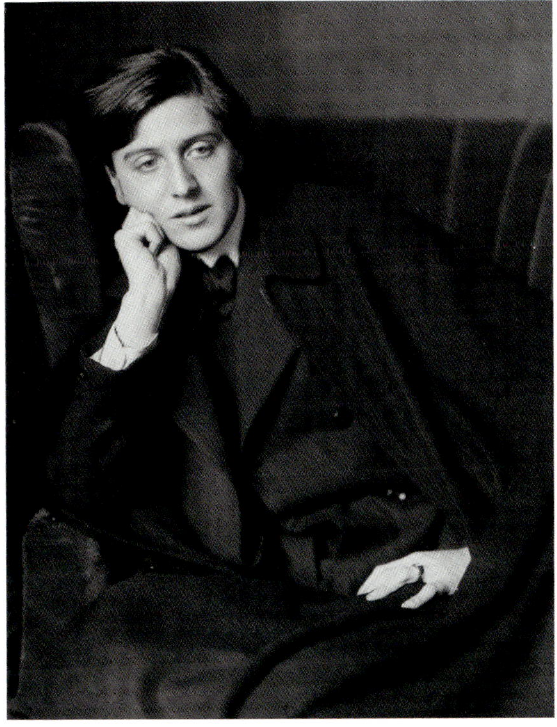

Alban Berg Studio of Madame d'Ora
(Dora Kallmus), Vienna 1909

The current focus of collecting is on the visual documentation of the history of Austria and photographic reportage in general. To this end, an agreement was reached in 2004 between the Austrian National Library and Austrian Radio (Österreichischer Rundfunk, ÖRF) for a million old photographs from the ÖRF Archive to be presented as a long-term loan to the Austrian National Library, where they are to be stored (and, if necessary, restored) and made accessible to users.

THE IMPERIAL FIDEICOMMISSUM LIBRARY

The Fideicommissum Library, the imperial family library of the House of Habsburg, comprises around 117,000 volumes. It originally came into being thanks to the bibliophilia and passion for collecting of Emperor Francis I and contains works of literature, history, technology, the natural sciences, geography and philosophy. In accordance with its status as a Fideicommissum, the library was maintained by the emperor's successors. Its holdings were substantially increased through the addition of the private libraries of several members of the House of Habsburg, including the empress Maria Ludovica (b. 1787, r. 1808–16), the emperor Maximilian of Mexico (b. 1832, r. 1864–67), the empress Elisabeth (r. 1854–98), and Crown

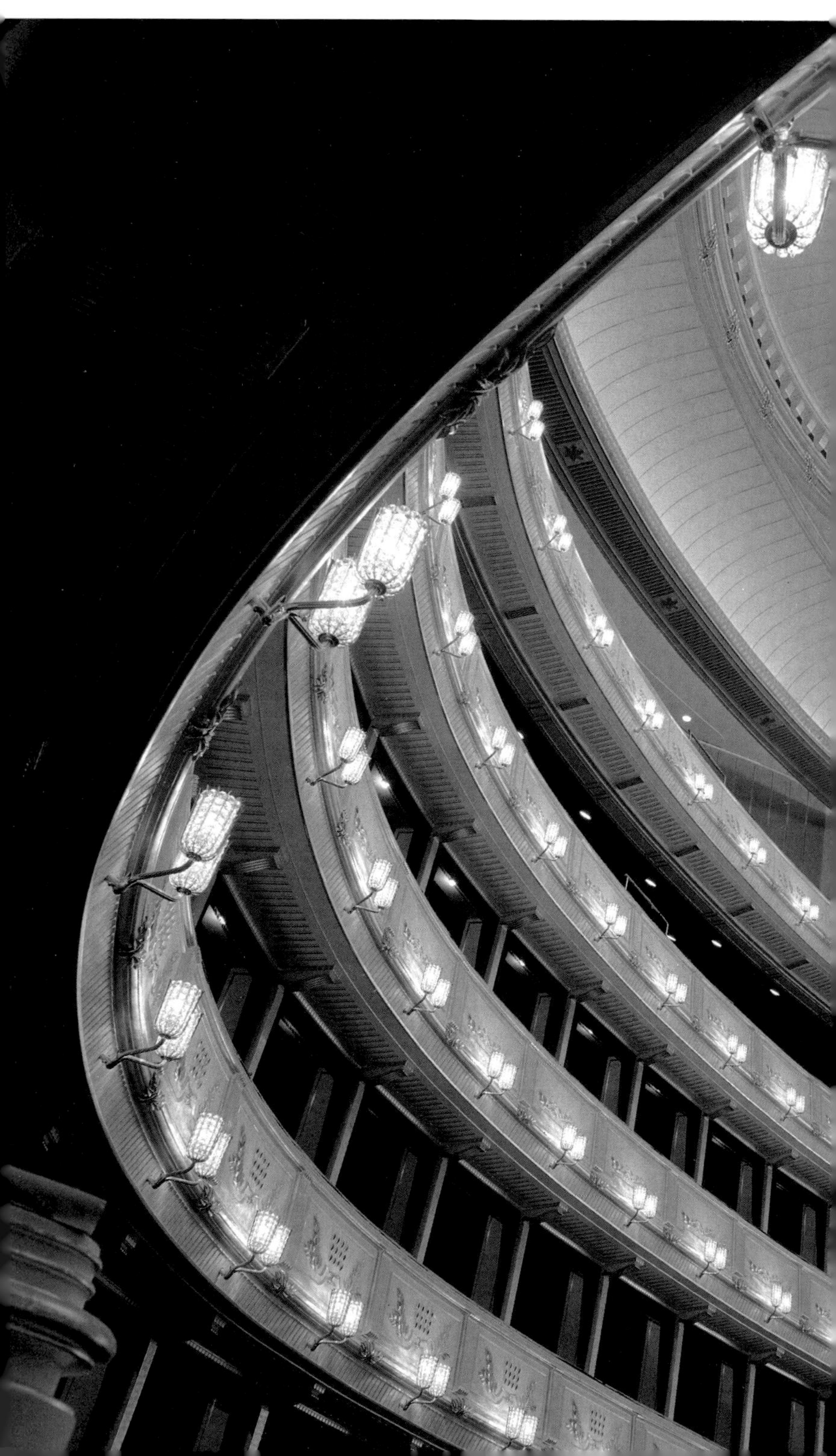

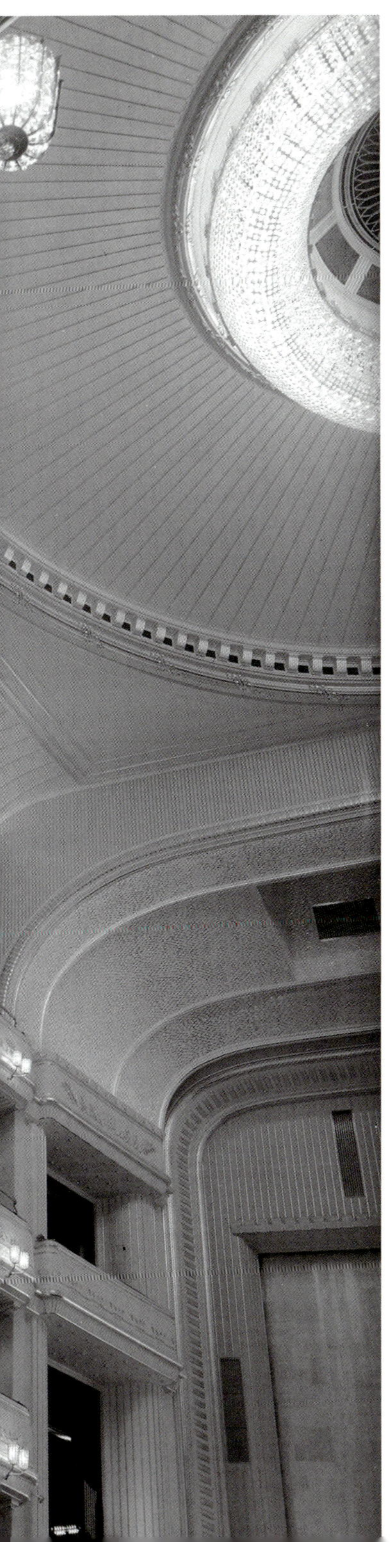

Prince Rudolf (1858–89). As a result, the Library provides an overview of the interests of the House of Habsburg during the last 150 years of the monarchy. A great many volumes are sumptuously bound and contain formal expressions of homage to the House of Habsburg, a common practice in the nineteenth century.

USING THE PICTURE ARCHIVE

In addition to the access to the Picture Archive's holdings available to users of the Reading Room, well over two million images can be accessed on the Internet and copies of them ordered in both analogue and digital form. Fifty thousand old photographs from the collections of the Austrian National Library and of co-operating institutions are currently accessible on the Internet at **www.bildarchiv.at** and **www.bildarchivaustria.at**.

Those seeking historical visual documentation on everyday life, politics, the bizarre, culture, sport, commerce, technology and many other subjects will find an enormous range of images that is constantly being enlarged. In the Picture Archive's Vienna Catalogue (*Wien-Katalog*) users may search for visual records of the city by district, street, building or monument; this collection also includes images of specific historical events.

Lucca Chmel, Viennese State Opera after the extension by architect Erich Boltenstern in 1955, black and white photograph

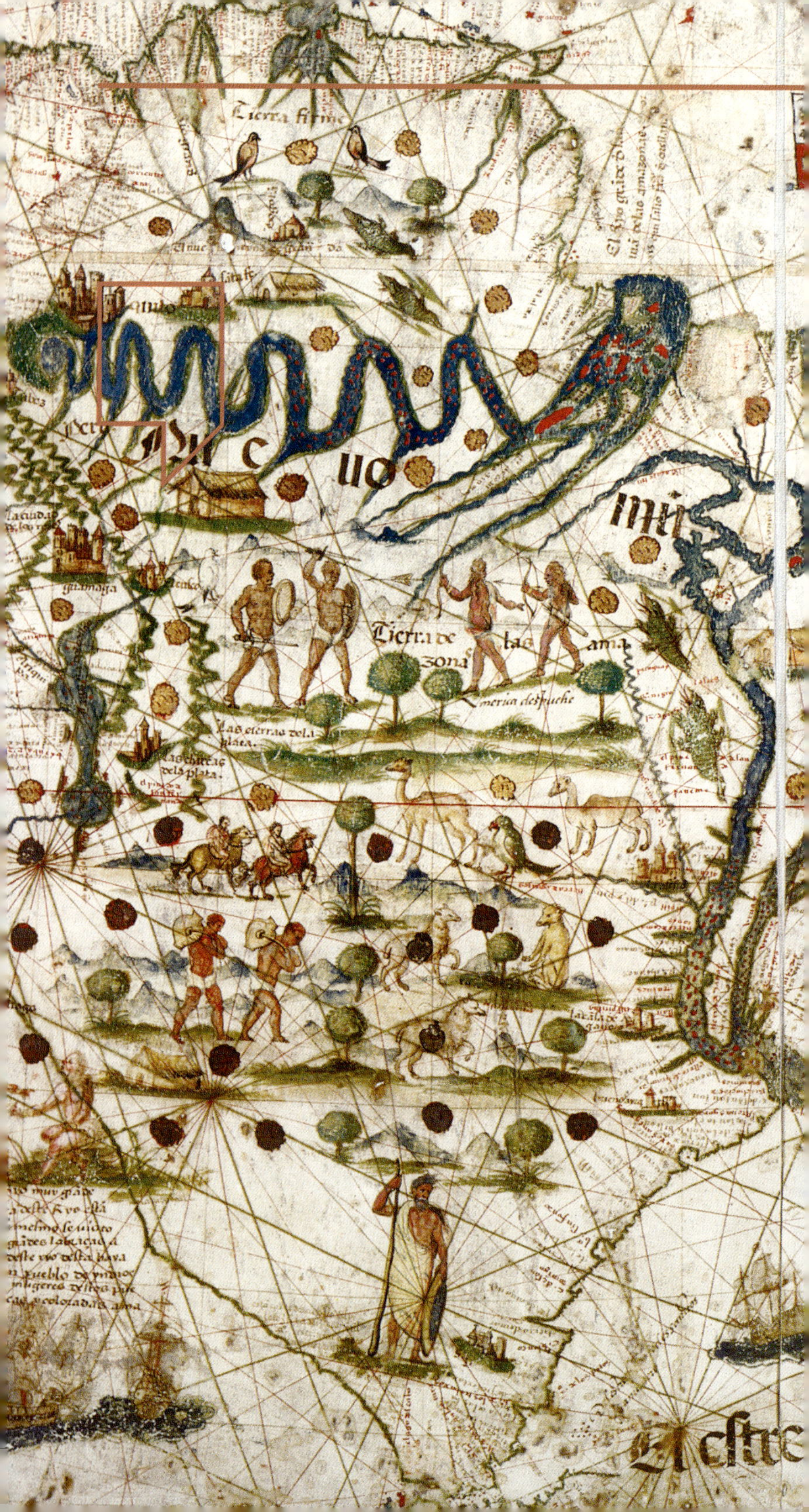

Tierra firme
El Rio marã d[e]
Tierra de zona
merica deñ puche
Lao tierras del la plata
Las minerias dela plata
A leste

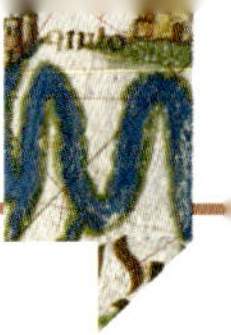

Map Department

The Austrian National Library's Map Department is regarded as one of the most important of its type in the world owing to its extensive and valuable holdings of old maps, city plans and atlases. Its purpose is to collect, and make available to users of its library, maps, plans, atlases, globes, topographical views (of both cities and landscapes) of any date, as well as scholarly literature of a geographical and cartographical character.

ON THE HISTORY OF THE MAP DEPARTMENT

Maps, atlases and books of a geographical character were already being collected by the Imperial Court Library in the sixteenth century. These holdings were significantly enlarged in the eighteenth century with two important acquisitions: the 324-volume atlas owned by Freiherr Philipp von Stosch (1691–1757) and the library of the late Prince Eugene of Savoy with its extensive holdings of geographical material of every sort.

1906 saw the foundation of a geographical collection within the Imperial Court Library in order to concentrate most of its maps, plans and related geographical literature. This subsequently became the Map Collection. In addition to more precisely targeted collecting, there now emerged a more scientific approach to processing the objects already in, or being added to, the collection. After the end of the First World War the Map Collection underwent a substantial enlargement with the absorption of maps, atlases and topographical views that had been part of the former Habsburg Fideicommissum Library, the Albertina Collection of Prints and Drawings, and the former Military Geographical Institute. The systematic extension of the collection of topographical views strengthened the holdings in terms of pictorial topographical sources. In recent years digitalized

Sancho Gutiérrez *Map of the World* made for Emperor Charles V, 1551, detail, see p. 116

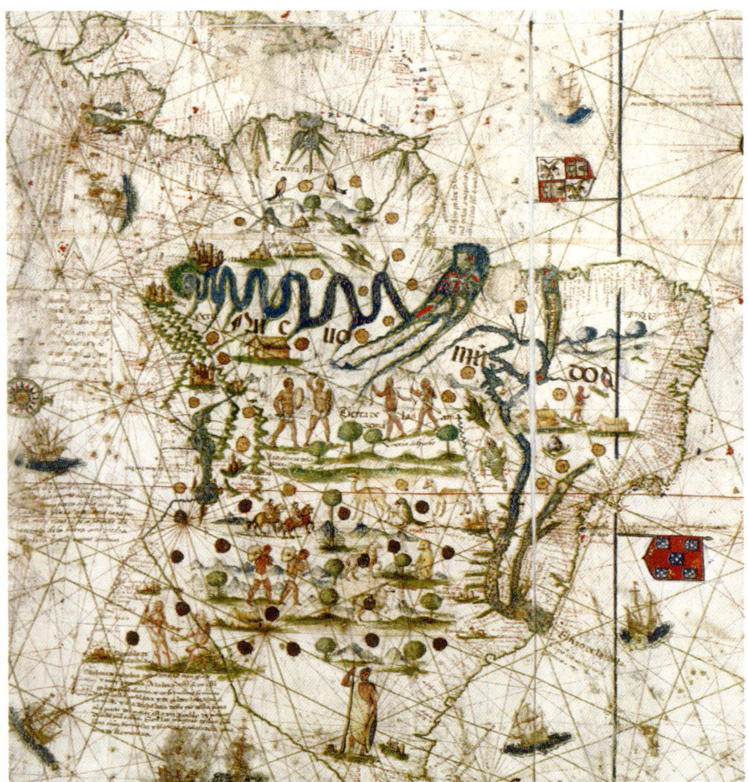

Sancho Gutiérrez *Map of the World* made for Emperor Charles V, 1551, 336 × 108 cm. Detail of South America with its coloured drawings

maps and atlases have also been collected. These can be used at a computer terminal in the Map Department Reading Room.

THE HOLDINGS OF THE MAP DEPARTMENT

As a result of centuries of collecting and conservation, the Austrian National Library's internationally regarded Map Department is well placed to offer its users access to an extensive range of cartographic material (maps, city plans, atlases, globes, relief maps, models of fortifications, topographical views (of both cities and landscapes), and items from its extensive holdings of geographical literature spanning several centuries. While the Map Department aims at universality, it has a regional emphasis on Central Europe, in particular the present-day territory of the Republic of Austria and the former territory of the Danubian Monarchy.

While the holdings of the Map Department as a whole are extremely rich, certain items are of exceptional interest and importance. Among these is the map of the world drawn on parchment in 1551 by the Spanish cartographer Sancho Gutiérrez (1515–80) for Emperor Charles V, a unique piece measuring 336 by 108 cm. This map records the great oceans as well as details of the various land masses, and its representation of the New World is of special interest.

Another notable item in the Map Department is the map published in Strasbourg in 1513 as the *Strasburger Ptolemäus*. This copy was bound together with an apparently unique map of the world produced by the celebrated German cosmographer Martin Waldseemüller (c. 1470–c. 1522).

Also of exceptional significance is the map of the world inscribed in Chinese characters made in the first half of the seventeenth century by the Jesuit priest Matteo Ricci (1552–1610). Only four copies of this map, measuring 365 by 165 cm and made up of several wood-cut prints, are known to have survived.

Indisputably, the item of greatest value to be found in the Map Department – it was added to the UNESCO register of 'world heritage documents' in 2004 – is the *Blaeu-Van der Hem Atlas*, a 50-volume collection of 2,400 superbly coloured maps, city plans and images, which epitomizes the cartographical ideals of the Baroque era. The atlas was compiled

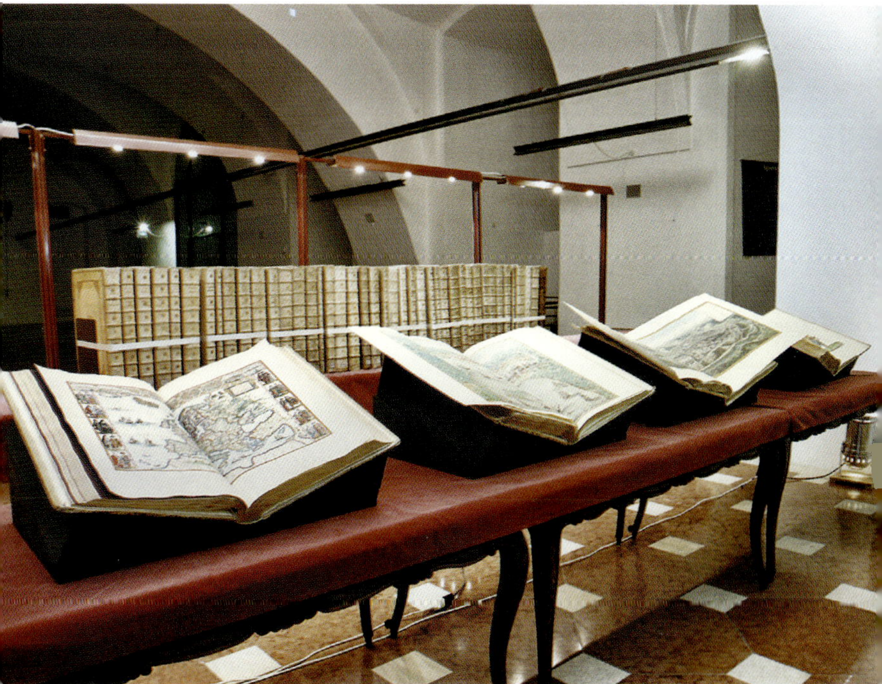

The Blaeu-Van der Hem Atlas mid-seventeenth century
This celebrated atlas of the Baroque period, comprising around 2,400 copperplate engravings and drawings was acquired by Prince Eugene of Savoy in 1730 for his own library.

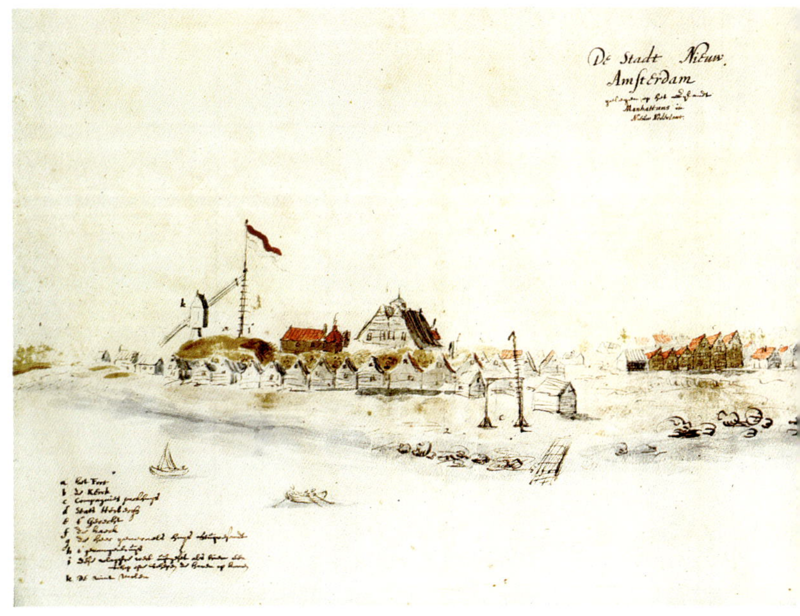

between 1662 and 1678 with great care, considerable expertise and at enormous cost, by an Amsterdam patrician, Laurens van der Hem (1621–78). It was based on the 1662 Latin edition of Joan Blaeu's 11-volume *Atlas Major*, to which Van der Hem then added printed maps, views and drawings made by other authors as well.

The *Blaeu-Van der Hem Atlas* was already a byword for excellence among map enthusiasts and collectors in much of Europe in the seventeeth century. In 1730 it was acquired at an auction by Prince Eugene of Savoy. Later his niece, Victoria von Sachsen-Hildburghausen, who had inherited his estate, agreed to sell it to Emperor Charles VI, along with the Bibliotheca Eugeniana, in return for an annual pension (see p. 117).

Among the numerous valuable city views to be found in the Map Department there are copper engravings and woodcuts of the sixteenth and seventeenth centuries, watercoloured engravings by Laurenz Janscha and Franz Ziegler, as well as original views of the Danube by Jacob Alt. Dating from the nineteenth century are pencil drawings of towns and castles in Tyrol by Johanna and Welf Isser, watercolours by the canon of Königsgrätz, Johann Venuto, and sketches from Greenland and Franz-Josef-Land by the Austrian polar explorer Julius Payer. Of exceptional significance, however, is the view of New Amsterdam made in 1650. This drawing in pen and ink and watercolour is regarded as the first on-the-spot visual record of the city later to become famous as New York.

Most of the older maps and city plans in the Map Department are currently being recatalogued. To this end, all the data required for an up-to-

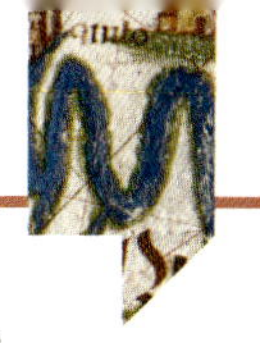

View of Nieuw Amsterdam c. 1650
Pen-and-ink drawing with watercolour

The first on-the-spot visual record of the city now known as New York

date catalogue record of each old map and every atlas will be assessed and incorporated into the Austrian Union Catalogue. The result will be a single, unified, consistent and high-quality card catalogue, which will eventually be freely accessible on the Internet.

From 2005 it will be possible to access via the Internet the catalogue for each of the 260,000 or more maps in the Map Department of the Austrian National Library, and to order by e-mail those items required for consultation in the Map Department reading room.

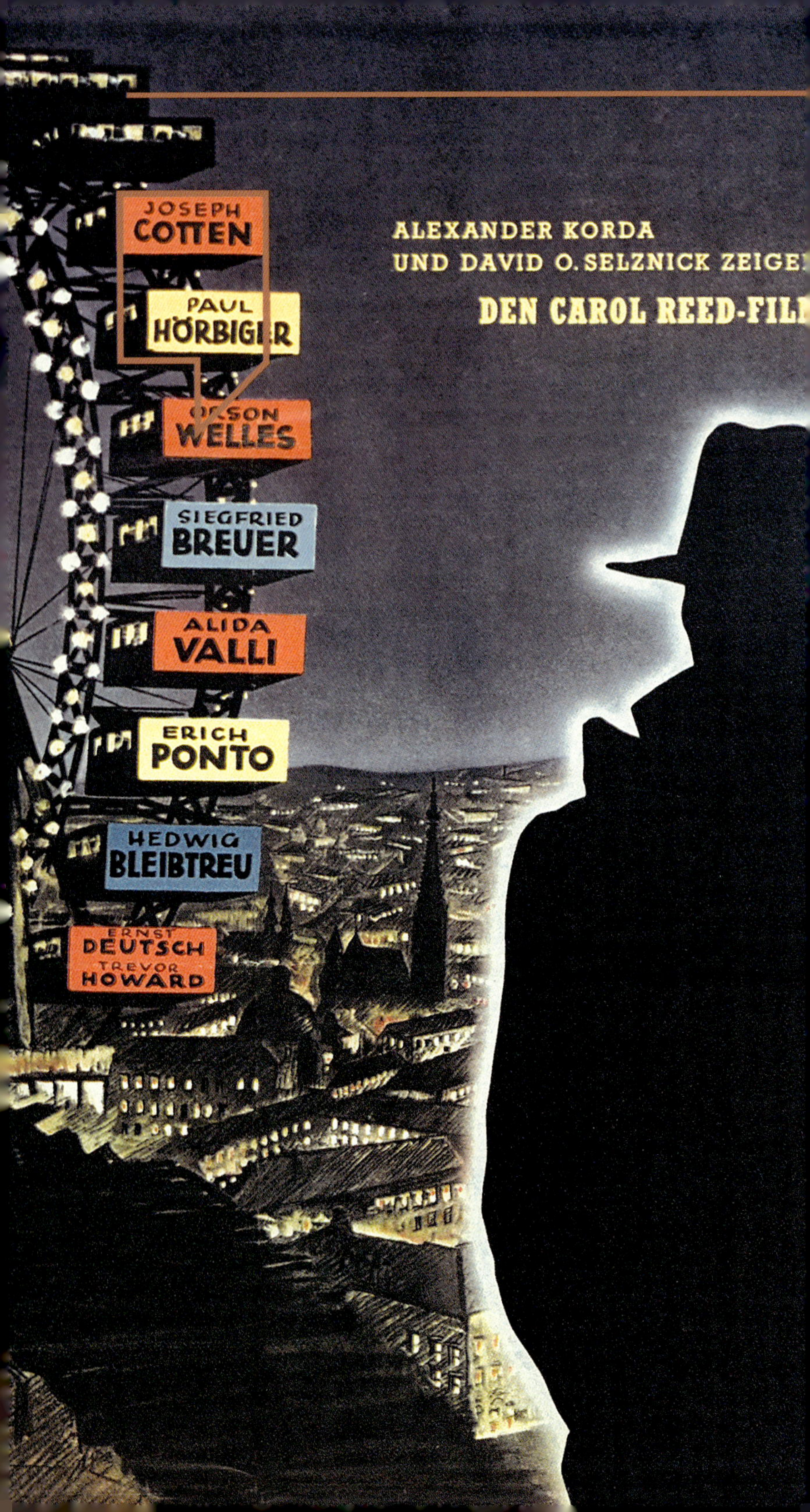

JOSEPH COTTEN
PAUL HÖRBIGER
ORSON WELLES
SIEGFRIED BREUER
ALIDA VALLI
ERICH PONTO
HEDWIG BLEIBTREU
ERNST DEUTSCH
TREVOR HOWARD
ALEXANDER KORDA
UND DAVID O. SELZNICK ZEIGEN
DEN CAROL REED-FILM

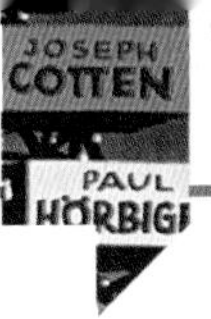

Department of Broadsheets, Posters and Ex Libris

The Department of Broadsheets, Posters and Ex Libris, established in 1995 as one of the ten special collections of the Austrian National Library, comprises over 350,000 items providing valuable source material for the study of Austrian history and politics as well as the history of art and of printing.

The collection stores and documents broadsheets and posters printed in Austria, a copy of which, in accordance with Austrian media law, must be deposited with the Austrian National Library. In the case of contemporary posters, the emphasis is on politics (notably, posters used in campaigns for national, regional and local elections) and cultural life (posters advertising theatrical and musical performances or museum and gallery exhibitions). The collection's holdings of bookplates are continuously expanding.

THE COLLECTION OF BROADSHEETS

A collection of broasdsheets, numbering around 10,000 items, had already been established by 1912. A broadsheet consists of a single sheet of printed matter addressing a particular subject intended to form public opinion. During the Reformation and Counter-Reformation and the subsequent Thirty Years War (1618–48), as also in other periods of revolution and war there was invariably a marked increase in the production of broadsheets. The holdings of the Collection of Broadsheets comprise the following categories: diverse single printed sheets and military recruitment announcements from the sixteenth to the nineteenth century, broadsheets relating to the Revolution of 1848 and those produced in Lombardy-Venetia from 1799 to 1866, and broadsheets printed in the years of the two twentieth-century World Wars and in connection with the electoral campaigns of the First and Second Austrian Republics.

Anonymous poster advertising the film *The Third Man*
detail, see p. 123

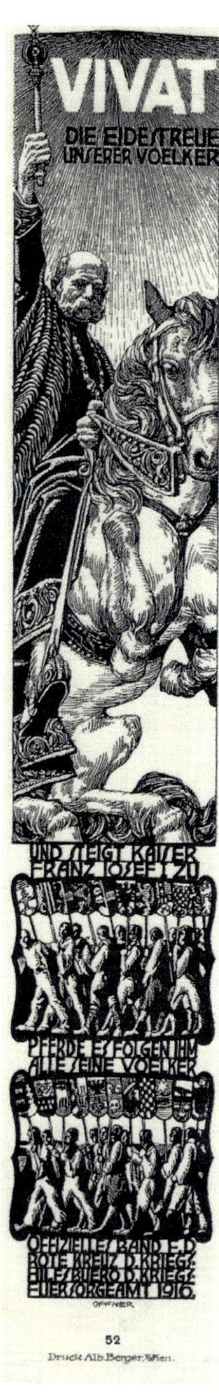

Alfred Offner '*Long live the sworn loyalty of our Peoples*' Vienna, Albert Berger, 1916

THE COLLECTION OF POSTERS

The foundations of the Austrian National Library's Collection of Posters were laid by Dr. Ottokar Mascha, who in 1917 donated his own important collection of early posters to the Imperial Court Library. In 1923 the 'War Collection' (of posters related to the First World War), initiated at the Library in 1914, was absorbed into the Collection of Broadsheets. This segment of the Collection of Posters, with its wide variety of subjects and artistic styles, supplies a comprehensive record both of the First World War as it progressed and of the patriotic propaganda issued in connection with it. In addition to posters it includes broadsheets, important official announcements, children's drawings, items bearing formal proclamations of loyalty to the House of Habsburg, food ration coupons and examples of *Vivat-Bänder* (silk ribbons designed by well-known Jugendstil graphic artists and sold for charity).

As a result of the obligation, imposed on publishers in 1918, to deposit with the Austrian National Library a copy of every broadsheet and poster for which they were responsible, and the absorption of copies previously deposited with the censorship authorities, it has been possible to assemble a comprehensive national record of these media.

Two valuable self-contained sections within the Collection of Posters are especially worthy of mention. Firstly, the collection of posters of the Jugendstil and Early Expressionist periods undertaken by Erhard Buschbeck (1889–1960). This includes designs by Egon Schiele (1890–1918) and Oskar Kokoschka (1886–1980) that are milestones in poster history. Secondly, the collection of over 3,000 film posters from 1910 to 1955 assembled by Joseph Gregor (1888–1960). With over 500 American posters for films made in Hollywood and over 1,000 posters for the silent cinema, this is among the most valuable film poster collections for those engaged in research in this and related fields.

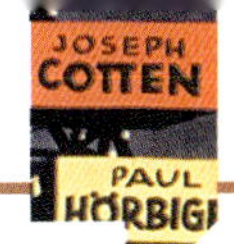

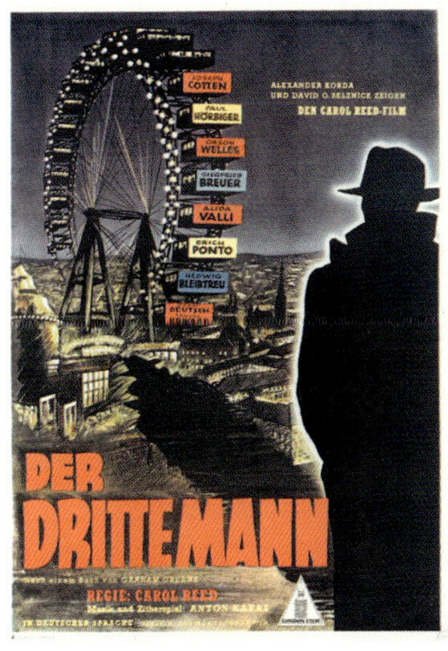

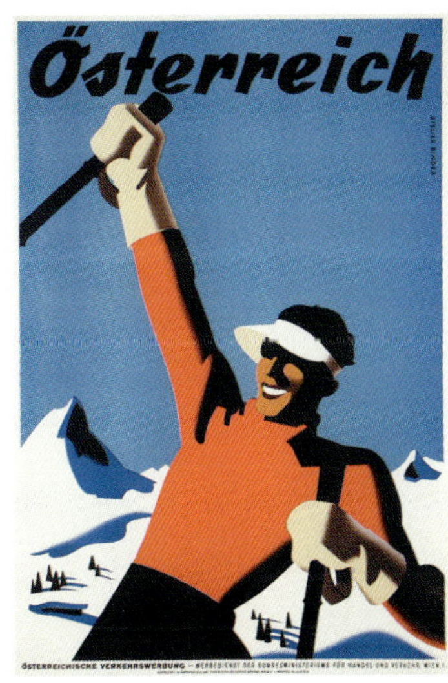

Anonymous *poster advertising the film The Third Man* Berlin, Druckhaus Tempelhof, 1950

Joseph Binder, travel poster for Austria, Vienna, Christoph Reisser, c. 1934

Egon Schiele, poster advertising the forty-ninth exhibition at the Secession, Vienna, Albert Berger, 1918

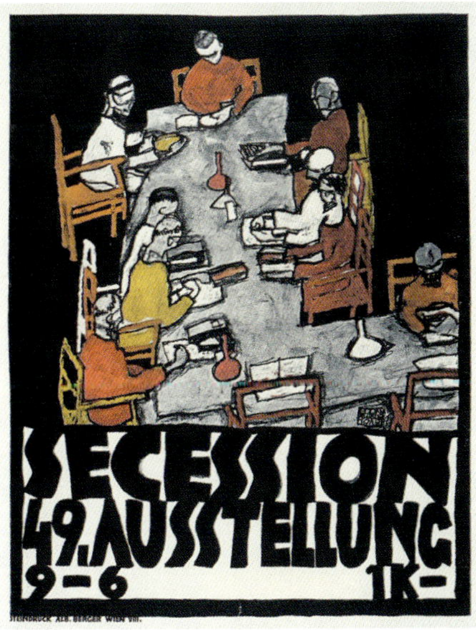

In 1998 the Collection of Posters was further enlarged through the acquisition of the Poster Archive of the Association of Austrian Commercial Artists. Comprising 1,300 posters, primarily of the period between around 1900 and the 1960s, this includes the work of the most important Austrian poster designers, among them Josef Binder (1898–1972), Ernst Deutsch (1883–1939), Hans Neumann (1888–1960) and Julius Klinger (1876–1942). This material testifies to the leading role played by Austrian graphic design in the inter-war period. This collection is named after the insurance company Donau-Versicherungen, which facilitated its acquisition.

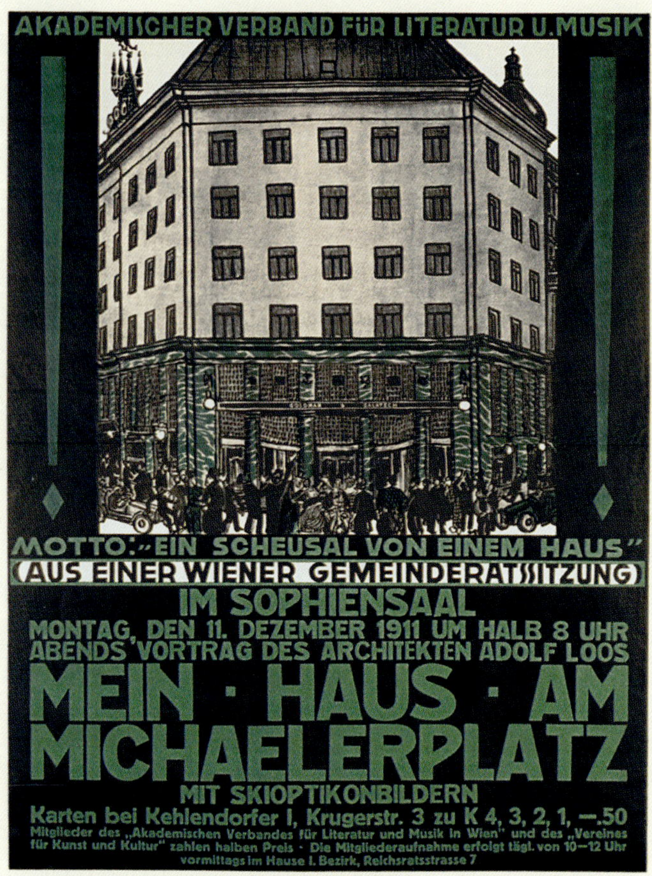

Urban Janke *poster advertising a talk* by the architect Adolf Loos, 'My House on Michaelerplatz', Vienna, Rosenbaum, 1911

THE COLLECTION OF EX LIBRIS (BOOKPLATES)

The Collection of Ex Libris comprises about 9,000 items spanning the period from around 1500 to 1850. A bookplate usually takes the form of a small sheet of paper bearing a name or initials and/or a coat of arms, and is affixed to the inside front cover of a book to signify ownership. Bookplates are known to have been in use since the thirteenth century: they were initially made by hand and, from the fifteenth century, also printed. Many of them also bore a curse on anyone who might think to steal the book or a warning to the prospective reader not to damage it.

The Austrian National Library's Collection of Ex Libris ultimately derives from two sources: the bookplates found in the books in the Imperial Court Library and those from Rudolf Benkard's collection which was acquired in 1930 and included over 6,000 items dating from the sixteenth to the eighteenth century, above all from southern Germany and Austria.

During the 1970s, as a result of new acquisitions and donations, the emphasis of collecting shifted to the first half of the twentieth century. The bookplate collections amassed by Hans Ankwicz-Kleehoven (1883–1962) and Franz Kubat (1894–1987), as also part of the estate of the Austrian copper-engraver Alfred Cossmann (1870–1951), were principally of Austrian, German and Swiss bookplates dating between 1900 and the 1960s. A further collection, assembled in what is now the Czech Republic, offers a good overview of bookplate production in the Eastern Europe between the two world wars. Since 1996 attention had also been focused on contemporary bookplates. The Austrian National Library's Collection of Ex Libris now numbers around 45,000 items.

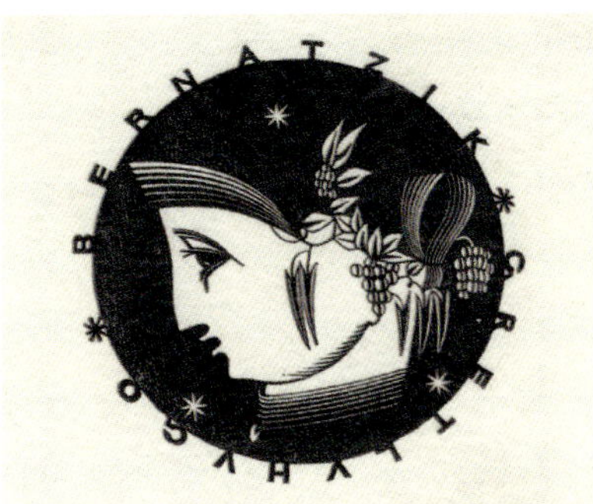

Dagobert Peche *book-plate for Gretl and Hugo Bernatzik* Woodcut

The Austrian National Library's Department of Broadsheets, Posters and Ex Libris regularly adds to its holdings. In recent years, for example, it has acquired the estates or advance bequests of Austrian graphic artists such as Wilhelm Jaruska (b. 1916), August Schmid (1913–98) and Alexander Exax (1896–1994), as well as the estate of the bookplate designer Otto Feil (1894–1985), and the archive of the book-binding workshop founded in 1873 by Hermann Scheibe. The evolution of Austrian graphic design in the twentieth and early twenty-first centuries is documented here through numerous fine examples in a variety of fields.

USING THE DEPARTMENT OF BROADSHEETS, POSTERS AND EX LIBRIS

The older items in the Collection of Posters can already be accessed through an image databank. More and more of the collection as a whole is being digitalized and, by 2005, all its catalogues will be accessible on the Internet. An Austrian National Library user's card (*Benutzungskarte*) offers access to the collection (which does, of course, have its own guidelines and regulations for users). Items in the collection's specialist library, which is a reference library, are immediately accessible, but access to broadsheets, posters and bookplates, as well as to material entering the collection as part of an artist's or collector's estate requires advance notification.

... wird überredet Tänzerin zu werden, ihre S...

...nützen — sie verläßt ihren Freund, den kleinen ...

...ch: ein (niedriger) niedriger Spiesser — Gespräch der Eltern üb...

...ucht: beide wünschen heimlich, dass sie einen ver...

...det. Irene wird Tänzerin.

Balletmeisterin.
Agent. Lokalbesitzer. — Fredy, ein Türstega, d...
...meisterin. Sie lernt einen Freunde kennen; einen
Rechtsanwalt, ein ~~~~~~~~~~~~~ Militär...
...offizier, ~~~~~~~~~~~~~~~~~~~~~~~~, # — — —
(...tistischen)

...amateurerfinder #

Rennbahn. (Mannequin) ✓ [Die Zeleg, der
                                    seiner für Pf...

... Sportplatz. (Eishockey)

...hönheitskonkurrenz. [Sie fühlt sich bereits M...
                              ...eine Schönheitskönigin

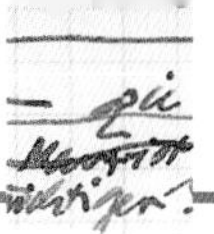

Austrian Literary Archives

The Austrian Literary Archives were established in 1989 and has been a fully functioning department of the Austrian National Library since 1996. It acquires the literary estates and autograph manuscripts of Austrian writers, as well as publishers' and editors' archives, dating from the twentieth century onwards. Its holdings are especially rich in the work of writers of the period after 1945. Another area of emphasis is literature produced in exile, above all the work of those forced to flee German-speaking Europe in the 1930s and 1940s. Contacts established with contemporary writers make it possible to secure examples of their work even within their lifetimes.

THE HOLDINGS OF THE OF THE AUSTRIAN LITERARY ARCHIVES

Around 110 entire or partial literary estates, material acquired during an author's lifetime, and other collections are preserved in the Austrian Literary Archives. Among the represented writers are:

Konrad Bayer (1932–64), Maxi Böhm (1915–82), Christine Busta (1915–87), Axel Corti (1933–93), Franz Theodor Csokor (1885–1969), Heimito von Doderer (1896–1966), Albert Drach (1902–95), Karl Farkas (1893–1971), Erich Fried (1921–88), Egon Friedell (1878–1938), Dietmar Grieser (b. 1934), Peter Handke (b. 1942), Josef Haslinger (b. 1955), Peter Henisch (b. 1943), Hermann Hesse (1877–1962), Ödön von Horváth (1901–38), Lotte Ingrisch (b. 1930), Ernst Jandl (1925–2000), Gert F. Jonke (b. 1946), Alfred Kubin (1877–1959), Anton Kuh (1890–1941), Alexander Lernet-Holenia (1897–1976), Friederike Mayröcker (b. 1924), Franz Molnár (1878–1952), Anreas Okopenko (b. 1930), Christoph Ransmayr (b. 1954), Gerhard Roth (b. 1942), George Saiko (1892–1962), Robert Schindel (b.1944), Karl Schönherr (1867–1943), Julian Schutting (b. 1937), György

Ödön von Horváth *Outline* detail, see p. 129

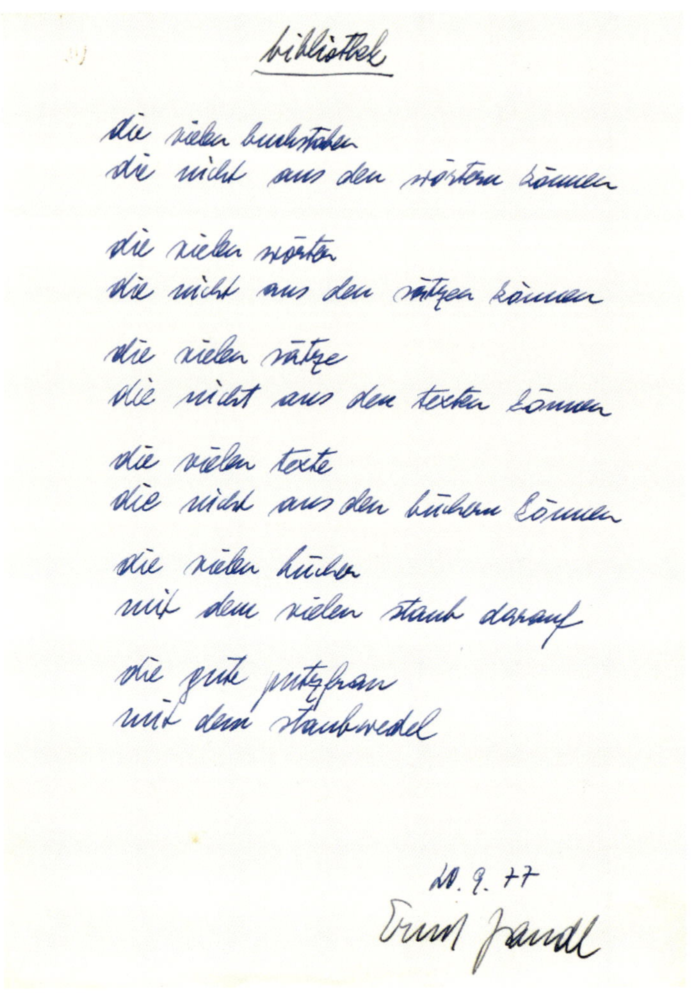

Ernst Jandl *The Library* 20 September 1977

Sebestyén (1930–90), Manès Sperber (1905–84), Hilde Spiel (1911–90), Friedrich Torberg (1908–79), Jakob Wassermann (1873–1934), and Dorothea Zeemann (1909–93).

The literary estates held in the Austrian Literary Archives contain literary works (autograph manuscripts, typescripts and corrected proofs), correspondence, biographical material (contracts with publishers, book reviews, press cuttings, and audio-visual material). These holdings are systematically processed and made accessible to users. They are supplemented by published material of particular relevance to the Archives' holdings.

An Austrian National Library user's card (*Benützungskarte*) allows access to the Austrian Literary Archives (which, of course, has its own user guide-

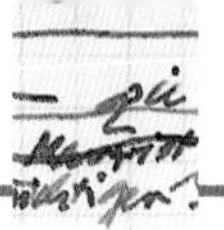

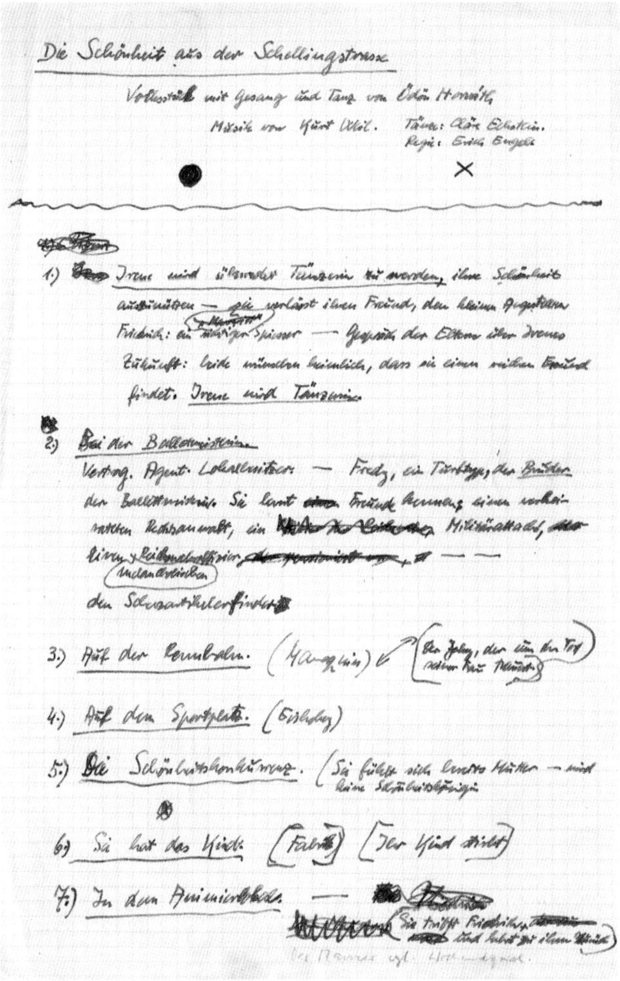

Ödön von Horváth outline of *The Beauty of Schellingstrasse*
a rough draft of his play *Tales of the Vienna Woods*

lines and regulations). Frequently used items and standard reference works are on open-shelf access. In general, other material can be delivered to users within two hours of request, although in the case of certain holdings, advance notification is necessary. Material may not be removed from the Archives.

Twice a year the Austrian Literary Archives organize events in its series of Archive Conversations, in which issues concerning the Archive, the Library and the study of literature are addressed. Two publications, *Sichtungen* (Sightings) and the magazine *Profile*, seek to offer a lively approach to authors and to the phenomena of literary life as well as addressing questions on the operation of the Archives.

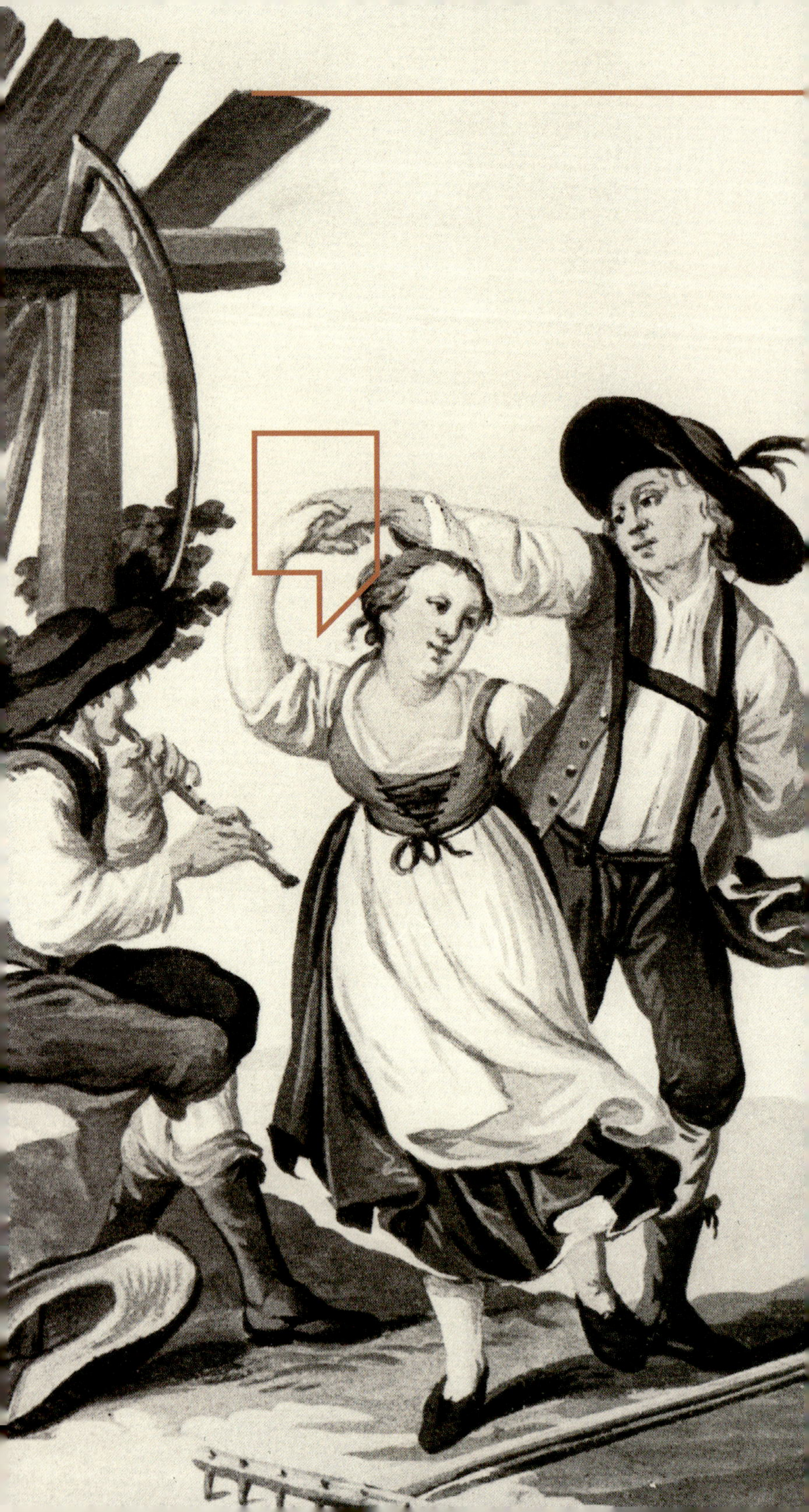

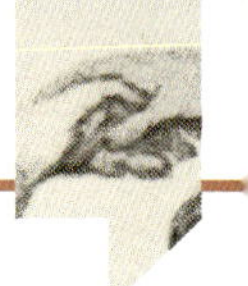

Archives of the Austrian Folk Music Society

The Archives of the Austrian Folk Music Society became part of the Austrian National Library in 1994, its remit being to document traditional forms of musical-poetic expression. In addition to manuscript records, of both words and melodies, the Library can lay claim to Austria's most extensive holdings of printed material on the subject of the folksong, folk music, folk dancing and folk poetry. The collection of recorded music embraces old 78 rpm and 33 rpm records, tapes and cassettes, CDs and digitalized formats. The collection also contains visual documentation and song sheets. It is housed in its own department within the Austrian National Library and is substantially aided by an association of supporters.

The Archives of the Austrian Folksong Institute has its origins in the project initiated in 1904 by the Austrian Ministry of Religion and Education to record and document all the national songs and dances, with their accompanying music, to be found in the territories of the Danubian Monarchy. After some uneven progress, this project issued in 1955 in the foundation of a Central Archive for Austrian Folk Song Collections, its purpose being to collect copies obtained from the nine folksong archives of the regions (*Länder*) of the Republic of Austria.

The Archive is used by numerous researchers and other interested individuals. A wide range of enquiries is received and answered, ensuring that the Archive's holdings are used productively and creatively. The most important songbooks, as well as standard reference works, are on open-shelf access, and further material ordered in the Archive Reading Room is supplied on request.

A substantial part of the catalogue of the Archive's holdings is accessible via the Internet through the combined database of folksong archives in Austria (Virtueller Datenverbund der Volksliedarchive in Österreich). By 2005 all holdings will be accessible via the Internet.

J. von Lederwash *a dancing couple* 1813, detail

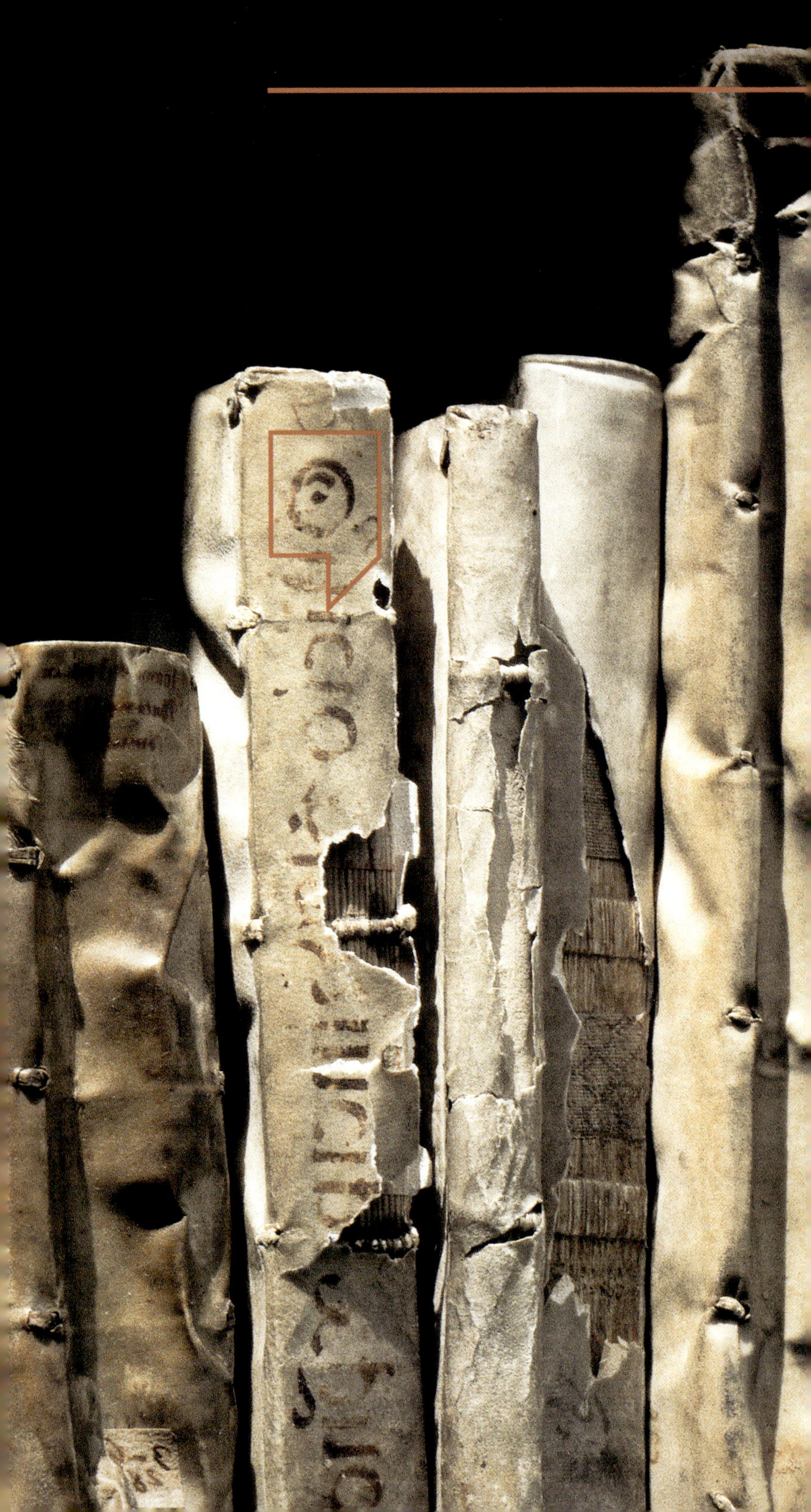

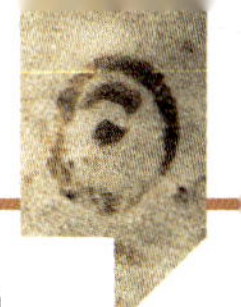

Institute for Conservation

The Institute for Conservation is responsible for the restoration and conservation of the enormous range of objects to be found in the collections of the Austrian National Library, for example: manuscripts, printed material, autograph texts, maps, globes, prints and drawings, watercolours, photographs, posters and newspapers. Thanks to the efforts of the Departments for the Conservation of Books, Paper and Photographic Material, the Library's holdings are preserved for the use and enjoyment of future generations and both the historic significance and their intrinsic artistic value maintained.

PRESERVATION OF THE HOLDINGS OF THE AUSTRIAN NATIONAL LIBRARY

| *Protective Conservation:*

It is essential that objects be stored so as to prevent any losses of their original substance. Carefully considered and maintained storage itself affords protection for the object by keeping it away from damaging external factors. Also of importance are protection against extreme changes in climate (temperature, humidity, etc.), the implementation of appropriate guidelines and regulations for users, advance planning of emergency procedures, and the use of robust and chemically stable protective containers and wrappings.

| *Conservation and Restoration:*

It becomes necessary to undertake conservation and restoration of an object when it is endangered by virtue of its current condition.

RISKS TO THE LIBRARY'S HOLDINGS

The materials used in book production – paper, leather, parchment and so on – are in themselves prone to change over time and they eventually become less resilient. Additional damage can be caused by the

Vellum covers damaged by dryness and light

production methods employed, for example insufficiently supportive bindings that reveal their inadequacies with the repeated opening and closing of a book. Related problems derive from poor quality materials, such as paper with a high wood-pulp content, which rapidly yellows and becomes brittle. Old, gall-iron inks can destroy the paper to which they are applied. Under certain conditions early film negatives can simply disintegrate.

External factors such as temperature, humidity, lighting and atmospheric pollution can create conditions in which the Library's holdings may age abnormally rapidly and thereby undergo drastic physical changes. High temperatures and high humidity provide optimum conditions for micro-organisms and injurious insects to flourish. The high energy-quotient of light leads to chemical damage. Poor storage materials such as paper and cardboard with a high wood-pulp content damage the substance of the objects they are intended to protect.

Inappropriate and careless handling of objects leads to serious mechanical damage, such as the loosening of a book's spine and the related weakening of its bindings, tears in paper, or finger-prints left on photographic prints or negatives. It is frequently necessary to deal with the damage caused by earlier repair procedures, such as the mending of tears with self-adhesive strips.

Various procedures are employed in the treatment of mechanical damage: book spines, for example, are strengthened with the addition of new leather; tears in paper are mended through the application of thin Japan paper; a high acid-content in paper is reduced through treatment with water; and the introduction of alkaline reserves protects paper from future damage by excess acid. The Library holdings are also protectively conserved through cleaning, the creation of acid-free protective containers, storage in better conditions or improved shelving. Substantial financial support for the restoration of the holdings of the Austrian National Library is provided by donations received in the context of the Book Sponsorship Scheme.

THE BOOK SPONSORSHIP SCHEME

The Book Sponsorship Scheme was instituted in 1990 with the aim of raising additional funds for the conservation of old objects in the collections of the Austrian National Library. Since that date over 4,500 book sponsors have made donations to support the restoration not only of valuable books, but also of posters, photographs, globes, manuscript scores, papyri and much more. Among those contributing to the initiative are many eminent individuals, including Hillary Clinton, Mikhail Gorbachev and Martin Scorsese, in addition to numerous corporate bodies.

Sponsors donate € 500 or more, receiving a certificate in acknowledgement of their generosity. The item restored with their support henceforth bears a label with their name. Contributions to the Book Sponsorship Scheme are tax deductible. For more information on becoming a book patron, visit www.onb.ac.at/about/nb/buchpt_fr.htm or **telephone (+43 1) 534 10 260.**

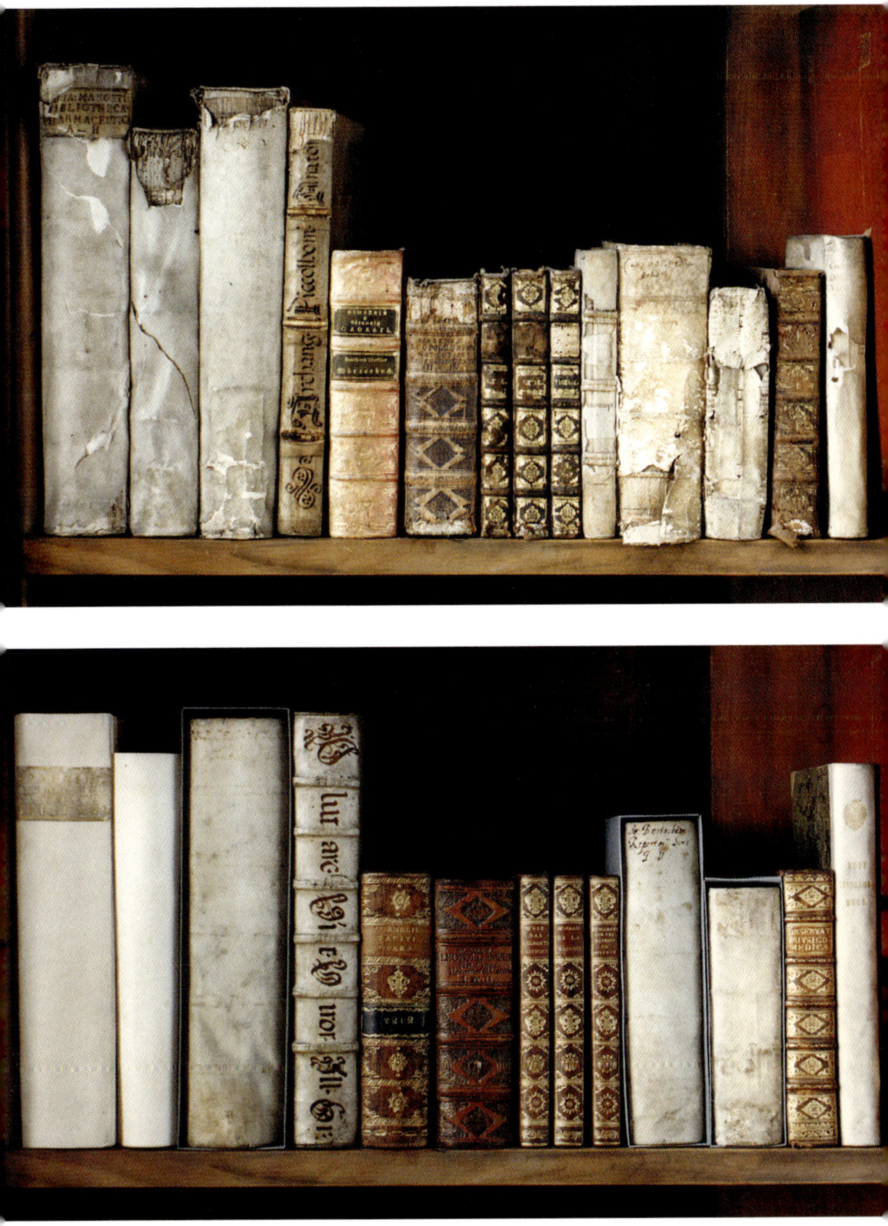

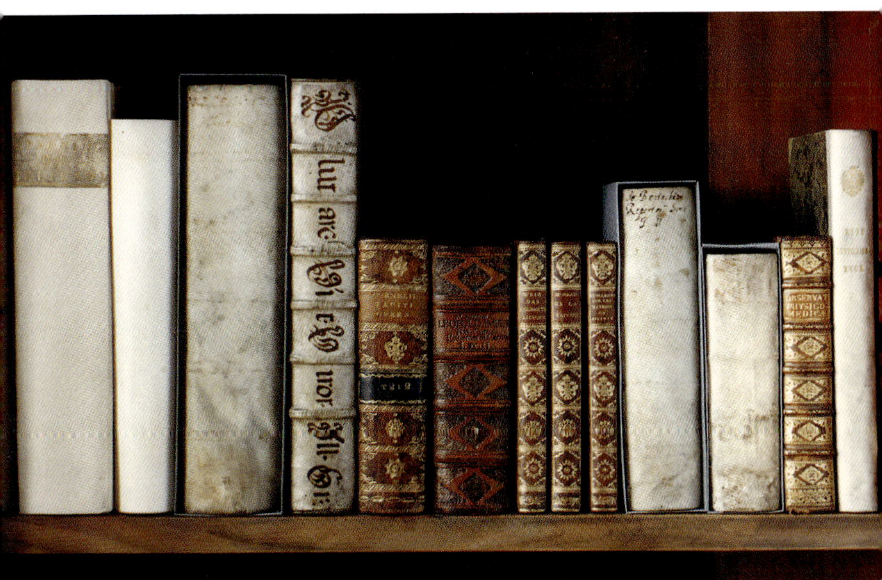

Books before and after restoration

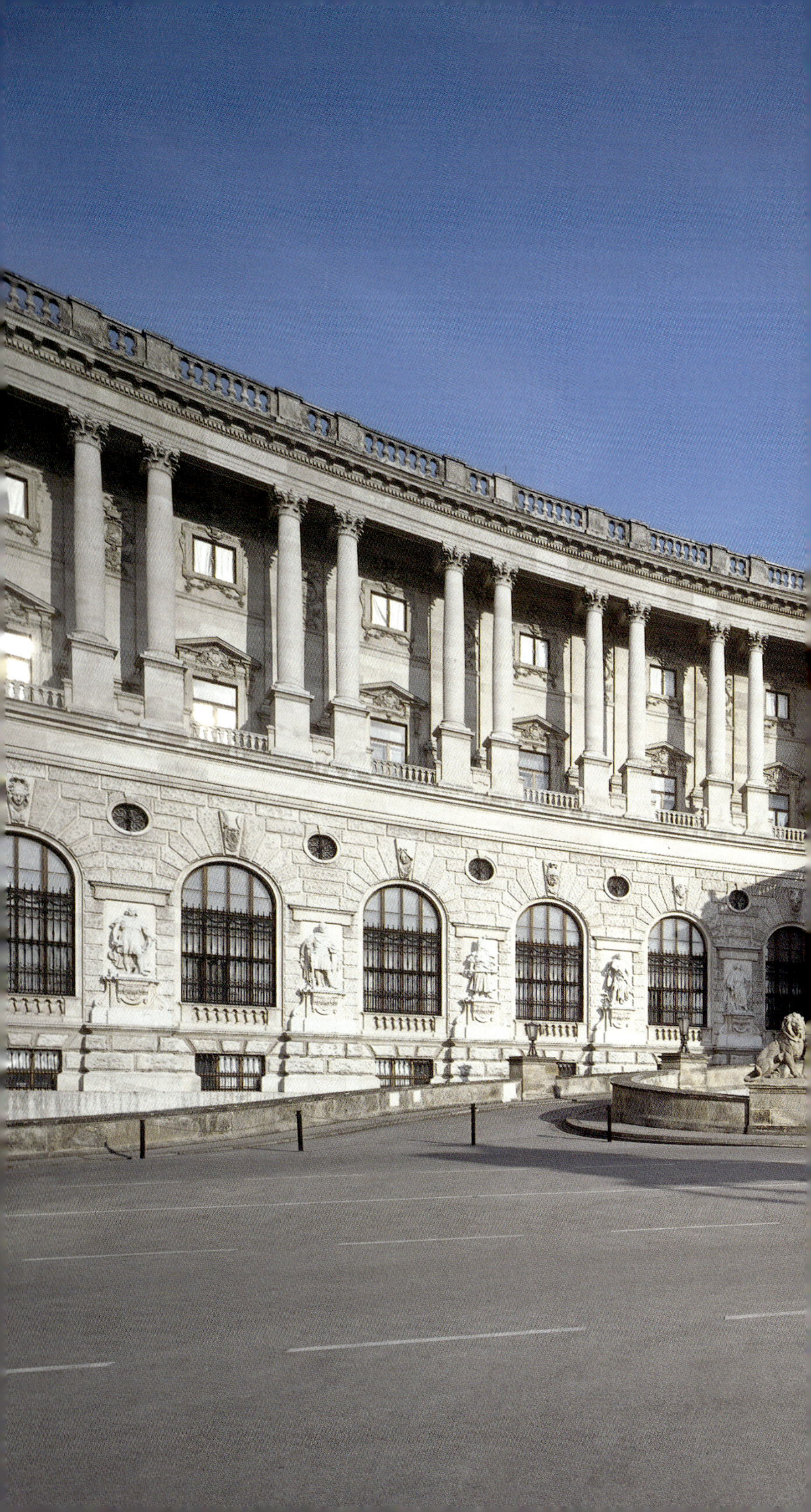

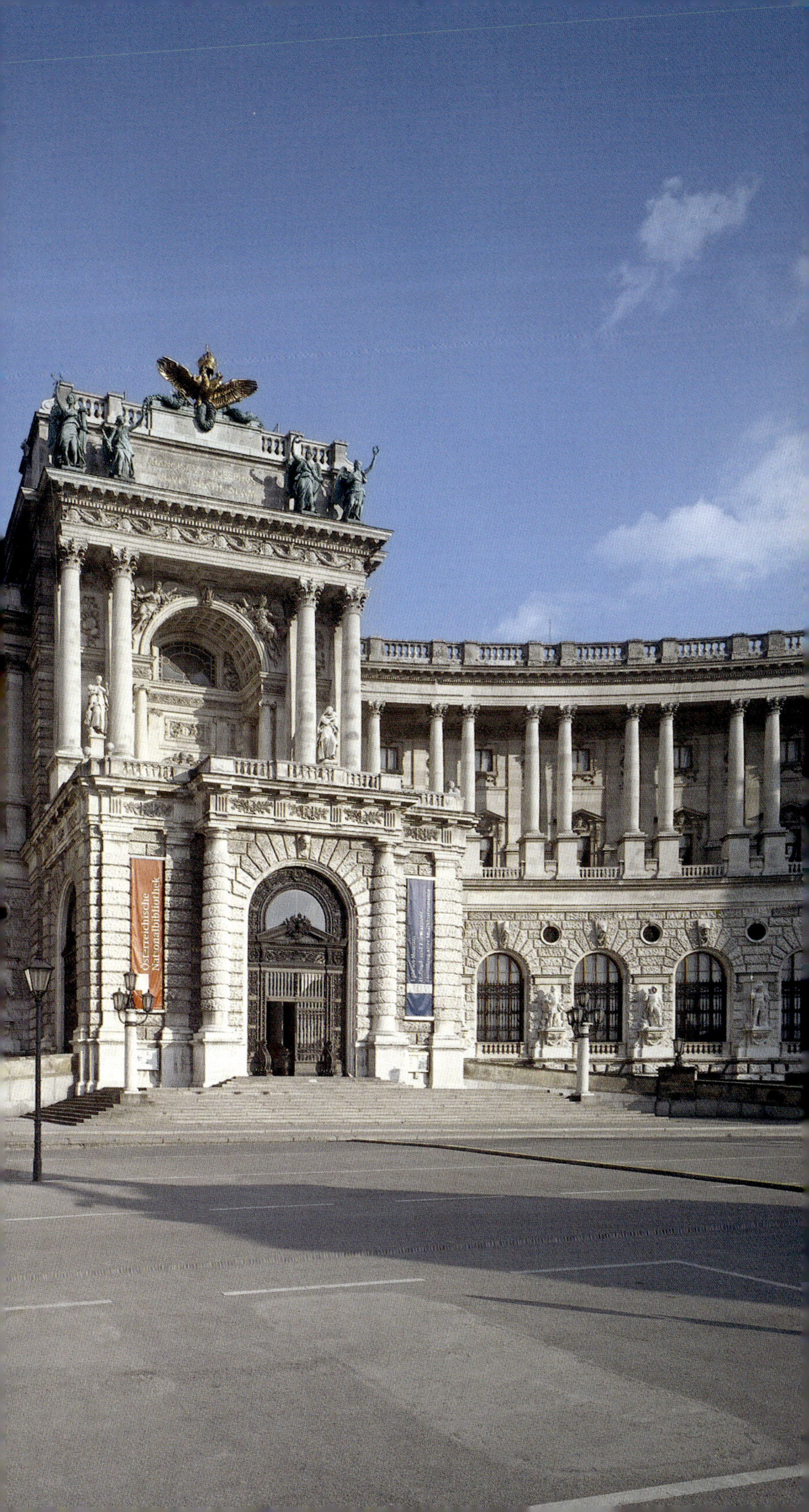

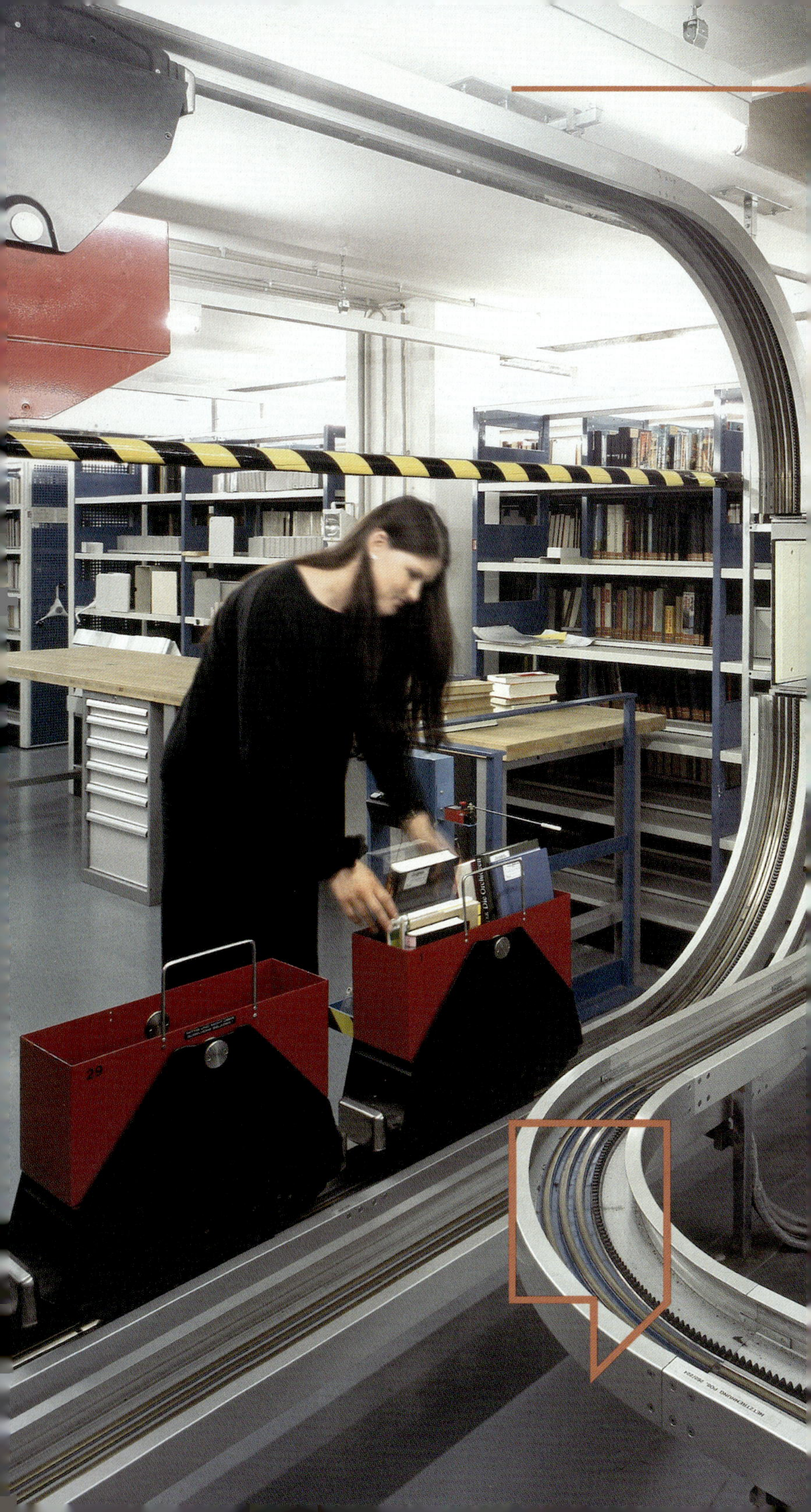

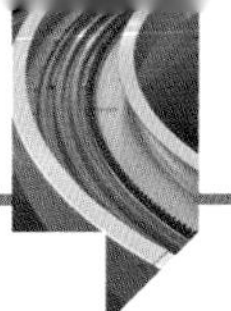

Modern Library

While incorporating a great range of museums and special collections, the Austrian National Library is also, and not least, a modern academic library. In its capacity as a centre of excellence committed to providing its users with services of the highest quality, it endeavours to meet the demands and expectations commensurate with the information society of the twenty-first century.

SERVICES FOR USERS

The services offered to users of the Austrian National Library are extremely diverse, ranging from those that may be regarded as traditional (access to its holdings in its various reading rooms, the provision of an academic information service, loan and inter-library loan facilities) to the most modern, such as rapid access to the Internet at computer terminals, various reproduction services and an increasing number of online services. In order to use the Austrian National Library, it is necessary to obtain a user's card (*Benützungskarte*). In principle, this is available to anyone over the age of fifteen and can be obtained for a period of a day (or a certain number of days) or a year.

IN-HOUSE SERVICES

The fact that around 800 individuals use the Austrian National Library's reading rooms every day demonstrates that the traditional library services, such as those indicated above, are still very much in demand – even though an increasing number of these are also available online. In addition to the reading rooms that form part of each of the ten special collections, the Austrian National Library provides its users with reading rooms and other areas accessible from Heldenplatz, the heart of

Book conveyer in the underground storage
The Neue Hofburg am Heldenplatz, the entrance of the modern library
(pp. 136/137)

the Modern Library. After the thorough renovation and modernization carried out between 2002 and 2004 – including the rearrangement and air-conditioning of the reading rooms, the provision of access for the disabled, and of a lounge for all readers in the foyer, these spaces have now assumed a modern, user-friendly appearance. In addition to quiet and comfortable desks and seating, the reading rooms offer a carefully selected range of standard reference works and frequently used published source material on open-access shelving. In the Catalogue Hall there are numerous computer terminals, at which users may search the Austrian National Library catalogue and access the Internet for related purposes.

The Newspapers and Periodicals Reading Room displays the current issues of over one hundred daily newspapers to which the Austrian National Library subscribes and of over 11,000 periodicals, a great many on open-access shelving.

In 1992 new underground storage was created, and this also houses an area in which users can consult outsize printed material, newspapers and microforms. Requests for material that the Austrian National Library is unable to accommodate through drawing on its own holdings can be met through the inter-library loan service.

Although the Austrian National Library is, of course, primarily a reference library, certain users, e.g. those preparing doctoral dissertations or scholars engaged in research, may arrange to make use of its lending library facilities, which will allow them to consult books outside the Library for a specific period of time.

Of particular importance among the services offered by the Austrian National Library is the assistance provided to those engaged in bibliographical research. This can be obtained from the Department of Academic Information (*Abteilung Wissenschaftliche Information*), which has at its disposal an enormous range of reference works. The Ariadne documentation service is specialized in enquiries related to women's issues and the *Informationsvermittlungsstelle/Elektronische Datenbanken und Recherchen* is devoted to research in online databases.

SERVICES AVAILABLE ONLINE

The Austrian National Library's holdings of printed material from 1501 to the present day is now catalogued in electronic form. Today's library users expect to enjoy the advantages of convenient international 24-hour access to a catalogue and the ability to order items for consultation in the reading rooms by e-mail. By 2005 the catalogue of each of the special collections will also be accessible via the Internet. At present the Austrian National Library receives over 50,000 book orders by e-mail every year. The online catalogue of printed material is supplemented, moreover, by a great many specialist databanks related to the special collections forming part of the Austrian National Library, such as those of manu-

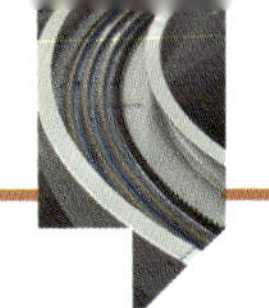

After thorough renovation and modernization, the Modern Library on Heldenplatz is now open to readers from Monday to Saturday.

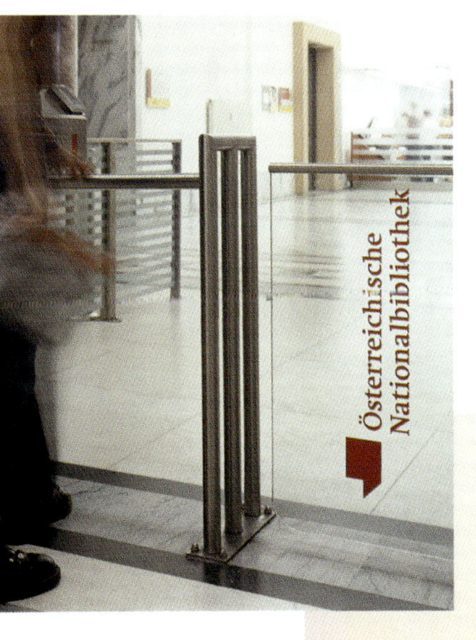

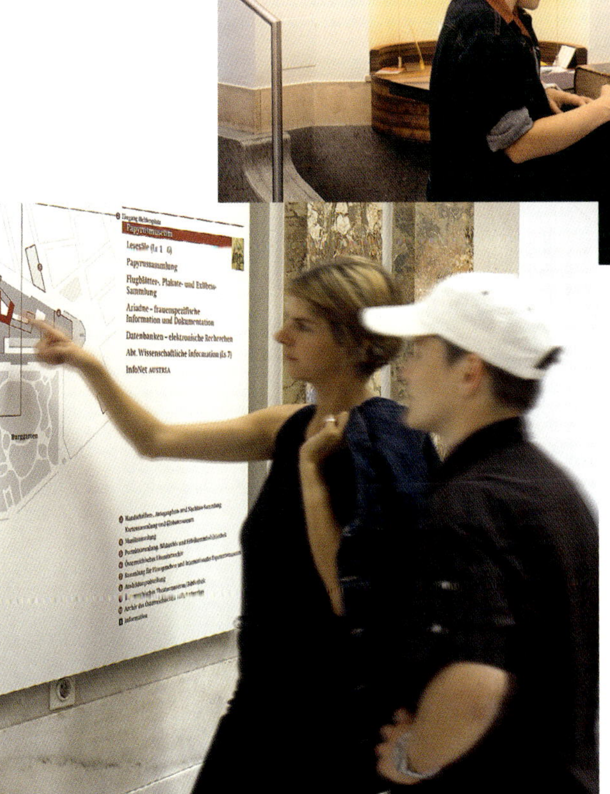

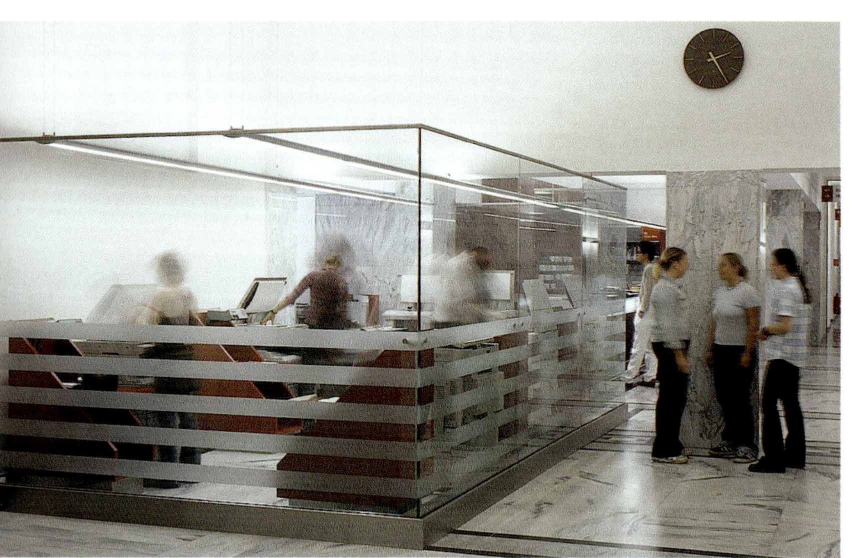

Copying area in the Main Reading Room

scripts and other autograph texts, of film posters, of articles from journals and collective publications on women's and gender issues (to be found in the aforementioned Ariadne databank), of the invented languages represented in the collection of the Esperanto Museum, and many more.

The databank InfoNet-AUSTRIA, the central guide to the special collections and their respective databanks, offers users access to over 900 Austrian documentation and information services.

Inter-library loan requests, reproduction orders, and research enquiries can all be sent to the Austrian National Library by e-mail.

Also worthy of mention is an entire series of online databanks and online publications, which the Austrian National Library is able to offer its users, in part via the Internet, and in part at computer terminals in its reading rooms. The latest addition to its online services, and one which is continuously being extended, is the virtual newspaper reading room: ANNO (AustriaN Newspapers Online). This makes an enormous range of older Austrian newspapers – from the *Wiener Allgemeine Zeitung* to the *Reichspost* and the *Wiener Zeitung* – accessible to users at any time.

Over 2,000,000 visits a year are made to the homepage of the Austrian National Library website at **www.onb.ac.at** – compelling evidence of the growing importance and broad acceptance of its services available online.

Reproduction Services

The Austrian National Library offers its users a great many reproduction services. In addition to the provision of standard photocopying machines in the Main Reading Room, it also meets requests for specialized photocopying, for copies from microfilm, for photography (especially of objects in the Picture Archive), for digitalized images, and for the loan of large-format transparencies for use in publications. Further special services include the provision of facsimile copies of newspapers published on a particular date (for presentation as birthday or anniversary gifts). These may, if desired, be supplied in a range of attractive presentation folders.

GUIDED TOURS

Tours of the reading rooms for school classes and other interested groups are, of course, also among the services offered by the Austrian National Library. These constitute an ideal introduction to how the Library functions and to the diverse services it can offer its users. Tours of the museums that form part of the Austrian National Library (State Hall, Papyrus Museum, Globe Museum) and of the various State Hall displays are also available, both for adults and children. Over 1,000 Austrian National Library tours take place each year. For further information on available tours, please contact the Public Relations Department (*Abteilung für Öffentlichkeitsarbeit*) of the Austrian National Library,
telephone +43 1 534 10 464
or send an **e-mail** to **oeffentlichkeitsarbeit@onb.ac.at**.

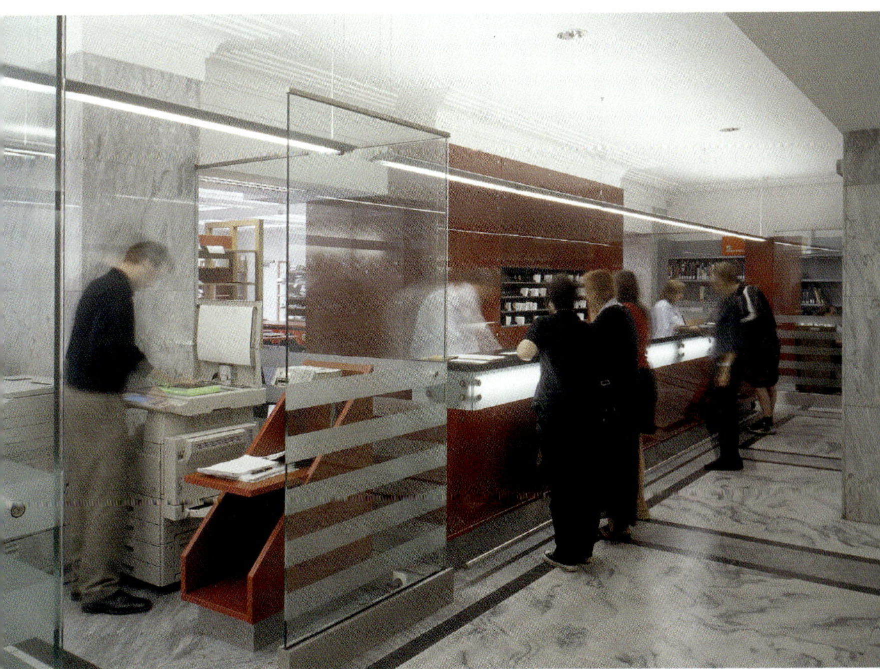

Issue desk in the Main Reading Room

New Acquisitions

The acquisition, cataloguing and display of objects entering the Austrian National Library's ten special collections is the responsibility of each department, but the acquisition of scholarly literature for the Library as a whole is the responsibility of the Department for the Enlargement and Development of the Library's Holdings. Inclusive of material published in new media formats, the annual total of new accessions is around 60,000 items.

New publications enter the collection of the Austrian National Library in three distinct ways:

| *Deposit copies:*

in accordance with the Austria media law of 1981, the Austrian National Library is entitled to receive a deposit copy, free of charge, of every work published or printed in Austria. It is the only library in Austria to enjoy this privilege. Following the amendment of this law in 2000, this ruling also applies to publications in electronic form. The Austrian National Library also receives a copy of all doctoral dissertations prepared at Austrian universities and other institutions of higher education. Over 50% of all new material entering the Austrian National Library collection each year arrives as a deposit copy.

| *Acquisitions:*

An annual budget of around one million euros is available for the acquisition of material published abroad. The Austrian National Library regularly acquires literature specific to Austria, works by Austrian authors that are published abroad, publications on the humanities (above all those that have a particular relevance to the holdings of the special collections), and those that cover intellectual history in general.

| *Exchange or Donation:*

The Austrian National Library maintains a lively programme of exchange with around 120 libraries, mainly in Europe and North America. Books are also donated to the Austrian National Library, both by private individuals and by institutions. Around 10% of the total of new material entering the Austrian National Library each year falls into these two categories.

Cataloguing New Acquisitions

The Austrian National Library belongs to the Austrian Library Association (*Österreichischer Bibliothekenverbund*), which currently has over fifty members. This arrangement introduces an advantageous element of synergy into the process of cataloguing new acquisitions in as far as data already available in the association's electronic catalogue, including that from abroad (e.g. the bibliographic data in the *Deutsche Bibliothek* or the British Library), may be directly appropriated.

This ensures that the cataloguing of all new acquisitions at the Austrian National Library follows the rules for alphabetic cataloguing in academic libraries that govern all members of the association. Cataloguing according to subject is then co-ordinated by an Austrian National Library department specializing in this area, which follows the international regulations for

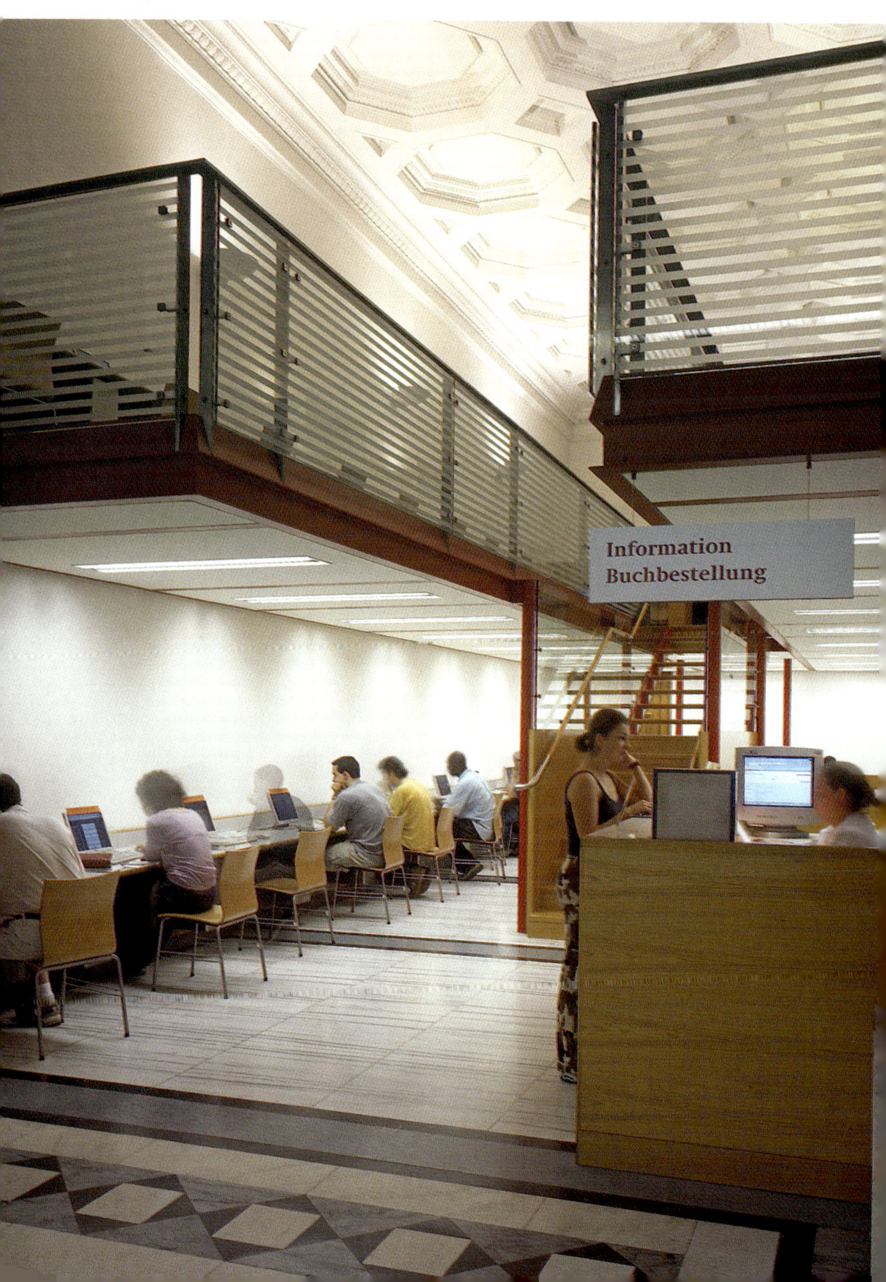

Computer terminals and information desk in the Modern Library on Heldenplatz

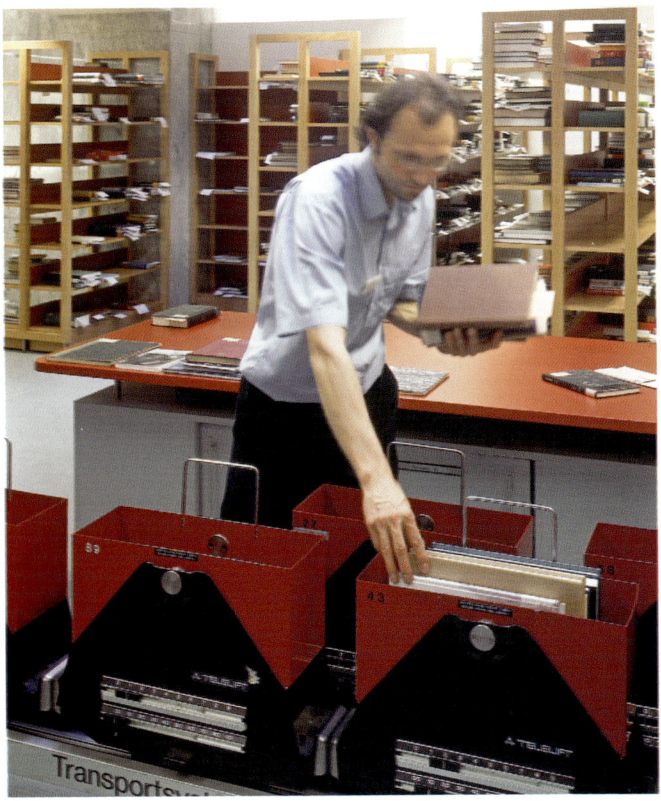

Books are conveyed from the underground storage to the issue desk

cataloguing. The interval between the arrival of a new publication and its availability to users of the Austrian National Library is around two months.

THE AUSTRIAN BIBLIOGRAPHY (ÖSTERREICHISCHE BIBLIOGRAPHIE)

The Austrian Bibliography has been continuously compiled by the Austrian National Library since 1946. It includes every new publication printed or published in Austria of which a deposit copy has been presented to the Library. Since 2003 the Austrian Bibliography has also been available in an online version, freely accessible at any hour of the day or night via the Internet: **http://bibliographie.onb.ac.at/biblio/**

NATIONAL AND INTERNATIONAL CO-OPERATION

An important aspect of the work of the Austrian National Library is its commitment to both national and international co-operation through its membership of numerous bodies. Among these are:

| *the Editorial Board of the Austrian Library Association*

| *the Austrian Editorial Board for Shared Corporate Data*

| *the Austrian Editorial Board for Data on Individuals*

| *the Austrian Editorial Board and Input Office for Titles in
the German Databank of Newspapers and Periodicals*

| *the European Bibliography for Research on Eastern Europe*

TRAINING AND HIGHER EDUCATION

In 1978 a training department was established within the
Austrian National Library to provide courses in library, information and
documentation studies. This department is devoted both to the primary
training and the higher education of academic librarians. Through a
series of workshops and seminars, the further education programme
"Brain Pool" provides prospective academic librarians with a thorough
and continuously updated introduction to every aspect of the field. In
co-operation with the University of Vienna, the Austrian National Library
also runs a university course leading to the qualification of master of
science in library and information studies. For further information visit
www.onb.ac.at/services/oenb-professionell_fr.htm
or **telephone + 43 1 534 10 357.**

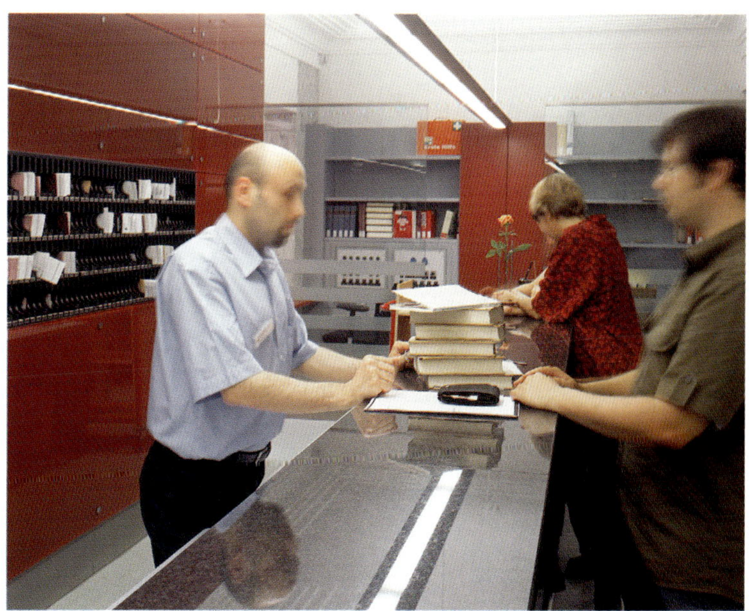

Issue desk in the Modern Library on Heldenplatz

The Society of Friends of the Austrian National Library

The Society of Friends of the Austrian National Library was founded in 1921 by the poet, dramatist and librettist Hugo von Hofmannsthal and the Burgtheater actress Hedwig Bleibtreu. It provides crucial practical and moral support for projects undertaken by the Austrian National Library. The Friends of the Austrian National Library finance new acquisitions and the restoration of objects in the Library's collections, sponsor larger conservation projects, and also supply the means, when required, for the wider publication of the Library's activities.

Members (contributing € 40 per year or more) enjoy diverse benefits in an exceptional setting:

| *Free entry to all museum departments of the Austrian National Library (State Hall, Papyrus Museum, Globe Museum and Esperanto Museum)*

| *Invitation to exhibition openings and other events at the Austrian National Library (lectures, readings, concerts, etc.)*

| *A discount of 15% on the purchase price of Austrian National Library publications (exhibition catalogues, the magazine biblos with its essays on books, the Library and writing in general)*

| *Free subscription to the quarterly ANL Newsletter with information on forthcoming events at the Library*

Supporters (contributing € 200 per year or more) enjoy the above-mentioned benefits and, in addition,

| *Access to the Austrian National Library reading rooms on Heldenplatz*

| *A mention by name on the homepage of the Austrian National Library website*

Sponsors (contributing € 400 per year or more) enjoy all of the above-mentioned benefits and, in addition

| *Free entry, with a guest, to the museum departments of the Austrian National Library and to all exhibitions*

| *A personal expression of thanks from the director-general of the Austrian National Library at its annual reception*

Patrons (contributing, in addition to the annual membership fee, a single donation of € 7,500 or more) receive a personal expression of thanks in a private meeting with the director-general of the Austrian National Library.

Three levels of corporate membership are also available (ranging from € 1000 to € 5000). The transferrable membership card gives access to all museums and reading rooms, as well as granting special conditions for renting the function rooms of the Austrian National Library .

All of the above-mentioned forms of contribution are tax deductible.

For further information, visit
www.onb.ac.at/about/gesfronb
or **telephone +43 1 534 10 202** or **-260**.

Corporate and Private Entertaining

The Austrian National Library's historic interiors offer an exclusive setting for events such as presentations, receptions, press conferences, lectures, symposia, formal dinners, and so on. The rooms in the State Hall wing and the Augustiner wing are available for hire both individually and in combination. The range of possibilities is wide, from a festive occasion in one of the most beautiful libraries in the world to gatherings of various sizes in easily adaptable modern spaces.

All of the following are centrally located within the historic architectural ensemble of the Viennese Hofburg:

State Hall Wing

| *Baroque State Hall: 436 m²*

| *Camineum (multi-functional hall): 374 m²*
Dinner seating for 340 guests; cinema seating for 450

| *Sala Terrena (multi-functional hall): 202 m²*
Dinner seating for 80 guests; cinema seating for 250

| *Atrium (multi-functional hall): 240 m²*
Dinner seating for 110 guests, cinema seating for 180

Augustiner Wing

| *Oratorium (small lecture hall): 117 m²*
Dinner seating for 100 guests; cinema seating for 130

| *Refectorium (only in combination with oratorium): 77 m²*
Dinner seating for 42 guests; cinema seating for 65

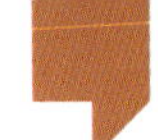

| *Van Swieten Hall (small lecture hall): 104 m^2*
  Dinner seating for 70 guests; cinema seating for 90

| *Lounge and Engelraum (cocktail reception) for 150 guests*

For further information and reservations, visit
www.onb.ac.at/about/nb/vermietung_fr.htm
or **telephone (+ 43 1) 534 10 262** or **-260.**

Sala Terrena (above) and Camineum (below)

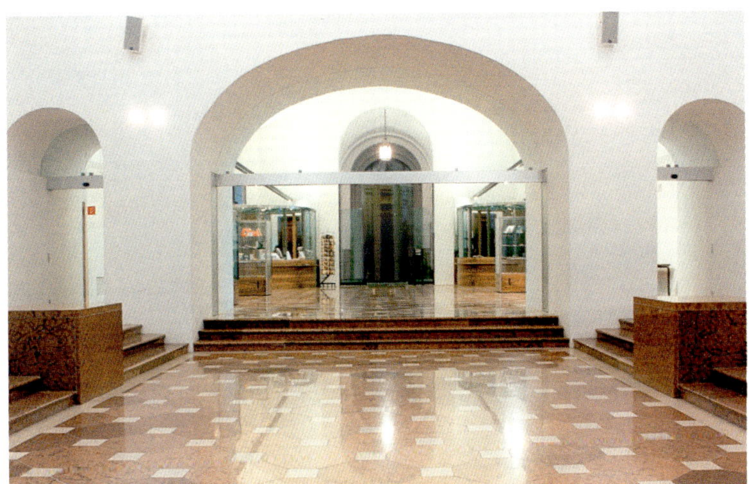

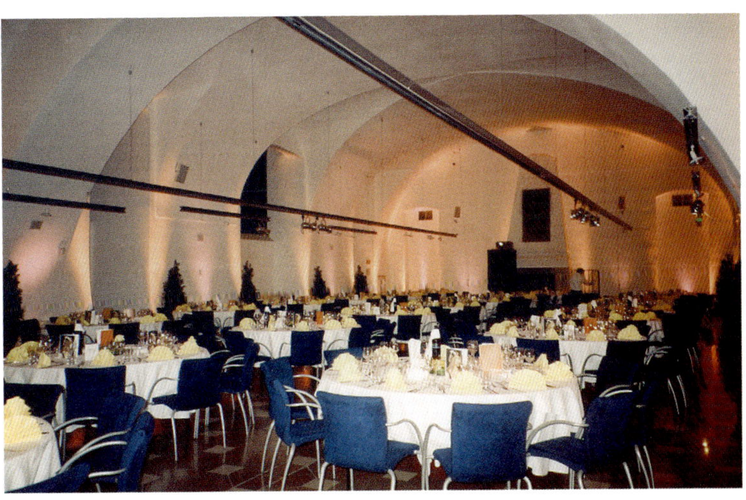

Addresses and other contact details

Main address	Josefsplatz 1, A-1010 Vienna, Austria
Postal address	Josefsplatz 1, P.O. Box 308, A-1015 Vienna, Austria
Telephone	(+ 43 1) 534 100
E-mail	onb@onb.ac.at
Internet	www.onb.ac.at
Opening hours:	For information on the opening hours of the various collections and services, telephone the section concerned or visit its website. Regularly updated information of every sort is included in the leaflet *Öffnungszeiten-Lageplan*, copies of which can be found throughout the Austrian National Library.

STATE HALL

Access	Josefsplatz 1, main entrance, first floor
Telephone	(+ 43 1) 534 10 394

PAPYRUS MUSEUM AND DEPARTMENT OF PAPYRI

Access	Heldenplatz, Neue Hofburg, central entrance
Postal address	Josefsplatz 1, P. O. Box 308, A-1015 Vienna, Austria
Telephone	(+ 43 1) 534 10 323 (Papyrus Museum)
	(+ 43 1) 534 10 425 (Department of Papyri)
Fax	(+ 43 1) 534 10 395
E-mail	papyrus@onc.ac.at
Internet	www.onb.ac.at/sammlungen/papyrus

GLOBE MUSEUM

From mid-2005: Globe Museum in Palais Mollard

Address	Herrengasse 9, A-1010 Vienna, Austria
Telephone	(+ 43 1) 534 10 710
E-mail	globen@onb.ac.at
Internet	www.onb.ac.at/sammlungen/globen/

Until mid-2005

Access   Josefsplatz 1, left entrance, third floor (lift)
Postal address   Josefsplatz 1, P.O. Box 308, A-1015 Vienna, Austria
Telephone   (+ 43 1) 534 10 297
Fax   (+ 43 1) 534 10 319

ESPERANTO MUSEUM AND DEPARTMENT OF PLANNED LANGUAGES

*From mid-2005: Esperanto Museum and Department of
Planned Languages in Palais Mollard*

Address   Herrengasse 9, A-1010 Vienna, Austria
Telephone   (+ 43 1) 534 10 730
E-mail   esperanto@onb.ac.at
Internet   www.onb.ac.at/sammlungen/esperanto/

Until mid-2005

Access   Arched entrance to Hofburg from Michaelerplatz,
                  Batthyany Stairs, third floor
Postal address   Hofburg, Michaelerkuppel, A-1010 Vienna, Austria
Telephone   (+ 43 1) 535 51 45

DEPARTMENT OF MANUSCRIPTS, AUTOGRAPHS AND CLOSED COLLECTIONS

Access   Josefsplatz 1, left entrance, first floor (administration),
                  second floor (reading room)
Postal address   Josefsplatz 1, P.O. Box 308, A-1015 Vienna, Austria
Telephone   (+ 43 1) 534 10
                  (+ 43 1) 534 10 341 and -288 (secretariat)
                  (+ 43 1) 534 10 289 (reading room)
Fax   (+ 43 1) 534 10 296
E-mail   han-slg@onb.ac.at
Internet   www.onb.ac.at/sammlungen/hschrift/

DEPARTMENT OF INCUNABULA, OLD AND PRECIOUS BOOKS

Access   Josefsplatz 1, main entrance, first floor
Postal address   Josefsplatz 1, P.O. Box 308, A-1015 Vienna, Austria
Telephone   (+ 43 1) 534 10 572 (secretariat)
                  (+ 43 1) 534 10 249 (reading room)
Fax   (+ 43 1) 534 10 250
E-mail   alt-bi@onb.ac.at
Internet   www.onb.ac.at/sammlungen/siawd/

DEPARTMENT OF MUSIC

From mid-2005: Department of Music in Palais Mollard

Address   Herrengasse 9, A-1010 Vienna, Austria

Telephone   (+43 1) 534 10 307
E-mail   musiksammlung@onb.ac.at
Internet   www.onb.ac.at/sammlungen/musik/

Until mid-2005
Access   Augustinerstrasse 1, fourth floor
Postal address   Josefsplatz 1, P.O. Box 308, A-1015 Vienna, Austria
Telephone   (+ 43 1) 534 10 314 | -315 | -316 | -317
Fax   (+ 43 1) 534 10 310

PICTURE ARCHIVE

Access   Heldenplatz, Corps de Logis (Ethnographic Museum),
                        second floor
Postal address   Josefsplatz 1, P.O. Box 308, A-1015 Vienna, Austria
Telephone   (+ 43 1) 534 10 337 (secretariat)
                        (+ 43 1) 534 10 329 (enquiries)
Fax   (+ 43 1) 534 10 331
E-mail   bildarchiv@onb.ac.at
Internet   www.bildarchiv.at
                        www.onb.ac.at/sammlungen/bildarchiv/
                        www.bildarchivaustria.at

MAP DEPARTMENT

Access   Josefsplatz 1, left entrance, third floor
Postal address   Josefsplatz 1, P.O. Box 308, A-1015 Vienna, Austria
Telephone   (+43 1) 534 10 297
Fax   (+43 1) 534 10 319
E-mail   kar@onb.ac.at
Internet   www.onb.ac.at/sammlungen/karten/

DEPARTMENT OF BROADSHEETS, POSTERS AND EX LIBRIS

Access   Heldenplatz, Neue Hofburg, central entrance,
                        second floor
Postal address   Josefsplatz 1, P.O. Box 308, A-1015 Vienna, Austria
Telephone   (+ 43 1) 534 10 213; (+ 43) 1 534 219
Fax   (+ 43 1) 534 10 214
E-mail   flu@onb.ac.at
Internet   www.onb.ac.at/sammlungen/plakate/

AUSTRIAN LITERARY ARCHIVES

Access   Arched entrance to Hofburg from Michaelerplatz,
                        Gottfried von Einem Stairs, second floor
Postal address   Josefsplatz 1, P.O. Box 308, A-1015 Vienna, Austria
Telephone   (+ 43 1) 534 10 327
Fax   (+ 43 1) 534 10 340

| E-mail | lit@onb.ac.at |
| Internet | www.onb.ac.at/sammlungen/litarchiv/ |

ARCHIVES OF THE AUSTRIAN FOLK MUSIC SOCIETY

Address	Operngasse 6, A-1010 Vienna, Austria
Telephone	(+ 43 1) 512 63 35
Fax	(+ 43 1) 512 63 13
E-mail	archiv@volksliedwerk.at
	office@volksliedwerk.at
Internet	www.volksliedwerk.at

INSTITUTE FOR CONSERVATION

Access	Josefsplatz 1, left entrance, ground floor (book restoration), mezzanine (administration, restoration of prints and drawings)
Postal address	Josefsplatz 1, P.O. Box 308, A-1015 Vienna, Austria
Telephone	(+ 43 1) 534 10 322 (administration)
	(+ 43 1) 534 10 345 (book restoration)
	(+ 43 1) 534 10 347 (restoration of prints and drawings)
	(+ 43 1) 534 10 236 (restoration of newspapers)
Fax	(+ 43 1) 534 10 321
E-mail	restaurierung@onb.ac.at
Internet	www.onb.ac.at/about/ifr

MODERN LIBRARY

Access	Heldenplatz, Neue Hofburg, central entrance
Postal address	Josefsplatz 1, P.O. Box 308, A-1015 Vienna, Austria
Telephone	(+ 43 1) 534 10 511 (enquiries)

PUBLIC RELATIONS

(press, guided tours, events, exhibitions organisation, sponsoring, book sponsorships)

Acces	Josefsplatz 1, left entrance, first floor
Postal address	Josefsplatz 1, P.O. Box 308, A-1015 Vienna, Austria
Telephone	(+ 43 1) 534 10/extension
Fax	(+ 43 1) 534 10 257
Press, events	(+ 43 1) 534 10 261 or -270
Hirings	(+ 43 1) 534 10 262 or -260
Guided tours	(+ 43 1) 534 10 464
Exhibitions organisation	(+ 43 1) 534 10 277
Sponsoring, book sponsorship	(+ 43 1) 534 10 260
E-mail	oeffentlichkeitsarbeit@onb.ac.at

Glossary

Archival Library
A library with holdings intended not only for present-day use but also for long-term preservation.

Author catalogue
A full listing, arranged alphabetically by author surname, of the holdings of a library.

Autograph text
A letter or other short text written by hand by the author him/herself.

Calligraphy
From the Ancient Greek term kalligraphia (beautiful hand-writing). Hand-writing executed with particular care and artistry. A calligrapher is a person especially skilled in this respect.

Camera praefecti
Office of the director-general.

Catalogue (of a library)
A complete, detailed listing of the items to be found in a library and of precisely where each is stored or shelved.

Catalogue entry
Formal description of a book, containing all the information required to identify it precisely: name of author, title, place of publication, publisher, year of publication, number of pages).

Codex (plural: codices)
From the Latin term codex (a thin, wooden writing tablet). In antiquity this term was used to indicate a set of such writing tablets covered in a thin wax layer and loosely tied together. The essence of this arrangement was preserved as the notion of the codex evolved. In the medieval period a codex was a set of parchment or paper pages with handwritten text, sewn together on one side with thread and then covered in a protective binding. The cover of the codex would be made of wood or a form of pasteboard. In the case of especially sumptuous codices, the cover might incorporate an ivory relief in a gold-leaf frame with decoration in enamel and precious stones. In the Late Middle Ages coloured leather came into use, but even blind-tooled leather bindings invariably had elaborate

embossed decoration. Very few manuscript texts from the medieval period have survived in their original binding.

Deposit copy

A copy of a book or other printed material deposited with a library, free of
charge, upon its publication, in accordance with the law requiring that
this be done so that the entire book production of a country is collected
and stored on one site. In most countries only the most important
libraries are entitled by law to receive deposit copies of every book published there.

Iconography

From the Ancient Greek term eikon (image).
The study of images. A method in art history concerned with enquiry into
the traditional meanings associated with specific image types (as opposed
to a focus on the evolution of forms and/or styles). From an iconographic
point of view, a knowledge of the thematic content of a visual representation, its significance in social or literary terms or in the context of
the history of religion, is regarded as essential to fully understanding a
work of art.

Iconology

From the Ancient Greek term meaning the 'word spoken' by an image.
Originally, a collection of iconographic elements (symbols, attributes,
etc.).

Illuminated manuscript

A manuscript decorated with, for example, small images or marginalia or
ornamented initial letters or a combination of these. Illuminations are
images added to a text to elucidate its meaning, just as illustrations may
supplement text in a printed book. An artist employed to illuminate a
manuscript was called an illuminator.

Incunabula

From the Latin term incunabula (cradle, baby's nappy). The term used
now for early printed material, that is to say material printed between
around 1450 (the invention of printing) and 1500. Incunabula are so called
because they date from the period when printing was still, so to speak, 'in
its infancy'.

Initial letter

From the Latin term initium (the beginning). The first letter of a word
within a text (usually at the beginning of a sentence or a chapter), which
is emphasized through its large size, distinct style and/or decoration. Decorated initials are above all to be found in manuscripts and incunabula.

Inter-library loan

An arrangement whereby an item not available in one library may be provided from the holdings of another, either for use in the Reading Room of
the first library or for loan to the user who has requested it.

Lending library

A library that lends a certain number of books to each user for consultation outside the library for a certain period of time.

Manuscript

From the Latin term manu scriptum (written by hand). Hand-written text of any sort intended for eventual dissemination or publication.

Microfiche

A miniaturized record of texts and/or images arranged in rows on a rectangular sheet of photographic film. This is inserted into an apparatus called a microfiche reader, which throws an enlarged version of each text or image on to a viewing screen.

Microfilm

A miniaturized record of texts and/or images arranged along a roll of photographic film. This is inserted into an apparatus called a microfilm reader, which throws an enlarged version of each text or image on to a viewing screen.

Microforms

A term encapsulating both 'microfiche' and 'microfilm'.

Miniature

From the Latin term miniare (to paint in red). An image added as an illustration to a manuscript or a book.

Morocco (binding)

Term for a type of book binding. Originally used with reference to a particular sort of goatskin, obtained from Morocco, from which book bindings were made.

Numerical sequence signature

The number, or 'signature', assigned to a book as it is accessioned (incorporated into the catalogued holdings of a library). Books are numbered in sequence as they are accessioned, and it is according to this number that they are stored, together with other books of approximately the same size. This is distinct from the way they are arranged in the case of open-access shelving.

Online catalogue

Catalogue of a library's holdings in electronic form, i.e. a catalogue accessible via the Internet. Online catalogues combine the data from pre-existing author and subject catalogues. Items may also be searched for under book title, publisher, year of publication and other categories.

OPAC

(Online Public Access Catalogue). A user-friendly online catalogue.

Open-access shelving

Books (usually standard reference works, arranged according to the various subject areas) are stored on shelving freely accessible to the users.

Palatina
Shorthand for Bibliotheca Palatina Vindobonenis (Palatine Library of Vienna). The name alludes to a connection between the Imperial Court Library in Vienna and the library established on the Palatine Hill in Ancient Rome by Emperor Augustus.

Palimpsest
From the Ancient Greek term palimpsestos (scraped away).
A term used for manuscripts from antiquity or the medieval period (in the form of parchment pages or papyrus rolls) that were rendered re-usable as writing surfaces by scraping or washing away earlier texts. Traces of the earlier layer(s) of text often remained visible. Today these texts can be rendered legible through the use of fluorescent photography.

Prefect
The original term for the individual placed in charge of the Imperial Court Library, in effect the Chief Librarian. Its modern equivalent at the Austrian National Library is director-general.

Printed material
Any form of mechanically reproduced material (text, image, musical score), singly or in combination, intended for general dissemination. Most frequently, a book.

Reference library
A library containing books that may be consulted only in its reading room(s).

Signature
The number assigned to each book, and recorded in its catalogue entry, to indicate precisely where in the library it is stored. With the exception of the special 'signatures' of books belonging in the State Room, Austrian National Library 'signatures' are numerical sequence 'signatures'.

Subject catalogue
A full listing of the books in a library arranged alphabetically according to their chief subjects.

Systematic shelving
Books are arranged on the shelves of a reading room so that those relating to the same subject area are grouped together. The advantage of this arrangement is that all the material available to users on open-access shelving that relates to a particular branch of learning is to be found in one place. The open-access material in the Main Reading Room of the Austrian National Library is an example of systematic shelving.

Union catalogue
A combined record of the holdings of several libraries. Its principal purpose is to provide information on the several libraries in which copies of a particular book may be found.

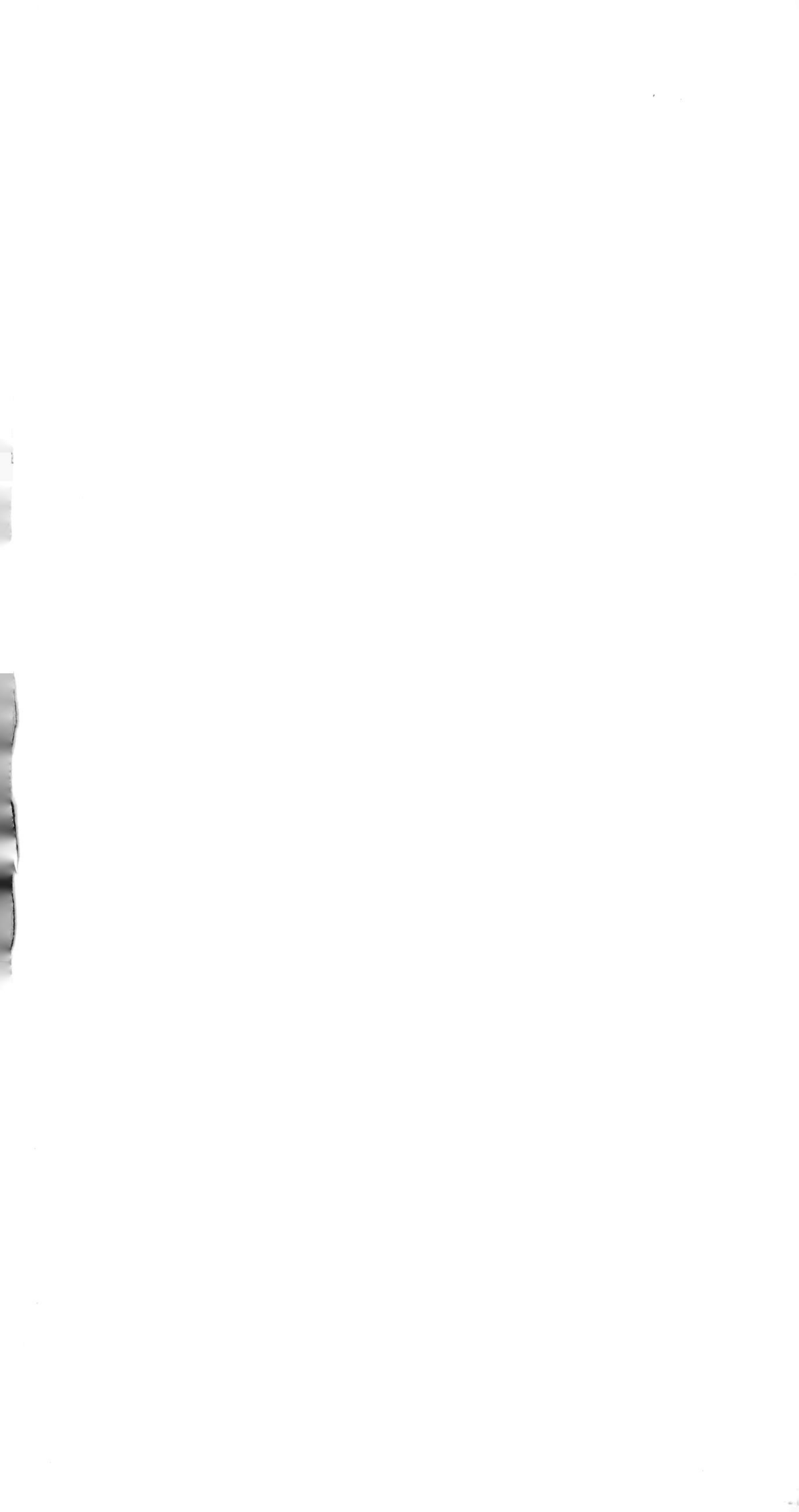